GCSE
BUSINESS
STUDIES
for Edexcel

Sue Alpin
Jan Cooper
Gerard O'Hara
Fiona Petrucke

GCSE BUSINESS STUDIES for Edexcel

Hodder Arnold

A MEMBER OF THE HODDER HEADLINE GROUP

Orders: please contact Bookprint Ltd, 130 Milton Park, Abingdon, Oxon
OX14 4SB. Telephone: (44) 01235 827720. Fax: (44) 01235 400454.
Lines are open from 9.00–6.00, Monday to Saturday, with a 24 hour
message answering service. You can also order through our website
www.hoddereducation.co.uk

British Library Cataloguing in Publication Data
A catalogue record for this title is available from the British Library

ISBN-10: 0 340 81656 2
ISBN-13: 978 0 340 81656 1

First published 2004

Impression number   10   9   8   7   6   5
Year   2008   2007   2006

Copyright © 2004 Sue Alpin, Jan Cooper, Gerard O'Hara, Fiona Petrucke

All rights reserved. No part of this publication may be reproduced or
transmitted in any form or by any means, electronic or mechanical,
including photocopy, recording, or any information storage and retrieval
system, without permission in writing from the publisher or under licence
from the Copyright Licensing Agency Limited. Further details of such
licences (for reprographic reproduction) may be obtained from the
Copyright Licensing Agency Limited, of 90 Tottenham Court Road,
London W1T 4LP.

Artwork by Marco Schaaf at NB Illustration.
Cartoons by Gustavo Mazali at Beehive Illustration.

Typeset by Tech-Set Ltd, Gateshead
Printed in Dubai for Hodder Education, a division of Hodder
Headline, 338 Euston Road, London NW1 3BH.

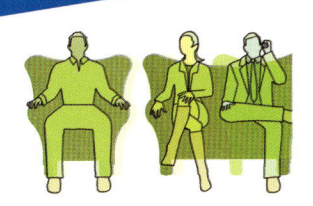

CONTENTS

Acknowledgements		vi
How to use this book		vii

Section 1 Business Activity and the Changing Environment
Unit 1	Introduction	2
Unit 2	Economic activity	11
Unit 3	Business objectives and judging success	15
Unit 4	Business activity and the external environment	22
Unit 5	Location	45
Unit 6	Types of business organisations	51

Section 2 Human Resources
Unit 7	Internal organisation	68
Unit 8	Communication	76
Unit 9	Recruitment and selection	88
Unit 10	Training	100
Unit 11	Motivation and rewards	105
Unit 12	Negotiation and consultation	117

Section 3 Accounting and Finance
Unit 13	Budgets	128
Unit 14	Cash flow and forecasting	132
Unit 15	Sources of finance	138
Unit 16	Revenue, costs and break-even analysis	145
Unit 17	Final accounts	154
Unit 18	Business performance and ratios	166

Section 4 Marketing
Unit 19	The market	176
Unit 20	Price	182
Unit 21	Promotion	188
Unit 22	Place	199
Unit 23	Product	207
Unit 24	Market research	213

Section 5 Production
Unit 25	Economies and diseconomies of scale	224
Unit 26	Methods of production	232
Unit 27	Productivity	237
Unit 28	Quality	243

Section 6 Assessment
Unit 29	Coursework	248
Unit 30	The examination papers	255

Index 256

ACKNOWLEDGEMENTS

The authors would like to thank the following people who have helped and advised in the preparation of this book: Alexia Chan, Llinos Edwards, Tessa Heath and staff at London Qualifications Ltd (formerly Edexcel). They would also like to thank John Alpin, Michael Cooper, Paul Petrucke and Jackie O'Hara, who have shown such patience and given tremendous support throughout.

The authors and publishers would like to thank London Qualifications Ltd for permission to reproduce examination questions from Edexcel past papers and the following institutions and individuals for permission to reproduce copyright illustrative material:

Advertising Standards Authority p. 197; BBC p. 97; Colin Cuthbert/Science Photo Library p. 241; Equal Opportunities Commission p. 97; Gamma/Katz pp. 229, 244; Getty Images pp. 46, 56, 78, 81, 154; Helen King/Corbis p. 113; Investors in People p. 114; Jacques M. Chenet/Corbis p. 39; Laif/Katz p. 201; ©Maggie Murray/Photofusion p. 211; Novosti/Topham p. 108; PA Photos p. 120; ©Paula Solloway/Photofusion pp. 95, 157; ©Phil Wilkinson/Topfoto p. 128; Reuters/Corbis p. 8; ©Robert Battersby/BDI Images Ltd pp. 57, 72, 176 (r&l), 203; ©Sally Lancaster/Photofusion p. 92; ©Topham/Chapman p. 149; ©Topham/Chris Clark pp. 138, 232, 234; ©Topham/ImageWorks pp. 23, 28, 41, 102, 168, 178; ©Topham/National Pictures pp. 6, 31; ©Topham/PA pp. 117, 195; ©Topham Picturepoint pp. 136, 182, 185, 186, 199; ©UPPA Ltd p. 191; WHSmith p. 82; William Whitehurst/Corbis p. 35.

HOW TO USE THIS BOOK

This book is divided into five sections to correspond with the Edexcel 1503 specification for GCSE Business Studies. Each section is further divided into units, breaking down the material in order to make it more manageable. There is an additional section on assessment.

The order in which the sections are to be approached will be decided by your teacher, but the authors recommend that all the units within each section are completed in the order shown in the book.

Diagrams and examples have been used frequently in this book. You should study these carefully to bring the subject matter to life; the images will show that the subject of Business Studies is happening all around us.

Task
There are plenty of tasks in each unit to help you to understand and apply your knowledge.

Extension task
These tasks are intended to give you more practice extending your understanding and consolidating the skill of application.

Exam tip
Tips and hints on how to do well in the examination

Past Paper
Actual examination questions selected from past papers at both foundation and higher levels. These will help you become familiar with the style and language used in the GCSE examination. Work on actual questions should also help you to choose the appropriate level of entry for the examination.

Revision Questions
Revision questions have been provided to enable you to check whether you have fully understood and learnt each unit. These questions should not take long to answer. Keep all your answers to help you when it comes to revising for the exam.

Key terms
Specialist words and terms are listed, with definitions, at the end of each unit. It is vital that you know and understand these.

Summary
This appears at the end of each unit and summarises the content of the unit.

GCSE BUSINESS STUDIES for Edexcel

Section 1
BUSINESS ACTIVITY AND THE CHANGING ENVIRONMENT

UNIT 1

INTRODUCTION

> ## What you will learn
>
> At the end of this unit you should understand:
> - what businesses do
> - how they do it
> - why businesses are important
> - where business is conducted
> - how decisions are made on what and how to produce
> - how decisions are made on who receives what.

WHAT DOES BUSINESS DO?

Business is about providing consumers with the products or services that they want or need. People set up businesses because they believe that they can make a **profit** by providing consumers with what they want and need. Profit is the total revenue of a business minus all of its costs (see Section 3, Accounting and Finance). Businesses do this in a difficult environment in which other organisations and individuals around them can either constrain their activities or help them to succeed.

Consumers want many things, but in order to survive they need the basic essentials of life:

Air is one of the few basic human needs which is not scarce and is free for people to use. We have to pay for all of our other basic needs, which are provided for us by businesses.

> ### Task
>
> For each need, with the exception of air, find the names of five businesses which provide them for us.

Once people have satisfied these needs, they start to want other items such as cars, televisions, holidays, fast food etc. People's wants are unlimited and depend on their personalities and experiences. Today people want things that ten or twenty years ago were not even dreamed of – such as mobile phones.

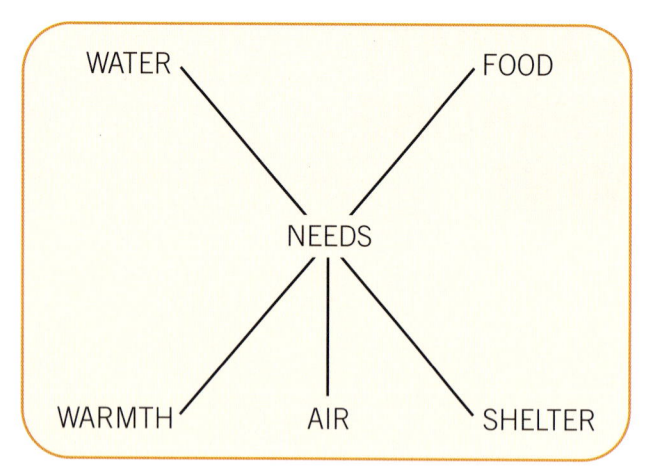

Figure 1.1 The basic essentials of life (WATER, FOOD, WARMTH, AIR, SHELTER → NEEDS)

> **Task**
>
> Write down ten things that people want today that they did not want twenty years ago.
>
> How many times have you heard the phrase, 'You can't have everything you want'? Why not? Think about something you would like to have but cannot and explain why you cannot have it. Think about something the school would like to have but cannot and explain why it cannot have it.

RESOURCES

Businesses provide us with our wants and needs by processing inputs into outputs. The inputs are the raw materials which a business uses and the outputs are the goods and services they produce. Businesses use resources, known as the **factors of production**, to satisfy our wants and needs. For convenience purposes we group these under four headings:

Land
This includes the land used to produce upon, as well as all of the natural resources we extract from the land and the sea. It refers to the raw materials which are obtained from farming, fishing, mining, quarrying and forestry.

Labour
This is the use of human skills, both physical and mental. Physical labour is when people use their hands to produce goods and services, such as a bricklayer or chef. Mental labour is when people use their minds, such as designer or solicitor.

Capital
Capital resources are those which have been produced by people to assist the production process, and include anything from a simple screwdriver to a chemical factory.

Enterprise
Entrepreneurs are the people who bring together and organise the factors of production to produce the goods and services which people want and need. Without these enterprising individuals, businesses would not exist and our wants and needs would not be met. These individuals take the risk that what they produce might not be sold at a profit and that they could lose everything they own.

It is also the function of the entrepreneur to coordinate the production process and decide which factors of production to use and in what combination. Some businesses are **capital intensive** and use more capital equipment (ie use a large number of machines in production) and little labour (eg chemical industry, car manufacturers). Other businesses are **labour intensive** (ie use a large amount of labour and little capital equipment, eg service industries such as the health service and post office). Which factor of production dominates depends on the type of business, its cost and its availability.

> **Task**
>
> Place the following resources under the headings land, labour, capital and enterprise:
>
> doctor, forest, coal, shop, owner of a corner shop, shareholder, computer, carpenter, van, bolt.

UNIT 1: INTRODUCTION

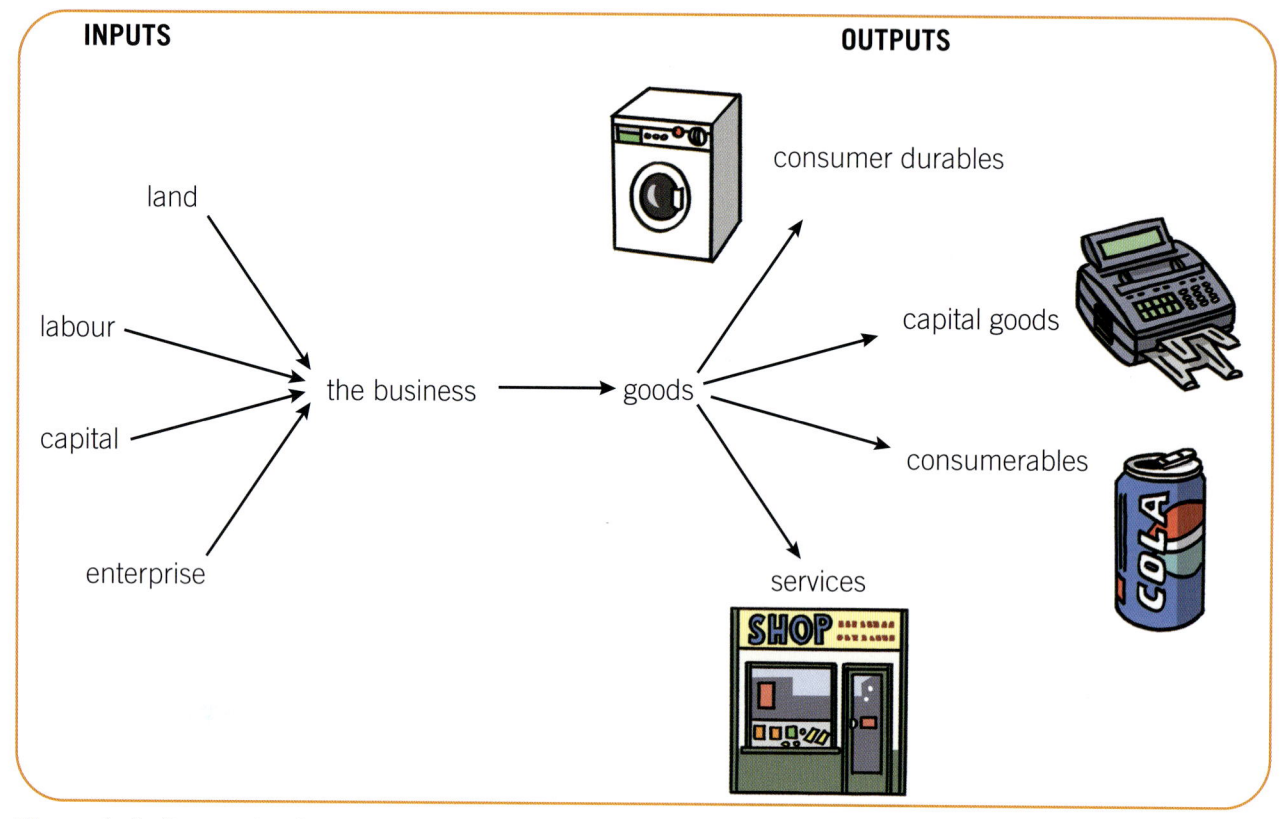

Figure 1.2 Processing inputs into outputs

CREATION OF WEALTH

Businesses are not only important because they provide us with our wants and needs. In the process of using resources to provide goods and services, they add value to those resources and create wealth. For example, when you buy a pine table from a furniture shop, it has already gone through a number of processes; at each stage value has been added to it, and wealth is being created through payment to the factors of production.

Firstly, the tree had to be grown and felled. This would then be taken to a saw mill where it would be cut into planks. A furniture manufacturer would buy the timber and make a table from it which they would sell to the retailer. The retailer would then sell the table. At each stage the money made from the production process will be used to pay the factors of production.

- If the table was sold for £500 and the furniture retailer had paid the manufacture £300, it has added £200 of value to the product. It would use some of this value added to pay the wages of shop assistants, pay the rent on the store, pay its heating and lighting bills and keep some of it for profit.
- The manufacturer paid the saw mill £100 for the timber, adding £200 to its value. The manufacturer will use this to pay workers' wages, various bills and make a profit.
- The saw mill bought the wood from the forestry company for £50. It would use the remaining £50 to pay wages, bills and make a profit.
- It cost the forestry company £20 to grow the tree. It would use this money to pay for its factors of production.

Stage	Value added (£)
Forestry Company	30
Saw Mill	50
Furniture Manufacturer	200
Furniture Retailer	200

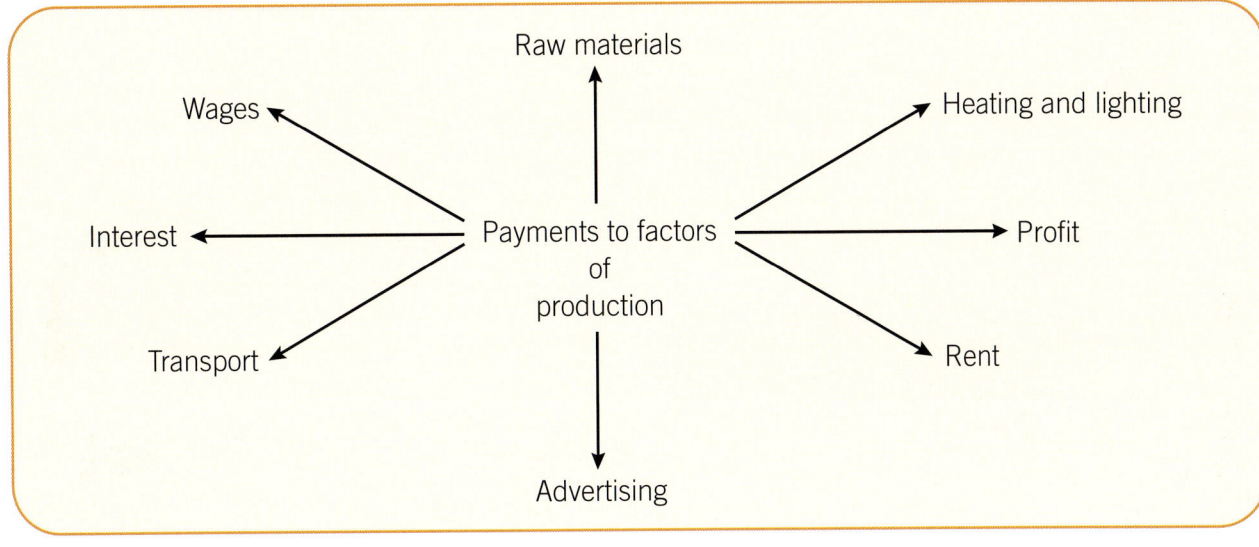

```
                    Raw materials
                         ↑
  Wages ←                              → Heating and lighting
                    Payments to factors
  Interest ←              of              → Profit
                      production
  Transport ←                            → Rent
                         ↓
                    Advertising
```

Figure 1.3 Payments to factors of production

Task

A furniture company has bought raw materials and service for £20 million. It has sold its finished furniture for £35 million, thus adding £15 million to the value of the raw materials. Of this £15 million, £5 million is used to pay wages and salaries, £1 million repays the mortgage on the factory, £2 million buys more capital goods, 2 million is paid to the government in taxes. This leaves a profit of £5 million.

With the aid of a diagram, show how much wealth the furniture company has created and how it has shared it out.

Task

List the different markets where you could buy the following products or services:

holiday to Ibiza, perfume, compact disc, earrings, pair of jeans, towels, refrigerator.

Markets can be local (eg corner shop), national (eg Tesco supermarket) and international (eg Nissan cars).

Task

Give an example of a business that operates:

1. in your local market cutting hair
2. in the national market selling and fixing exhaust pipes for cars
3. in the international market selling petrol.

THE MARKET

Businesses need somewhere to sell their goods and services, and consumers need to know where they can buy them. Where businesses sell and consumers buy goods and services is known as the **market place**. Any location or any form in which buyers and sellers can meet is known as a market; it can be anything from an open air market to the internet.

The market is not only important in that it allows a buyer and a seller to meet. It also helps to decide the price of goods and services. In some markets, the price of the product is determined by the seller. In other markets, buyers and sellers might haggle over or negotiate the price. Buyers may also compete among themselves, bidding up the price until only one buyer is left.

> **Task**
>
> Who fixes the price:
> 1. in a furniture shop
> 2. in a house sale
> 3. in an antiques auction
> 4. of a second hand car
> 5. for servicing the central heating?

Figure 1.4 Who is fixing the price in the antiques auction above?

Market forces

The market is also very powerful because it decides what resources will be used and how they will be used. In the market, buyers have money to spend. They choose which goods or services to spend their money on, from the millions that are on offer. Each time they buy a good or service they are sending a message to the seller saying that is the good or service that they want. If a business is providing goods or services that buyers want then they will probably get a large reward – an increase in profits. Profit is important in the market place. If the business *is* making a large profit, it will want to provide more of that good or service and will therefore need to use more resources and pay for more factors of production. However, if a business is *not* making a profit, it will not be able to pay the factors of production and will have to stop providing that good or service. The resources they have been using will be transferred to those businesses which are doing well.

Some markets are very competitive, with many businesses providing goods and services (eg clothes shops), others are dominated by a few (eg supermarkets) and some are monopolist, where only one company provides that good or service (eg local water companies).

ECONOMIC PROBLEM

If resources were unlimited, everyone could have all of their wants and needs. However, resources are limited in a number of ways:

- Land – there is a fixed amount of land on which to build houses, factories and grow food. Many natural resources such as coal and oil are running out and cannot be replaced
- Capital – businesses have only a certain amount of finance to invest in capital equipment
- Labour – only a certain number of people are available for work and certain skills are in short supply
- Entrepreneurs – not everyone can be Richard Branson or Bill Gates

Although resources are in short supply, our wants and needs are not. We could all produce a long list of goods and services that we would like, but the resources to buy them are limited.

There are two costs involved when an individual or business makes a decision to buy something. There is the **actual** money cost, ie the actual amount of money that an individual or business wants for providing that good or service, and the **opportunity** cost, ie by spending money on one good or service you are giving up the opportunity to buy other goods or services. Unless you are very lucky or do not want much (highly unlikely), you will not be able have all the goods and services you would like. Choices therefore have to be made. The true cost of deciding to buy *one* good instead of another is the satisfaction or pleasure you have given up by not buying the *other* good. For example, you use your wages from your Saturday job to save up to buy a new mobile phone, but in saving your money you are giving up the satisfaction you would have received from using the money to go to the pictures with your friends. This is known as the opportunity cost. Opportunity cost is also important for businesses, which constantly have to make choices, such as should they increase the wages of workers, invest in a new computer system or give the shareholders a greater share of the profit.

Task

Mr and Mrs Wardle have saved £2000 to go on their first holiday abroad in two years. Just before they leave, the central heating system breaks down and needs to be renewed. They cannot afford to do both.

Egan Enterprises Ltd has to decide whether to use its profits to meet a 5% wage demand by the workers or pay a higher dividend to the shareholders. They have not made enough profit to do both.

Nodlob council has £20 million to spend on education or creating jobs. It needs to build a new school or a business park to attract new businesses. It cannot afford to do both.

Look at the three situations above and in each case:

- explain why a choice has to be made
- make a choice and explain why you chose that option
- explain who might be affected by your choice.

Exam tip

This section deals with ideas rather than facts and is therefore difficult to understand. However, you need to memorise the key terms – wants, needs, resources, factors of production, land, labour, capital, enterprise, wealth, market forces, scarcity and opportunity cost.

ECONOMIC SYSTEMS

All countries, societies, businesses and individuals face the same problem – the wants and needs of the people are infinite but the resources to meet them are limited. Choices have to be made. An economy is a system set up by people to help them answer the following questions:

- Which goods and service are going to be made?
- How will those goods and services be made?
- Who will receive those goods and services?

How these questions are answered will vary depending on the economic and political system in that country. Three systems can be identified:

Free market economy

In this system all resources are owned and controlled by private individuals, and production and distribution takes place through the markets. There is no government or taxes. Consumers decide what should be produced by buying those goods or services that they want or need from businesses. In order to meet this demand, businesses have to pay for the factors of production. Having to make a profit in order to survive dictates how a good is produced, and businesses need to be efficient and cost-effective so that they can make as large a profit as possible. They need to ensure that they are supplying the goods and services consumers want at the right price and the right quality, or they will go out of business. Who obtains these goods and services depends on an individual's income. Those individuals on a high income will be able to buy more goods and services than those on a low income.

Advantages
- Incentive for entrepreneurs to be successful as they keep all of the profits.
- Incentive for businesses to be efficient so that they can compete and make more profit.
- Wide choice of goods and services for consumers.
- Markets are responsive to changes in consumer demand.
- Competition helps keep prices down and encourages new ideas.

Disadvantages
- Only those with money have their wants and needs satisfied.
- Unequal distribution of wealth between the rich and the poor.
- Goods such as street lighting and the defence services will not be provided as people will not pay for them, in the hope someone else will provide them and they will benefit.
- Only those people who can afford them will have access to education and healthcare.
- Some businesses may become monopolies and charge any price they like.
- No social security system. If people are unable to work because they are too old or sick, they will have to rely on their family or charity to help them.

There are no examples of free market economies in the world.

Planned economy

In this system what, how and who is decided by the state or government. Resources are owned by the state and it is the state that sets the price of goods and services. The government controls all businesses and appoints planners who decide what is going to be produced and how.

The role of business is to carry out the orders of the state. For example, the planners will set a target for a shoe company of how many shoes it has to make. They will tell them what raw materials to use and how many workers they can employ. Who receives the goods and services is also determined by the government, and is usually on a first come, first served basis.

Advantages
- Everyone has free access to public services such as education, health and housing.
- Everyone who is capable of working will have a job. Those incapable of working will receive social security benefit.
- Resources are allocated first to those areas which are deemed important, ie housing, education and health.

Disadvantages
- Difficulties in coordinating every aspect of the economy lead to shortages.
- Everyone works for the state, so wages are similar. There is therefore no incentive to work hard or develop a career.
- As there is no profit motive or competition, businesses do not need to be inventive or efficient.
- Goods produced are of a standard design.
- Few luxury items are produced as resources are used to provide public goods.
- Black markets and corruption dominate as people attempt to get the goods and service they want.

Figure 1.5 Queuing for bread in a planned economy

At one time, a number of countries such as Russia and China adopted a planned system. Today, however, there are very few, because this system is unable to provide consumers with their basic needs or satisfy their wants, and there are no incentives for individuals to work hard and be successful.

Mixed economy

In practice all economies are a mixture of free enterprise and state control. Countries try to achieve the benefits of both systems, ie the efficiency of the free market with the social benefits and fairness of a planned economy.

In a mixed economy, businesses make decisions on what and how to produce, but the government intervenes in the market to try to influence and control those decisions, eg laws, grants, taxes. The government will also control resources more directly if they feel that the whole of society will benefit from them, eg health, education, defence, social security.

A mixed economy is one in which some resources are controlled by the state and some by private individuals – private and public sectors exist together. The mixture of an economy depends upon the political persuasion of that country and what the people believe in. The USA believes that government intervention and ownership of resources should be kept at a minimum, whereas China believes that the government should play a major role in deciding what, how and who.

Revision Questions

1. Which of these is a factor of production?
   a) inflation
   b) demand
   c) profit
   d) land

2. People who buy products are known as:
   a) sellers
   b) consumers
   c) producers
   d) employees

3. Materials used and people employed are examples of:
   a) training
   b) resources
   c) induction
   d) economies

4. Which of these is not a need?
   a) shelter
   b) cars
   c) food
   d) warmth

5. An economy which has both a private and public sector is:
   a) mixed
   b) planned
   c) market
   d) traditional

Task

Draw up a table to show which of the following goods and services are produced in the market sector and which in the state sector of the UK economy:

education, television sets, gas cookers, health care, army, roads, cars, petrol, police.

Exam tip

In this section a number of technical business terms have been used. It is important that you learn these terms, as the examiner will test your knowledge of them more than your understanding. However, the better you understand the terms, the easier they will be to remember.

Summary

In this section you should have learnt how important businesses are in our lives. They provide us with the items that we want and need and also give us the means to obtain them. In providing us with our wants and needs, businesses have to use resources which we call the factors of production. Unfortunately, resources are scarce and people's wants are infinite, so decisions have to be made on which goods and services to produce and who will get them. A system known as an economy therefore has to be put in place to help us make these decisions. The true cost of rejecting one want or need for an alternative is known as the opportunity cost.

Key terms

Business activity – individuals or groups of individuals who provide goods and services

Capital goods – equipment that is used in the production process to help make other goods, eg robots on an assembly line

Capital intensive – a system of production where capital is the main factor of production

Consumer – a person who buys goods and services

Consumerables – single-use goods which have to be used in a short space of time, eg food

Consumer durable goods – goods bought by consumers which will last for more than one year, eg washing machine

Factors of production – resources which are used in the production of goods and services: land, labour, capital and enterprise

Goods – physical items that are produced by business activity

Labour intensive – describes a business which uses labour as the main factor of production

Market – a place where buyers and sellers meet

Needs – what is essential for life

Opportunity cost – satisfaction or benefit that could have been gained from an alternative use of a resource

Services – non-physical products such as a haircut or loan

Value added – the value that is added to a good or service as it goes through the different stages of production

UNIT 2

ECONOMIC ACTIVITY

What you will learn

At the end of this unit you should understand:

- the differences between primary, secondary and tertiary activity
- how each sector is linked
- why the number of people employed in the tertiary sector has increased while the numbers in primary and secondary have fallen.

TYPES OF BUSINESS ACTIVITY

Business organisations can be classified into three main types of activity:

1. primary
2. secondary
3. tertiary.

Primary activity is the first stage of the production process and involves the extraction of natural resources from the land and the sea. This sector provides the raw materials for the manufacturing sector and includes farming, fishing, mining, quarrying and forestry.

Secondary activity involves turning the raw materials into finished goods. This sector includes any business which is involved in manufacturing, assembling, processing, constructing and refining.

Tertiary activity involves providing a service for either businesses or for individuals. Services for businesses include banking, insurance, retailing, transport and warehousing. These services allow the primary and secondary sectors to work more efficiently. Services for individuals can range from hairdressing to teaching.

Task

Place the following list of occupations under the headings of primary, secondary, tertiary.

postman, builder, pop star, sales assistant, coal miner, bus driver, window cleaner, fireman, civil servant, fruit picker, estate agent, oil rig worker, bank clerk, air steward, butcher, insurance broker, car assembly worker, wine importer.

Figure 2.1

> **Exam tip**
>
> You must be able to define and give examples of each type of activity.

CHAIN OF PRODUCTION

Primary activity (extraction of raw materials), secondary activity (turning raw materials into manufactured goods) and tertiary activity (providing services) are linked together in a chain of production, and are all inter-dependent on each other. Some products go through many stages of production, while for others the chain is a great deal shorter. In the production of shoes, a number of clear stages can be seen.

Figure 2.2 Chain of production for shoes

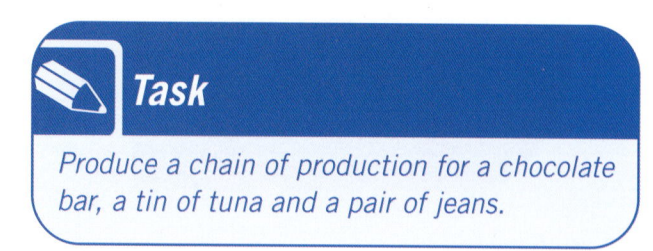

TABLE 2.1 Changing trends in employment in economic activity

Year	Primary	Secondary	Tertiary
1700	75%	15%	10%
1900	15%	55%	30%
2000	2%	28%	70%

As we can see from the above table, the number of people employed in the primary and secondary sectors has fallen, while the numbers employed in the tertiary sector have risen. There are a number of reasons to explain this trend.

- Increased use of machinery means fewer workers are needed in the primary and secondary sectors.
- Raw materials have run out.
- Cheap imports from other countries.
- Lack of investment in new factories and technology.
- Markets lost as other countries developed their own industries.
- High wages in the UK resulted in manufacturing companies locating in other countries where wages are lower.
- As people's income and leisure increases, they spend more time and money on services such as health care, leisure, tourism, travel, pensions, mortgages and others, leading to more workers being needed in these areas.

The increase in the number of workers in the tertiary sector and the decline in the number of workers in the secondary and primary sectors is known as **deindustrialisation**.

> **Task**
>
> Produce a chain of production for a chocolate bar, a tin of tuna and a pair of jeans.

Revision Questions

1. The manufacturers of furniture are in which sector of industry?
   a) tertiary
   b) secondary
   c) economic
   d) primary

2. A farm shop is in the .... sector of industry.
   a) tertiary
   b) public
   c) secondary
   d) primary

3. Farmers today employ fewer workers than they used to. This is because of:
   a) high unemployment
   b) government regulations
   c) improved technology
   d) the European Union

4. Companies that make aircraft are in the .... sector of industry.
   a) primary
   b) secondary
   c) tertiary
   d) financial

5. The primary sector of industry includes which one of the following business activities?
   a) providing furniture for a show house
   b) wiring houses
   c) selling houses
   d) providing the material for making bricks

Task

Frosty Fingers is a frozen food manufacturer which is in the secondary sector of production. It uses services provided by the tertiary sector.

1. a) State what is meant by the term secondary sector. (2)
   b) Select three services in the tertiary sector which would support Frosty Fingers. (3)
   c) Explain how two of the services you have selected would support Frosty Fingers. (6)

Past Paper

Harbon Estates Ltd is a property development company that buys land and develops it. Its current development is a housing estate called 'Sleepy Hollow'. The houses have been built by Delta Homes plc, a national construction company and are being sold by Fuller & Brandon, a local estate agent. Permission to build has been granted by the local authority.

Assess how primary, secondary and tertiary production activities are, or have been linked as a result of the 'Sleepy Hollow' development. (8)

Edexcel, 1999, Foundation

UNIT 2: ECONOMIC ACTIVITY

Exam tip

The examiner will be testing you on three areas in this section: your knowledge of terms, the reasons why the employment structure has changed, and how the three activities are linked.

Summary

In this section you should have learnt how business activity can be grouped under the three headings of primary, secondary and tertiary. Also, how each activity is linked to the others through the chain of production, and how the employment structure of the UK has changed over time as a result of a number of factors, eg deindustrialisation and an increase in the demand for services.

Key terms

Chain of production – the various stages a product goes through before being sold to a consumer

Deindustrialisation – the process in an economy whereby the primary and secondary sectors decline in importance while the tertiary sector becomes more important

Economic activity – any work for which people get paid

Primary activity – economic activity that involves the extraction of natural resources from the sea and land

Secondary activity – the manufacturing of products from raw materials

Tertiary activity – the provision of services which help to support the other two sectors of economic activity

UNIT 3

BUSINESS OBJECTIVES AND JUDGING SUCCESS

>> **What you will learn**

At the end of this unit you should understand:
- the main objectives of businesses
- why businesses set themselves objectives
- how businesses can judge if they have achieved their objectives.

WHAT IS AN OBJECTIVE?

An objective is a target that an organisation or individual can work towards achieving. It should be:

Specific
Measurable
Achievable   } SMART
Realistic
Time related

Businesses set objectives for themselves just as you might set yourself an objective, eg make the school football team, achieve five GCSEs at grade C, or be a pop idol.

The main objective of any business is to survive. In order to achieve this, it has to set itself the objective of making a profit. If a business fails to make a profit, it will not be able to pay wages, bills, buy raw materials, invest in new machinery or borrow money. It will eventually go out of business. Although these are the main objectives, there are others:

- Profit maximisation – aim to make the highest amount of profit possible based on sales, costs and investment.
- Market share – businesses will try to be the biggest in their market by having the highest value of sales. For example, if a software games company has sales of £100 million and the total sales for software games was £400 million, it would have 25% of the market share. By increasing its market share, it will gain increased economies of scale (see Unit 25) and have greater power over its competitors, suppliers and consumers.
- Customer satisfaction – by providing consumers with what they want at the right price and of the right quality consumers will keep using the business and help it to grow and expand.

Figure 3.1 Wealth creation

- Wealth creation – businesses attempt to make money for their owners, managers and workers by increasing dividends to shareholders and increasing wages and salaries of employees.

> **Task**
>
> Read each of the statements below and decide which of the above business objectives it refers to:
>
> 1. Our objective is to increase sales by 10% next year.
> 2. We aim to increase the dividend to shareholders by 5%.
> 3. We must increase profits by 5% for the next two years.
> 4. We will reduce the price of our products by 2%.
> 5. If we do not reduce our prices to match our competitors', we will lose customers.

Mission statement

Many businesses today set out their objectives in a **mission statement**. This describes the main objectives of the business in a clear and precise way so that owners, employees and customers understand them.

> **Task**
>
> 1. Identify the main business objectives from the mission statements in Figure 3.2 below.
> 2. Find out if your school has a mission statement. Use it to identify the main objectives of your school. Do they differ from Nodlob's objectives?
> 3. Use your school's mission statement and those below to help you produce your own mission statement.

Stakeholders

Businesses set out to achieve certain objectives, but may find that conflict arises between the different people who have a stake in the success of that business. For example, you may find that your objectives in Business Studies differ from those of your teacher! Any person or any group that has a stake in the success of a business is known as a **stakeholder**. In a school the main stakeholders are the parents, pupils, teachers, local authority and ancillary staff.

Nodlob School

Our aim is to encourage all pupils to take advantage of the opportunities offered by the school to attain their full potential in all areas of school life — the academic, the social, the physical and the personal — so that they are ready both to play a productive part in a democratic society and to move forward to the next stage of education, training or career with confidence, as young people of responsibility and judgement.

Body Shop

To tirelessly work to narrow the gap between principle and practice, whilst making fun, passion and care part of our daily lives.

Figure 3.2 Examples of mission statements

In a large business, the owners, managers and workers are likely to be different people with different objectives. The owners will want the largest possible return on their investment, which will be achieved by the business maximising its profits. Workers are interested in how much they earn and better working conditions, which will mean an increase in costs and a lowering of profit. Managers' salaries may be linked to sales, therefore they may be more concerned with increasing the size of the business rather than profit. For other interested groups the image of the business may be important, eg the business will spend large amounts of its profit ensuring that it is seen to be environmentally friendly.

The objectives that the business adopts will depend on which group has the most power. However, it is in the interests of all groups that the business is successful, so this may result in a mixture of objectives. To keep everyone happy, it may aim to make enough profit to please the shareholders, give the managers expensive company cars and pay higher wages to the workers than those employed in similar businesses.

> **Task**
>
> *Identify the personal objectives of someone setting up their own business. Describe how these maybe similar or different to those objectives outlined above.*

Public sector enterprises

Business objectives differ according to the type of ownership and who owns the business. There are two types of ownership, private and public, which will be explained in more detail in the next section. The objectives of business in the public sector (eg local council swimming baths, the BBC) may differ from the private sector in that they are not necessarily expected to make a profit. Their main objective is to provide a high quality service which benefits the community. The BBC's objectives are to entertain, inform and educate the nation; the local swimming baths aim to provide a place where people can learn to swim so that they will be safe and secure when they are near water. These enterprises may be expected to cover all of their costs from what they earn, or make a certain level of profit for investment purposes, but many run at a loss because of their benefit to the public.

Figure 3.3 The swimming baths – a public service

> **Exam tip**
>
> *Remember that different stakeholders have different objectives, and that this can lead to conflict between them.*

> **Task**
>
> *Identify the main objectives of a local authority leisure centre and describe the benefits it brings to the local community. Do you think it should run at a profit or loss? Explain your decision.*

JUDGING SUCCESS

Businesses set themselves objectives which they hope to achieve if they wish to be successful. Businesses need to be able to measure their objectives to judge if they have been successful or not. There are a number of ways in which a business can measure how successful it is.

Survival/profit

If a business continues to trade, it is surviving and has therefore achieved one of its main objectives. However, for most businesses merely surviving is not enough and they wish to make a profit. Businesses judge how successful they are by the size of the profit they make and whether or not that profit is more or less than previous years. Businesses may also judge their success by comparing how much profit they make with how much similar businesses make. Businesses use accounts to measure their profit and to find ways to increase their profitability (see accounts ratios in Unit 17).

Size and growth

Another way a business can judge if it is being successful or not is to measure by how much the firm is growing and whether or not it is increasing in size. There are four main ways of measuring how large a business is:

1. The number of people it employs.
2. The total value of the business's output/sales.
3. The amount of money the business has invested in capital equipment.
4. The stock market value, ie the number of shares issued multiplied by the value of each share.

It is recognised that a business is large if it scores highly in at least two of the above criteria. A business with a large amount of capital equipment and a high value of output would be considered large even if it employed only a few workers, eg chemical companies.

A business needs to keep a measurement of the above factors. If any of them are increasing, the business is growing in size and it is achieving success.

Turnover

Turnover is the amount of a good or service a business sells. It is calculated by multiplying the price of the good or service by the number sold.

Figure 3.4 Will every business grow to its full potential?

A business can measure its success by whether or not it is increasing its turnover from year to year. It can boost turnover either by increasing its sales or by charging a higher price.

Number of employees
A business can measure its success by the number of new jobs it creates or the number of people it employs.

Shareholders
Shareholders are individuals who invest in a business by buying shares in that business in return for a share of the profit, which is known as a **dividend**. The higher the dividend the shareholder receives the more they regard the business as being successful. For example, if business ABC pays a dividend of £50 for every £1000 worth of shares, and business XYZ pays a dividend of £100 for every £1000 worth of shares, then business XYZ is judged to have been more successful.

Consumer satisfaction
Businesses aim to sell high quality goods or services that consumers want and at a price they are prepared to pay. A business can judge if it is producing a high quality good or service and charging the right price by the reactions of its consumers. If the good or service is not of a high quality or the price is wrong, then consumers will stop buying it. If consumers are satisfied with the quality and the price of the good or service, then they will continue to buy it and the business can judge itself as having been successful.

Clearly many of these objectives and measurements of success are linked. If, for example, business XYZ is producing a good or service that consumers want, then its turnover will increase and so will its profits. XYZ will want to make more profits so it will expand the business by employing more workers and/or investing in more capital equipment. The more profit it makes, the higher the dividend it will be able to pay to its shareholders. XYZ has therefore achieved a number of its objectives and can be judged to have been successful in a number of ways.

If a business achieves any of the above objectives, it can say it has been successful. However, which of the above criteria it considers to be the most important depends on the individual business.

Revision Questions

1. Survival is a business ....
   a) promotion
   b) point of sale
   c) cost benefit
   d) objective

2. If a company sets growth as a business objective, this is known as
   a) expulsion
   b) reduction
   c) expansion
   d) depreciation

3. If a business was so successful that it caused a competing company to close down, it would have increased its
   a) liability
   b) ownership
   c) franchise
   d) market share

4. Last year Laura Smith achieved one of her main business objectives. What was this?
   a) to make a profit
   b) to keep machines in good working order
   c) to have a holiday
   d) to promote health and safety

5. Which of the following would a business use to measure how successful it was?
   a) turnover
   b) depreciation
   c) specialisation
   d) interdependence

Task

XYZ Ltd is a small clothing company that supplies a range of sport clothing to a number of retail outlets in the UK. A large order for a new range of sports wear has been received. The size of the order requires an increase in the normal level of output. The directors must choose between two alternative ways of increasing output:

- take on more employees and keep the existing equipment
- replace existing equipment with automated machinery.

1. a) State two objectives the directors would consider when deciding between increased staffing or investment in new automated machinery. (2)
   b) Explain the two objectives you have identified. (2)

The directors must decide between the two alternatives.

2. a) State which alternative you consider to be the most suitable for the company. (1)
   b) Give two reasons for your choice. (4)
   c) Briefly describe how the directors could put your chosen alternative into practice. (3)

Past Paper

A major business objective for Fuller & Brandon estate agents (a partnership) is survival, and for Harbon Estates Ltd, a property development company, it is profitability.

1. Explain how each business could achieve its objective. (6)

2. Identify and explain two ways in which these businesses can measure their success. Use a different measure for each. (6)

(Edexcel, 1998, Higher)

Exam tip

You need to learn the main business objectives and how they are measured, but you must also be able to select and apply them to different business types and situations.

Summary

If a business is going to be successful, it needs to set itself objectives and develop strategies that will help it to achieve those objectives. The business then needs to put in place some way of measuring how successful it has been in achieving those objectives. Businesses are therefore no different from individuals who set themselves targets, develop action plans and then have some way of judging whether or not they have achieved those targets.

Key terms

Dividend – part of a business's profits which is a reward to the shareholders for investing their money in the business

Market share – the proportion of the total sales of a market that a business holds

Profit – what is left after all of the costs of making and selling a good or service have been taken away from the sales revenue

Public services – those services which are provided for the public by the state, either free of charge or below the market price, eg National Health Service, education

Stakeholder – an individual that has an interest in the success of a business

Turnover – the value of sales over a period of time: number of sales × price

UNIT 3: BUSINESS OBJECTIVES AND JUDGING SUCCESS

UNIT 4

BUSINESS ACTIVITY AND THE EXTERNAL ENVIRONMENT

What you will learn

At the end of this unit you should understand:
- what is meant by the business environment
- the difference between internal and external environment
- the external factors that affect businesses
- how businesses are affected by the external environment.

In this section we will be looking at the effects which organisations and individuals have on a business and its ability to achieve its objectives. Businesses are influenced by both **internal** and **external** factors. Internal factors are those which can either help or constrain a business but over which they have control, such as finance, production, marketing and human resources. External factors are those factors outside of a business's control that have an effect on a business and its ability to achieve its objectives.

Task

Place the following factors under the correct heading of internal or external:

inflation, suppliers, unemployment, competitors, controllable, tax, population size, new technology, location, costs, advertising, uncontrollable, pressure group, environmental laws, workforce, training.

POLITICAL
National and local government policy and laws
National and local government spending and taxation
European Union
Pressure groups

BUSINESS

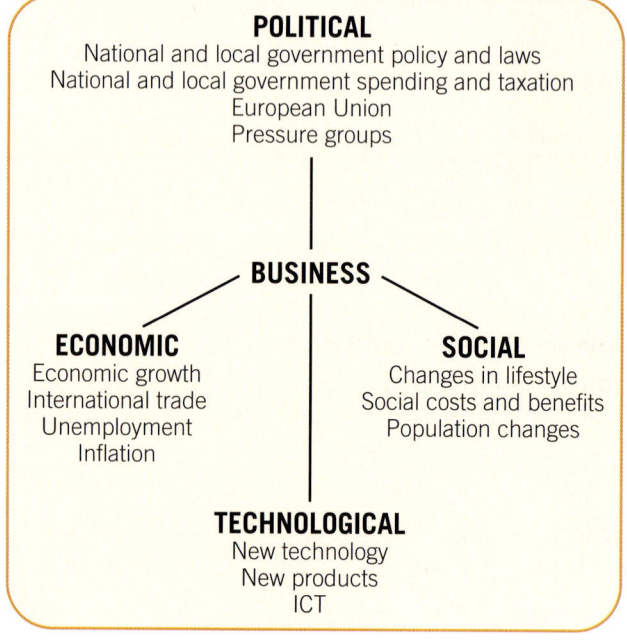

ECONOMIC
Economic growth
International trade
Unemployment
Inflation

SOCIAL
Changes in lifestyle
Social costs and benefits
Population changes

TECHNOLOGICAL
New technology
New products
ICT

Figure 4.1 External factors affecting business

The above factors can best be remembered as PEST. These factors provide opportunities for and impose constraints upon businesses and their ability to achieve their objectives.

POLITICAL INFLUENCES

Decisions made by central and local government affect businesses. Like businesses, governments have objectives which they hope to achieve. These objectives can be grouped as either social or economic.

Social objectives

- Ensure that people feel safe and secure by providing defence and law and order.
- Ensure that people have access to health care and decent housing.
- Ensure that the population is educated.
- Improve the quality of life of the population.

Economic objectives

- Aim for full employment.
- Maintain a low level of inflation.
- Achieve a stable balance of payments.
- Improve the standard of living of the population.

It is very difficult for the government to achieve all these objectives at once, so choices have to be made. In order to achieve its objectives the government can adopt three main types of policy:

1. Monetary – changes in the money supply and interest rates.
2. Fiscal – changes in taxation and spending.
3. Direct controls – legislation.

Monetary policy

The government controls the amount (supply) of money in the economy by controlling the banking system. The government attempts to influence the amount of money that the banks lend, who they lend it to and the price they charge (interest rates). One of the main purposes of using monetary policy is to reduce **inflation**. To do this, the government will increase **interest rates** which will reduce the amount of money people will borrow, which will then reduce the demand for products. Businesses will have to reduce their costs when demand falls, in order to attract buyers with lower prices.

Lower inflation will help consumers and businesses because neither will have to pay as much for the goods and services they want. For example, the raw materials which a business requires will fall in price and thus reduce the costs to the business; this will mean higher profits for the business or they may pass the savings onto the consumer in the form of lower prices. However, increasing interest rates will also have a harmful effect on businesses and consumers. Consumers will suffer as they will have less money to spend because their mortgage and credit card payments will increase. Businesses will suffer because the demand for their goods and services will decrease and the cost of their loan repayments will go up. Both of these factors will affect the business's profits.

If, on the other hand, the government wishes to reduce unemployment by increasing demand, it will reduce interest rates. People will borrow more money which they will spend on buying goods and services. To meet the increase in demand businesses will have to employ more people and unemployment will fall.

So, although the government is constantly trying to make the best decisions for the economy, consumers and businesses, its actions can have both helpful and harmful effects.

Figure 4.2 Shoppers spending money

> **? Past Paper**
>
> Harbon Estates property development company has built a housing estate called Sleepy Hollow. As the sale of properties in Sleepy Hollow goes ahead, interest rates rise.
>
> Assess two effects on Harbon Estates Ltd of a rise in interest rates. (6)
>
> *(Edexcel, 1998, Foundation/Higher)*

Fiscal policy

The government attempts to influence demand in the economy through its spending and taxation policy. If the government lowers taxes, people will have more money to spend on goods and services. This will increase demand which means businesses will have to produce more and will therefore need to employ more people. Clearly if the government increases taxes, it will have the opposite effect.

There are a number of taxes the government can increase or decrease. These can be either **direct** (taken directly from income or profit) or **indirect** (placed on goods and services).

Direct taxes

- Corporation tax – a tax paid by companies on their profits.
- Income tax – a tax paid by private individuals on the amount they earn. However, sole traders and partnerships are taxed at income tax rates rather than at corporation tax rates.
- National insurance – paid by both employer and employee as a proportion of an employee's income. This revenue contributes towards the social security system, eg job seeker's allowance.

Indirect taxes

- Value added tax – this is payable at each stage of production on the value added by the business. This tax is usually passed on to consumers through higher prices.
- Excise duties – these are additional taxes on top of VAT placed on certain goods such as alcohol, tobacco and petrol.
- Customs duties – additional taxes on imported goods.

If the government increases indirect taxes, this makes goods and services more expensive and will usually lead to a fall in sales. If the government increases direct taxes, businesses and consumers will have less money to spend and this will lead to a fall in demand for goods and services.

The government can also influence demand through its spending policies. If the government increases its spending on building more roads, schools and hospitals it will need to employ people to help build them and work in them. This will help reduce unemployment and mean people will have more money to spend on goods and services.

The government informs the country of its spending and taxation intentions every year in its budget.

> **Task**
>
> Find out the current rates for the following taxes and say what effect they will have on businesses:
>
> - corporation tax
> - income tax
> - value added tax.

Direct controls

The government can also affect businesses through legislation and policies which have a direct influence on businesses and their decisions. For example, through its regional policy the current government is attempting to influence businesses to locate in areas of high unemployment by offering incentives such as tax breaks, employment subsidies and rent-free or low-rent premises. The government also tries to encourage businesses to employ and train the young and unemployed through schemes such as the New Deal; the government will help towards paying the starting wages of any young or unemployed person a business takes on. Another direct control is minimum wage and maximum working hour's legislation, which sets the minimum wage any business can pay its workers and the maximum number of hours they can make them work.

The government also helps businesses by offering them guidance and information. It helps small businesses by providing advice and guidance on European Union developments. As support for those businesses which export, the government, for a fee, guarantees to pay for any losses a business may incur in the process of exporting goods.

> **Task**
>
> Find out the current rates for the minimum wage and maximum number of hours that can be worked in a week. Describe and explain the effects they will have on businesses.

Local authorities

Local authorities are layers of local government such as county or district councils. Representatives of local government are known as councillors and they are elected by the local people to represent them and their interests. Local authorities provide services such as education, leisure, housing, refuse collection and social services. They are funded by central government, council and business taxes, and revenue they receive from the services they offer.

Local authorities influence businesses in a number of ways:

- They are responsible for the upkeep of the infrastructure of the area, ie maintaining the roads, police and fire services.
- They offer grants and loans to businesses to locate in their area.
- They enforce laws which affect businesses, such as consumer protection and planning permission for new buildings or changes in use of existing businesses.

Local authorities will attempt to assist businesses as much as possible, because businesses create jobs and bring revenue into an area which the local authority can use to improve the social welfare of the local population.

Planning permission

One of the biggest influences local authorities have on businesses is the granting or denying of planning permission.

If a business wants to build a factory, office block or shops, it has to obtain permission from the local authority. The same applies to a business which wants to change the use of a building, eg from a clothes shop to a restaurant. Planning decisions are taken by councillors who are advised on policies and decisions by appointed planning officers. At one time there were long delays in dealing with planning applications and many were rejected. Today the planning process has been speeded up and local authorities work in partnership with local businesses. By speeding up the process and looking on applications more favourably, local authorities recognise that they will attract more businesses to the area, which will create more jobs, increase their revenue from business taxes and help boost the local economy.

Many business people and individuals object to planning permission as they believe that it is local government interference and that they know what is best for their business. However, planning permission exists to encourage economic growth while at the same time protecting the environment and the heritage of an area.

Legal environment

The government and the European Union (EU) have introduced many laws which affect the relationship between business, consumers and the environment. The main purposes of these laws are:

Figure 4.3 Health and safety in the workplace

1. To protect consumers from unfair practices.
2. To protect workers in the workplace.
3. To make sure that there is free competition between businesses so that they do not gain an unfair advantage over their rivals.
4. To protect the environment.

Consumers and the law

To stop businesses from providing misleading information about or selling faulty goods or services, the government has passed a number of laws to protect consumers.

Trades Description Act

This makes it a criminal offence to describe goods and services incorrectly. If a watch is described as being shock-proof, water-resistant and made in Switzerland, then that is exactly what it must be.

Sale of Goods Act

When you buy a good you enter into a legal contract with the seller. It is the seller and not the manufacturer who must deal with any complaint you may have. The seller must make sure that the goods that are sold are of a satisfactory and merchantable quality. This means that they must be as described, they must not be damaged or broken, and must be able to do what they are supposed to do. If a pair of walking boots is described as being of real leather, water-proof and strong enough to last for 1000 miles, they should be made of leather, keep your feet dry and last for that distance.

Supply of goods and services

This has the same purpose as the Sale of Goods Act, but also applies to services.

Figure 4.4 Consumer rights

Weights and Measures Act
This act makes it illegal for a business to sell short measures or goods which are underweight. A pint of beer should be a pint of beer and 500 grammes of sausages should be 500 grammes of sausages. Inspectors have the right to test weighing and measuring equipment to ensure that they are correctly calibrated.

Consumer Protection Act
Businesses are liable for any damage which their defective goods might cause. The act ensures that goods are safe to use and not likely to cause injury or loss of life, eg faulty gas heaters.

The Food and Drugs Act
It is a criminal offence to sell food or drink which is unfit for human consumption, or on which the labelling wrongly describes the contents or misleads people about the quality or nutritional value of food.

Consumer Credit Act
This states that any business giving credit must be licensed. Consumers must know how much extra they are paying in interest, and there must be a 'cooling off' period during which goods bought on credit can be returned.

Unsolicited Goods and Services Act
Businesses are prevented from delivering unordered goods and then demanding payment.

Fair Trading Act
This act set up the Office of Fair Trading whose main aims are to:

- inform consumers of their rights
- prosecute businesses which break the law
- recommend to the Monopolies and Mergers Commission any businesses that need to be investigated.

Most consumer legislation is enforced by local councils through departments such as the Trading Standards Department and Environmental Health Department. By introducing these laws, the government is forcing businesses to accept their responsibilities to consumers. Compliance with these laws will lead to increased costs for businesses but will ensure they gain consumer satisfaction by providing high quality products and high standards of service.

> **Task**
>
> Produce an advert for a pair of trainers. Annotate your advert to show which consumer laws it is obeying and how.

Employment and the Law
To ensure fair treatment of workers and responsible behaviour by employers and employees in the workplace, the government has introduced a number of laws.

Health and Safety at Work Act
This law requires employers to be responsible for the health, safety and welfare of employees in the workplace by ensuring that equipment is safe, that employees know how to handle, store and transport articles and substances, and that they are correctly trained and supervised in all of the above.

Factories Act
Offices, shops and factories must provide the minimum requirements for safety, such as adequate lighting, toilets and fire escapes.

Sex Discrimination Act
It is illegal to discriminate against anyone because of their sex or marital status with regard to recruitment, terms and conditions of service, training, promotion and dismissal.

Race Relations Act
It is also illegal to discriminate against someone on the basis of race, ethnic group or colour.

Redundancy Payments Act
Employees who have worked for a business continuously for five years part-time or three years full-time are entitled to redundancy pay of one week for every year worked.

Figure 4.5 A man and woman doing the same job

Equal Pay Act
An employee who does similar work to someone of the opposite sex is entitled to equal rates of pay and conditions. This act is meant to give men and women equal pay for the same job.

Employment Protection Act
This act protects employees against unfair dismissal. Before an employee can be dismissed, employers must follow an agreed discipline procedure. For minor offences (eg lateness), employees will receive a written or verbal warning. Offences which can lead to instant dismissal (eg theft) will be listed.

Competition and the Law
The main legislation influencing the conduct of businesses is competition policy. These laws and controls ensure that businesses are run legally and fairly.

Restrictive Trades Practices Act
Businesses are prevented from:

- agreeing to fix prices, eg petrol companies agreeing on a set price for a litre of petrol
- restricting output, which would reduce supply and therefore artificially inflate the price, eg farmers agreeing to limit the amount of milk they supply
- dividing the market up between them, eg supermarkets agreeing to stay out of each others areas.

Resale Prices Act
It is illegal for manufacturers to fix the price at which retailers can sell their products. Manufacturers can recommend a price but not enforce it, eg supermarkets are allowed to sell jeans at lower prices than those recommended by the manufacturer.

Fair Trading Act
This act set up the Office of Fair Trading and the Monopolies and Mergers Commission. Their roles are to ensure that competition takes place between businesses and to stop restrictive practices.

The Monopolies and Mergers Commission investigates businesses which wish to merge and result in a monopoly being created. A monopoly situation is one where one business controls 25% or more of the total supply of a particular product or service. A business having such control could limit supply, raise prices and offer a poor quality product or service. This would leave the consumer with two choices – either buy the good or service or go without. This situation is clearly against the public interest and would result in both consumers and businesses suffering. To guard against this, the government will intervene through the Monopolies and Mergers Commission to make sure that any merger or monopoly that is against the public interest does not go ahead.

Many privatised businesses such as British Telecom have a monopoly. The government has attempted to ensure that other businesses are free to compete in the telecommunications business so that prices are driven down and quality is driven up for consumers. The government has also set up organisations to monitor these businesses and deal with any complaints from the public; eg Oftel investigates British Telecom, Ofwat investigates water companies.

It is important that businesses operate in a controlled or competitive market to stop dominant businesses from charging low prices in order to price out their competitors. This would mean less choice for consumers and could lead to that business dominating the market and disregarding consumers' views. Competition also ensures that businesses have to minimise their costs and invest in developing better and new products in order to survive.

Environment and the Law

Today the government, consumers and businesses are much more aware of the environment and how we are damaging it. Some of the main environmental concerns are global warming, acid rain, depletion of the ozone layer, loss of wildlife and natural habitats, air, land and water pollution. Many of the causes of these problems are the activities of businesses in providing consumers with their wants and needs.

Greater environmental awareness of consumers means that many businesses are adopting more eco-friendly practices to ensure that they maintain consumer loyalty. To help protect the environment the government has introduced the following acts:

The Environmental Protection Act

Under this act businesses have to ensure that they are using those methods which will best reduce the amount of land, air and water pollution. Failure to do so will result in fines.

Clean Air Act

The emission of smoke from factories and homes is controlled.

The European Union

It is not only the UK government which influences businesses but also the European Union. The European Union is a market of 350 million people, currently made up of 15 member states. The United Kingdom joined the EU (formerly known as The European Economic Community) in 1973 in order to gain from free trade between the member countries. This means that there are no quotas or tariffs on goods and services traded between countries in the EU. However, a common external tariff is placed on all goods and services which are imported into the EU. In 1992 a Single European Market was created which allowed businesses to take advantage of three important freedoms:

1. Freedom of movement of people and labour – UK residents can live and work anywhere in the EU.
2. Freedom of movement of goods and services – UK businesses can sell their goods and services anywhere in the EU without red tape or tariffs.
3. Freedom of movement of capital – no limit on how much money financial institutions or individuals can take in and out of other EU countries.

? Past Paper

Docdel plc is a car dealership. Customers buying cars from Docdel plc have legal protection. Explain how the following Acts protect these customers:

- Sale of Goods Act
- Trades Description Act (6)

(Edexcel, 1997, Foundation)

Resort hotels are part of the business activities of Flyaway plc. Some of the hotels are based in the United Kingdom.

Explain how United Kingdom government legislation controls Flyaway plc's relationship with the hotel employees and customers. (11)

(Edexcel, 2001, Higher)

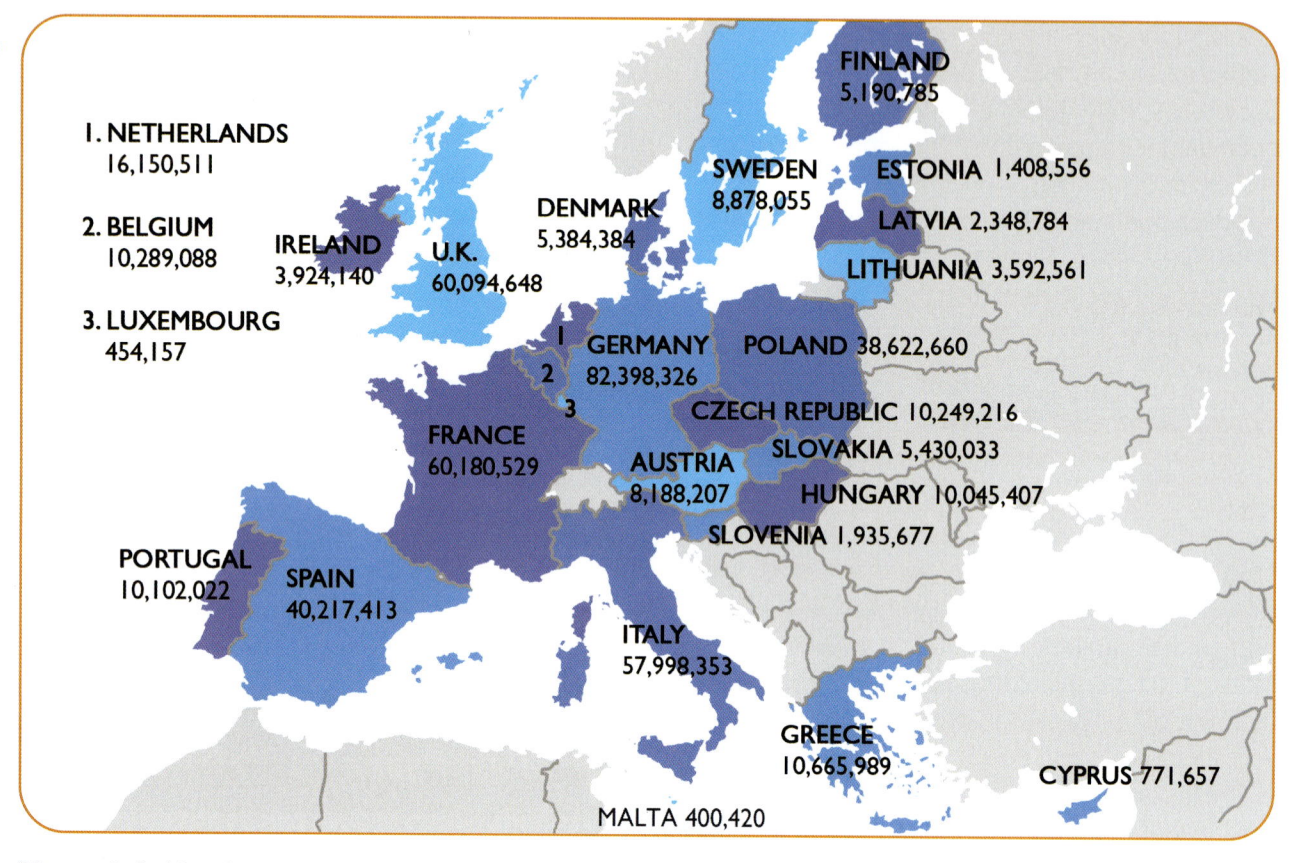

Figure 4.6 Member countries of the European Union

There is a wide range of rules and regulations placed on all businesses trading in the EU, some of which benefit UK businesses while others cause problems. Some benefits of membership include the following points:

- Businesses have access to a large single market which may result in greater sales and increased profit.
- There is protection from competition from non-EU members.
- There are grants and loans available to improve infrastructure, relocate businesses to areas of high unemployment and help with training.
- Merger opportunities may arise with other EU businesses.

However, there are also drawbacks:

- Greater competition may mean inefficient businesses lose their share of the market and go out of business.
- Increased EU regulation leads to more bureaucracy (red tape) which increases costs.
- Laws to protect consumers against additives in foods and ensure greater competition can lead to an increase in costs.
- Huge subsidies paid to farmers as part of the Common Agricultural Policy lead to higher taxes.

Single currency

All of the member states of the EU, with the exception of the UK, Greece, Sweden and Denmark, have joined the European Monetary Union. This is where all the countries taking part have agreed to a single currency called the euro. The prices of goods and services in those countries will be given in the euro. The advantages of joining the single currency are:

- Travellers, tourists and businesses will save money as they will not have to pay commission to change their currency into other currencies.

- It will be easier to compare prices between countries, eg compare the price of cars in France with those in Germany.
- Stability for businesses. If exchange rates fluctuate, businesses do not know how much goods from abroad will cost or how their goods will be priced in foreign countries.

The disadvantages are:

- Businesses have to convert all of their prices, tills and cash machines to the new notes and coins.
- Some businesses may take advantage of this change and charge higher prices.
- It takes time for businesses, consumers and workers to get used to the new currency.
- Floating exchange rates allow countries to devalue their currency (eg the price of the pound would go down compared to other currencies) in order to make their exports more competitive.

There is much debate about whether or not the UK should be in Europe or join the single currency. Many people believe that the EU brings many benefits to businesses and offers greater protection for consumers and workers, and the UK should therefore be taking a more active and enthusiastic role in the EU. However, many other people believe that the UK is losing the ability to govern itself and make its own decisions. They believe that the EU interferes too much in the running of businesses and people's lives, and that decisions which affect both businesses, consumers and workers are being made by 'faceless bureaucrats in Brussels'.

Task

Produce a poster which shows either the reasons why the UK should be in the EU and the single currency, or the reasons why it should not.

Pressure groups

A pressure group is a group of people with similar views and beliefs; the group forms an organisation which tries to influence government, businesses and individuals. They can be local, national or international. A local pressure group might be a group of anxious parents who are objecting to the local school closing. An example of a national pressure group is the National Society for the Prevention of Cruelty to Children (NSPCC), which brings pressure to bear on the government about children's issues. An international pressure group is Friends of the Earth (FoE), which has made governments, businesses and individuals aware of the damage being done to the environment.

To achieve their aims, pressure groups use a number of methods:

- organising public meetings
- advertising their cause
- distributing leaflets and posters
- lobbying local councillors and MPs
- organising boycotts of products
- organising petitions and presenting them to local/national government
- organising demonstrations or sit-ins.

The main weapon of pressure groups is publicity. Businesses do not like negative publicity as it gives them a bad image and could lead to consumers boycotting their products, thus reducing their sales and profits. On the other hand, if they respond to

Figure 4.7 A demonstration by Friends of the Earth

pressure placed on them, their costs may increase which will reduce their profits.

Businesses also know that being seen to be eco-friendly and socially aware is a good marketing tool, so they will have their own publicity campaigns to persuade consumers that they are responding to the concerns of pressure groups.

> **Task**
>
> **Campaign Against the Incineration of Rubbish (CAIR)**
> The local community have just become aware that an Industrial Waste Company (IWC) wishes to build an industrial waste incinerator in the village. You and other local people want to stop this from going ahead. Describe and explain the steps you would take to stop the incinerator from being built.

ECONOMIC INFLUENCES

Economic growth

A country can measure how well it is doing by measuring how much it has earned. It does this by adding up the total value of goods and services it has produced. This is known as the Gross Domestic Product (GDP). Although the UK's GDP is constantly increasing, it does fluctuate.

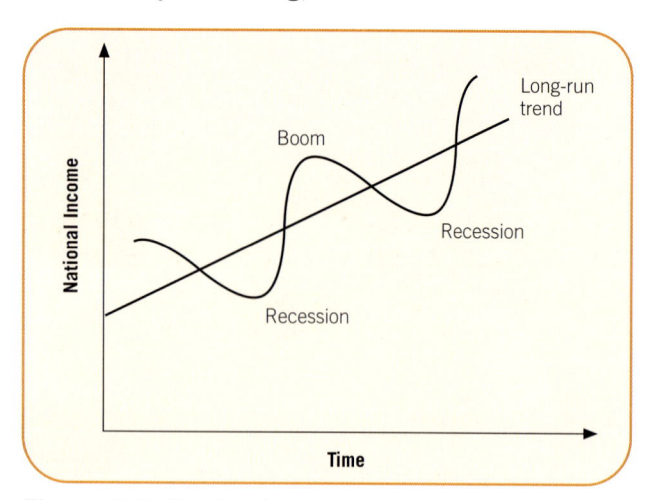

Figure 4.8 The business cycle

Figure 4.8 shows that the economy goes through booms and recessions. The effects of these fluctuations on business are clear. During booms, when economic growth is high, demand for goods and services is also high which means increased sales and therefore increased profits. During a recession, when economic growth is slow, demand for goods and services is also low; sales decrease so there is increased competition for consumers which places a downward pressure on prices and therefore a business's profits. Some businesses will make losses and go out of business during a recession.

Inflation

Inflation occurs when there is a general increase in the price of goods and services. The government measures inflation by taking a 'basket' of goods and services which are bought by most people each month and monitors their price from one month to the next. Items which are included in this basket are: bread, milk, petrol, heating and lighting. If inflation is said to be at 5%, it means that on average goods and services are 5% more expensive than the previous year. Governments try to keep inflation low as rising prices can affect businesses in a number of ways:

- The price of raw materials will increase, which will mean an increase in business costs and therefore a reduction in profits.
- Higher prices will lead to consumers buying less or buying cheaper imports, which will result in a decrease in sales and profits.
- The price of goods and services which are exported will increase, which will make them less competitive. Those businesses which sell their goods and services abroad will see a fall in sales and profits.
- Businesses are reluctant to invest in times of high inflation as they are unsure of what might happen to their sales and costs. They therefore become cautious about going ahead with any major investment projects.
- The wage bill for businesses will increase as workers demand larger pay increases to keep up with inflation.

In order to help businesses, the government attempts to keep inflation low mainly through the use of monetary policy.

> **Task**
>
> Find out the current rate of inflation. Is the current rate good or bad for businesses? Explain your answer.

Unemployment

Unemployment occurs when people who want jobs cannot find them. There are a number of causes of unemployment:

- Structural – the structure of the economy changes. For example, coal mines have closed, causing many miners who do not have the correct skills to do other type of work to become unemployed.
- Seasonal – people who work on short-term contracts are unemployed at certain times of the year, eg fruit pickers, holiday representatives.
- Frictional – when people are between jobs, ie they have left one job and are waiting to start another.
- Cyclical – unemployment that occurs when the economy is in a recession and there is a lack of demand for goods and services.

If there is high unemployment in an area then people without jobs will not have much money to spend. People in work may be worried about losing their jobs and will be unwilling to spend money. This will lead to a decrease in demand, which will result in a fall in sales and a reduction in profits.

However, high unemployment can also help businesses as it gives them a wider choice of employees and makes existing employees more cooperative to changes in working practices as they will be worried about losing their jobs. In an area of high unemployment, a business will receive a large number of applicants for new jobs. They will even be able to offer low wages and still attract applicants. If employees are worried about losing their jobs, they will be less likely to ask for higher wages or improved working conditions.

> **Task**
>
> Find out the current level of unemployment in your area. Describe and explain the effects this will have on local businesses.

International trade

International trade occurs when businesses buy and sell goods and services from other countries. Goods and services which are bought *from* other countries are known as **imports**, and goods and services which are sold *to* other countries are known as **exports**. The advantages of international trade for a country are a wider selection of goods and services for consumers at competitive prices, and larger markets for UK businesses. The record of the UK's trade with other countries is known as the **balance of payments**.

> Balance of payments
> = revenue from exports − spending on imports

A balance of payments *surplus* means that a country is earning more from its exports than it is spending on its imports. A balance of payments *deficit* means it is spending more on imports than it is earning from its exports.

International trade offers both threats and opportunities for businesses. Opportunities include the following factors:

- Businesses will benefit from increased sales and higher profits by selling in more markets.
- Rather than rely on UK suppliers, they may import more competitively priced supplies from abroad.

The threats include:

- Competition from foreign businesses may take sales away from UK businesses.

Figure 4.9 International trade

- Language problems.
- Knowing and obeying a different country's laws.
- Costs of selling abroad, eg transportation, overseas depots, sales agents.
- Lack of knowledge about foreign markets and consumers.
- Fluctuations in exchange rates.

Just like individuals or businesses, the country has to pay its way and make sure that what it spends can be paid for out of its earnings. If the country's balance of payments is in deficit, then the difference between the value of imports and exports has to be made up by borrowing from other countries. Just like individuals or businesses, the country cannot keep borrowing to make up the shortfall, so over time exports have to equal imports. The government tries to help and encourage businesses in a number of ways:

- Putting up barriers to trade so it is more difficult for foreign businesses to sell their goods and services, eg quotas, tariffs, embargo.
- Giving subsidies to UK businesses to help them compete with foreign businesses.
- Information and advice on foreign markets through the British Overseas Trade Board.
- Organising trade fairs in foreign countries which promote UK goods and services.
- Offering an insurance scheme which guarantees any losses a business may incur from trading in another country.
- Favourable exchange rates.

Exchange rates

Businesses which sell goods and services abroad want to be paid in their own currency. A British business selling car parts to a French car company will want to be paid in pounds; a French car company selling cars to a UK car dealership would want to be paid in euros. Businesses therefore have to be able to buy other currencies. The price of one currency in terms of another is known as the **exchange rate**. If you go to France for a holiday you would need euros. If you spent £100 and received 200 euros, this would mean an exchange rate of £1 = 2 euros. The same concept applies to businesses.

As with most goods and services, the price of currencies depends on demand and supply. If the demand for a country's currency is high because that country has sold a large number of exports and/or many people are going on holiday there, then the price of that currency will increase. If the demand for the currency is low for the opposite reasons to those above, then the price of that currency will fall. If you study the tables in the tasks below you will see the effects of changes in the exchange rate on businesses.

Task

Chidley Clothing Ltd is a British company that makes and sells jeans to many countries, including France. They sell their jeans for £100.

Exchange rate	Price of jeans	Price in France
£1 = 4 euros High	£100	400 euros
£1 = 3 euros	£100	300 euros
£1 = 2 euros	£100	200 euros
£1 = 1 euros Low	£100	100 euros

1. Which exchange rate would Chidley Clothing Ltd prefer? Explain your answer.

Chidley Clothing's biggest rival is Houston Clothing, an American company that makes and sells jeans to many countries, including the UK. They sell their jeans for $100.

Exchange rate		Price of jeans	Price in UK
£1 = $4	High	$100	£25
£1 = $3		$100	£33
£1 = $2		$100	£50
£1 = $1	Low	$100	£100

2. Which exchange rate would Chidley Clothing prefer this time? Explain your answer.

If the value of the pound is £1 = $2, this means that a good which cost £1 to produce in the UK would sell for $2 in the USA. If the pound fell to £1 = $1, this would mean that it would now sell for $1, resulting in exports revenue decreasing. If we take the same changes in exchange rates and look at what happens to imports, we can see that a good costing $2 to produce in the USA would sell for £1 in the UK. After the fall in the value of the pound that $2 good would now cost £2; the cost of imports would rise. UK businesses would therefore prefer to see exchange rates low, as the price of their goods and services will become cheaper and make them more competitive. Also, as the exchange rate falls, imports will become more expensive and encourage UK consumers to buy UK products. The only disadvantage to this is that if UK businesses import raw materials these will become more expensive, thereby increasing costs.

In general, a *lowering* of the pound means that UK exports are cheaper; UK businesses should sell more and imports will become more expensive, so consumers will buy fewer imported goods and more British. Equally, a *rise* in the value of the pound will make UK exported goods and services more expensive so less will be sold, and imports cheaper so more will be bought.

Figure 4.10 Foreign currencies

Exam tip

When answering questions, remember that political and economic factors are both an opportunity and a threat to UK businesses.

Past Paper

The sales director of Nocha Ltd (the ice cream manufacturer) wants to promote and sell the company's products abroad. The directors are seeking advice from the UK government to help them to export their products.

1. a) Explain why the sales director will find it easier to export to another member of the EU, rather than to a country outside the EU. (3)

UNIT 4: BUSINESS ACTIVITY AND THE EXTERNAL ENVIRONMENT

b) Analyse two problems which the sales director must overcome when promoting and selling the company's products overseas. (6)

c) State three reasons why the UK government would want to support the sales director's plan to export. (3)

d) Describe one other way in which the UK government influences Nocha Ltd. (4)

SOCIAL INFLUENCES

Society and businesses have a big influence on each other. Businesses not only influence people and their lives but are also influenced by people and their lifestyles. Social influences on businesses come under two headings:

- demographic
- lifestyle.

Demographic effects

Demography is the study of a country's population. Changes in the size and structure of a country's population will clearly have a big effect on business activity.

If a country's population is increasing due to an increase in the birth rate, a fall in the death rate or a higher number of immigrants than emigrants, the effects on business will be:

- an increase in demand for goods and services
- an increase in the amount of labour available
- an increase in investment by businesses to meet the increase in demand.

On the other hand, a fall in population will have the following effects:

- a decrease in demand for goods and services
- a decrease in the amount of labour available.

If the population is increasing, more goods and services will be demanded. To meet this increase in demand businesses will have to employ more workers and invest in more capital equipment. If demand increases, sales will increase and businesses will make more profit. If businesses have more workers to choose from, they will be able to select the right person for the job; because more people will be looking for work, businesses will be able to place a downward pressure on wages and therefore keep control of their costs. If the population is declining, then the opposite will happen.

Population structure

The structure of a country's population also has a big effect on businesses. The structure of a population can be shown in a population pyramid. This shows what percentage of people are in each age group and gender.

Businesses are interested in the number of people in each age group and gender because it will determine the demand for their goods or

Figure 4.11 Demand and supply of goods and services

services and the types of goods and services they should be offering. For example, in the UK the largest age group is the over-50s, who are known as the 'baby boomers', the generation who were part of the baby boom after the Second World War. If this is the largest age group then this will be the largest market segment. Businesses will therefore gear their goods, services and marketing campaigns to this market segment. Walk into a high street music shop and you will notice the number of compact discs that are on offer from artists whose records originally came out on vinyl! Sales of compact discs of artists who attract 10–20-year-olds are down because this age group is at its smallest since the 1960s. The music industry has changed and is aiming its products at the older generation.

If the birth rate is increasing, the demand for nappies and other baby products will increase, resulting in the sales and profits of those businesses involved in providing goods and services for babies and mothers. A more elderly population will mean a higher demand for goods and services that the elderly use, eg retirement homes.

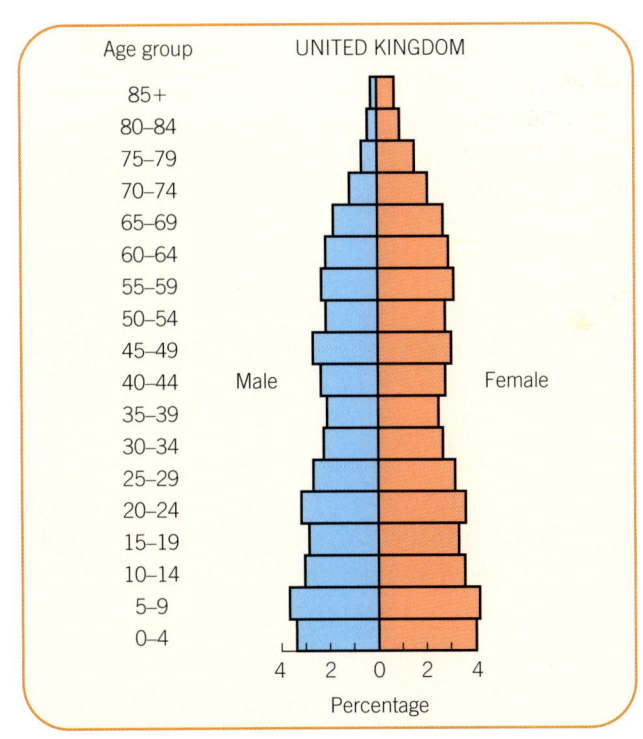

Figure 4.13 Population structure

Task

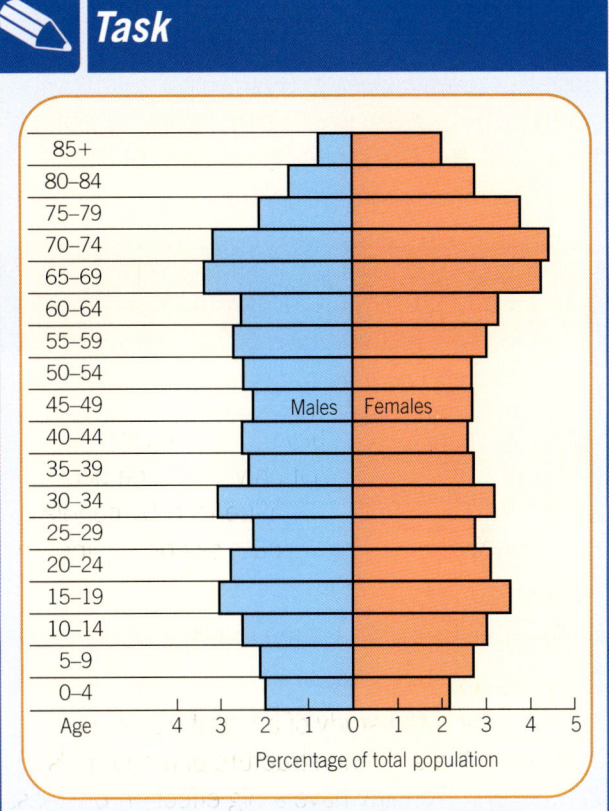

Figure 4.13 Skater Park or indoor bowling green?

Study the above population pyramid for an area in the UK. A local leisure company is deciding between opening a skater park for teenagers or an indoor bowling green for the over 50s in this area. Using the information in the population pyramid, say which one you would choose and why.

The size and structure of the population in a local area will also have an effect on business. For example, the population of the north east of England is declining, mainly due to the loss of jobs in the traditional industries of mining and shipbuilding. Young people are moving, mainly to the south east, in the search for work; older people, because of their age and ties to the region, are not. The effect of this internal migration on the north east is that the overall demand for goods and services is falling, but in particular those which the 18–30 age group demand, resulting in a fall in sales and a reduction in profit which may lead to those businesses closing. Businesses will therefore locate in those areas where demand is highest, eg the south east. The social consequences of this population movement for both areas are very high.

> **? Extension task**
>
> *Describe and explain the effects of the movement of population from the north east to the south east on the people and businesses in both areas.*

Lifestyles

The way people behave when they buy goods and services influences businesses. People's beliefs, values, tastes and attitudes are constantly changing, and businesses have to react to these changes or go out of business. For example, people are more aware of the environment and the exploitation of less economically developed countries. Businesses recognise the importance of having a good image and are therefore showing more social responsibility and being more environmentally aware.

A good example of this is The Body Shop, which is against animal testing for products, pays a fair price for resources bought from underdeveloped countries, ensures that the pay and conditions of workers of its suppliers are of an agreed standard, and uses recyclable materials in its packaging. Although adopting these policies has increased the cost of their products and made them more expensive than their competitors, Body Shop has seen the demand for its products increase because people want to show that they care for the environment and their fellow human beings. The Co-op bank is another organisation which advertises that it will not invest in projects which damage the environment or exploit the less economically developed countries.

Figure 4.14 Social issues

Nike is a business which is having to publicly explain and justify the wages and conditions of the workers in its factories in less economically developed countries, because it is worried that consumers may boycott their products.

People's attitudes change over time. For example, at one time society held that a 'woman's place was in the home'. This is no longer the case as women become more and more prevalent in the workplace. This has led to a wider choice of workers for businesses and also means an increase in demand for those businesses which provide childcare.

Education, travel, television and cinema can also change people's tastes and fashion. However, what is popular one month may well be out of fashion the next. This is particularly true of the clothing businesses that have to keep up with current trends and fashions or see their sales fall. It is difficult for businesses to spot changes in tastes, but those that do will see their sales increase and profits rise. Other businesses will jump on the band wagon and start offering similar goods or services.

> **Task**
>
> List five products that you bought last year but which are no longer in fashion. Describe what has happened to the businesses which supply those products.

Social costs and benefits

Any action we take has costs and benefits for both ourselves and those around us. For example, when a person is deciding to take up smoking they weigh up the costs and benefits to themselves of smoking and then make a decision. These are the private costs and benefits because they are private to the individual. However, if they decide to smoke, this decision will affect other people. These are known as the **social costs and benefits** because they affect people in the community socially.

> **Task**
>
> Produce a table of the costs and benefits smoking brings to a private individual and the social costs and benefits of smoking to the community as a whole.

Business decisions have an effect on the business (private costs and benefits) and the community (social costs and benefits). A business may believe that its only interest is in making a profit and that the local community interests are of little importance, but a business needs planning permission before it can expand, build or change the use of buildings or factories. It is therefore important for a business to be aware of the costs and benefits to the community if it wishes to minimise local objections to its plans and gain planning permission.

If, for example, a business which makes glass ornaments decides to expand its business by building a new factory, there are costs and benefits to the business and society. The private costs and benefits to the business can usually be calculated financially, ie the cost of building the factory and the profit made from the new factory. The costs and benefits to the community are called the social costs and benefits and are more difficult to calculate in financial terms. Some of the social costs and benefits of building a new factory are presented in the table below.

> **Task**
>
> An industrial waste company (IWC) wants to build an industrial waste incinerator on an area of open space next to a primary school and housing estate. The new incinerator will create over 200 new jobs in an area of high unemployment and solve the problem of what to do with the domestic, industrial and health waste generated by the town.

TABLE 4.1 Social costs and benefits of building a new factory

Costs	Benefits
Loss of open, green space – damage to wildlife	Increase in jobs for local people during construction and in the new factory
Pollution, visual and air – ugly factory buildings, fumes and gases from factory	Local businesses will benefit from improved trade
Increased traffic	Pleasant landscaped grounds

Write a letter to the planning committee explaining why they should give you permission to build the incinerator. Remember to come up with counter arguments or measures to appease any local objections.

If you were the planning committee, what might be your decision? Write a letter to the company informing them of the decision you have come to and why.

? Past Paper

Some local residents are unhappy about losing green belt land and have formed the 'No Sleepy Hollow Here', pressure group to campaign against the development. Despite this opposition, the local authority has given Delta Homes plc permission to build the housing estate on this land.

1. Explain three reasons why the local authority might have given Delta Homes plc permission to build on this land. (6)

(Edexcel, 1998, Foundation)

The 'Sleepy Hollow' development is located in green belt land, previously used for agriculture.

Many local residents were against this housing development. They formed the 'No Sleepy Hollow Here' pressure group. The local authority granted planning permission because it was keen to see the development take place.

2. Examine the likely costs and benefits of the 'Sleepy Hollow' development for:
   - the local community
   - the local authority. (12)

(Edexcel, 1998, Higher)

TECHNOLOGICAL INFLUENCES

Technological developments have resulted in the growth of some businesses and the decline of others, and have forced industries to adapt. Two of the main technological developments that influence businesses are new products (eg mobile phones) and new processes (eg automated assembly lines).

New products create new demand. Many of the products we use every day are relatively new, such as mobile phones, satellite television, computers and electronic games. New products lead to increased sales and larger profits. Whole new industries have been created, opening up new markets and creating new jobs. However, the introduction of new products has led to some products becoming obsolete, for example, what has happened to those businesses which used to make typewriters? It is important that businesses invest in research and develop new products if they are to compete with other businesses, open up new markets and create new jobs.

New production techniques such as Just in Time, Computer Aided Design (CAD), Electronic Point of Sale (EPOS) and use of robots in the assembly process have benefited businesses in a number of ways:

- Reduction in storage space and costs as materials are available at the right place and the right time.
- Increased output as new technology and techniques allow businesses to increase production.
- Increased labour productivity as new techniques and technology means individual workers can produce more.
- Increased quality as robots produce products of a high standard time after time.
- Automation has led to a decrease in the number of workers and a reduction in costs. Robots do not need tea breaks or holidays and can work for 24 hours per day.

New technology and new techniques are expensive to buy and install, and therefore can initially

Figure 4.15 An example of new technology

increase costs. The use of robots in the factory and the introduction of new information and communication technology in the office have led to many factory workers and office staff becoming redundant. However, the demand for skilled workers who can manage and control new technology has increased.

Businesses and the government are putting increasing amounts of money into education and training to equip the workforce with the skills that will be in demand as the rate of technological change increases.

E-commerce

E-commerce, or selling on the internet, is regarded by many as the new industrial revolution and it is believed that any businesses that do not trade online will be left behind by their competitors. Over the last ten years the number of people buying and selling on the internet has increased. Businesses put details of their products on their websites; customers can then browse through either a particular product range to see who offers the best deal or through the products of a particular business. If a customer wishes to buy a product, they can order it online and pay using their credit or debit card. Once the products have been ordered and paid for, they are then delivered. The most popular online products are books, music, holidays and foodstuffs. The benefits to businesses of selling in this way are:

- Small businesses that produce specialist goods can sell them anywhere in the world, thus increasing their market.
- Costs can be reduced because the cost of downloading information is paid for by the internet user not the provider, so items such as sales brochures no longer need to be produced.
- Sales staff are no longer needed as the information is online instead.

Task

Try and find out the names of as many businesses as you can that offer online shopping. Include their online addresses and what they sell.

Past Paper

The National Farmers' Union communicates with farmers and other interested people through its website, which has an e-mail facility.

What are the advantages to farmers of communicating electronically via the website and e-mail? (5)

(Edexcel, 2002, Foundation)

Task – Case Study

Read the case study and find as many external influences as you can. Place each one in one of the four categories – PEST. Explain what effect these have had on business.

A DYING INDUSTRY!

Smoking could soon be banned in all public places across the European Union, Brussels warned. Legal action against bars or restaurants which allowed customers to light up was, 'simply a matter of time' said health commissioner David Byrne. In Britain there are around 14 million smokers and almost 5,000 people work in the tobacco industry. Tax on cigarettes brings in £7 billion a year.

Restaurant owners say a ban would cost them £346 million and lose more than 45,000 jobs. But Mr Byrne believes that that has to be balanced against the 120,000 smokers who die each year, the £1.7 billion cost to the NHS and the danger to non-smokers. He said, 'There is clear evidence now that there's a correlation between passive smoking and health-related diseases. The adoption of measures to prevent the exposure of the public to the effects of tobacco is desirable. The less smoking there is in public places, the better. I would support measures that move in that direction.'

A representative from the pressure group ASH agreed, 'If we are to stop smoking altogether, we must get the message across to children that smoking is not socially acceptable but the opposite, so hopefully those children will think twice before starting to smoke and will not have to use nicotine patches or chew nicotine gum when they want to give up smoking'.

Smoking is considered a cultural right in European countries such as Spain, Greece and Italy, where up to 40% of teenagers are hooked. Mr Byrne said, 'One must always be sensitive respecting cultural traditions but, when you are dealing with something fundamental like health, you have to try and see to what extent you can change opinion.'

New York has banned smoking in its 13,000 bars. Owners, who face a £250 fine, say business has dropped by up to half. Britain has already outlawed tobacco advertising. However, the tobacco retailers are fighting back and have collected signatures on a petition for fair play on tobacco taxation and are to lobby parliament to reduce tax on cigarettes. They say that falling sales and consumption may result in a cutback of production and unemployment in the industry.

Revision Questions

1. Grants are paid to farmers by:
   a) customers
   b) suppliers
   c) government
   d) partnerships

2. The National Farmers' Union acts for teachers as:
   a) co-operative
   b) pressure group
   c) chain of command
   d) span of control

3. Gillens Ltd has to pay ………… on most of its purchases.
   a) income tax
   b) council tax
   c) corporation tax
   d) value added tax

4. Changes to an existing building would require ………… permission.
   a) trade union
   b) planning
   c) competitors'
   d) trading

5. Each year Cutrite plc has to pay corporation tax to the:
   a) shareholders
   b) bank
   c) employees
   d) government

6. Building work at a new leisure centre caused dirt, noise and heavy traffic. These are known as:
   a) social benefits
   b) private costs
   c) private benefits
   d) social costs

7. People who object to the building work at the leisure centre could form a:
   a) pressure group
   b) trade union
   c) franchise
   d) co-operative

8. Safety standards for making teddy bears are set by government:
   a) taxes
   b) laws
   c) grants
   d) contracts

9. If Just Jeans Ltd was the only company making jeans in the United Kingdom, it would be a:
   a) hierarchy
   b) delegation
   c) monopoly
   d) pressure group

10. Employees making jeans at Just Jeans Ltd are protected by the:
    a) Consumer Protection Act
    b) Health and Safety at Work Act
    c) Sale of Goods Act
    d) Trades Descriptions Act

11. Consumers who buy food products are protected by the:
    a) Equal Opportunities Act
    b) Data Protection Act
    c) Equal Pay Act
    d) Food and Drugs Act

12. The tax shown on an invoice is:
    a) corporation tax
    b) income tax
    c) council tax
    d) value added tax

13. People who change how a business operates are known as:
    a) a pressure group
    b) a monopoly
    c) advertisers
    d) franchisers

UNIT 4: BUSINESS ACTIVITY AND THE EXTERNAL ENVIRONMENT

Exam tip

This unit contains a great deal of information and technical terms to learn. You also need to know how PEST affects businesses. Remember to think about costs, demand, sales and profits.

Summary

Businesses have to operate in a harsh environment. All those factors which have an effect on business but over which a business has no control are known as the external environment. These can be grouped under the headings political, economic, social and technological (PEST). These factors can either provide opportunities for or constraints on businesses in a number of ways:

- increase or decrease costs
- increase or decrease demand and sales
- increase or decrease profits.

Even if a business has a successful product, competitors might introduce a better one in the future and take away their sales. The government might pass laws which restrict what they can do. Changes in the size or the movement of population can affect their sales. Successful businesses will find solutions to these problems. They adapt how they operate to conform to government regulations and laws. They provide products which appeal to consumers, are of a high quality and are produced efficiently.

Key terms

Balance of payments – a record of the money coming into and leaving a country in exchange for goods and services over a period of time

Boom – a period of time when the economy is growing at a fast rate

Demography – the study of population

Exchange rate – the price at which one currency is changed for another

Inflation – an increase in the general level of prices in an economy

Infrastructure – the built environment, such as roads, factories, power lines

Interest rate – the price an individual or business pays for borrowing money

Quotas – limit on the number of goods allowed into a country

Recession – a period of time when the economy is slowing down, demand and output are falling

Tariff – a tax placed on imports

UNIT 5

LOCATION

>> **What you will learn**

At the end of this unit you should understand:
- which factors influence the location of businesses
- why the correct location of a business is important.

CHOOSING THE RIGHT LOCATION

One of the most important decisions a business has to make, whether they produce goods or services, is where to locate. Making the right decision will have a big influence on the success of the business. There are a number of factors which a business has to take into account before making its final decision on where to locate, but the ideal location is where costs are at a minimum.

Some of the factors shown in Figure 5.1 are more important to some businesses than others. It is important for you to learn these factors, and be able to select and apply those factors which will have the biggest influence on the location of different businesses.

Nearness to market

Service industries such as shops need to be located where their customers can easily get to them, eg dentist, florist, bank, restaurant. A manufacturing company will locate next to the user of its products, eg a business which makes parts for cars may locate next to a main car manufacturer, as this will cut down on transport costs. Large cities tend to attract bulk-increasing businesses. These are businesses where the output/finished product is more expensive to transport than the raw materials, so they need to located near to their market in order to reduce transport costs. An example is the brewing industry, which uses barley and hops as its raw

Factors affecting BUSINESS LOCATION:
- Nearness to market
- Safety
- Availability of labour
- Location of other businesses
- Cost and availability of land/premises
- Nearness to raw materials
- Regional factors
- Transport cost
- Communications
- Utilities
- Industrial inertia
- Goverment incentives

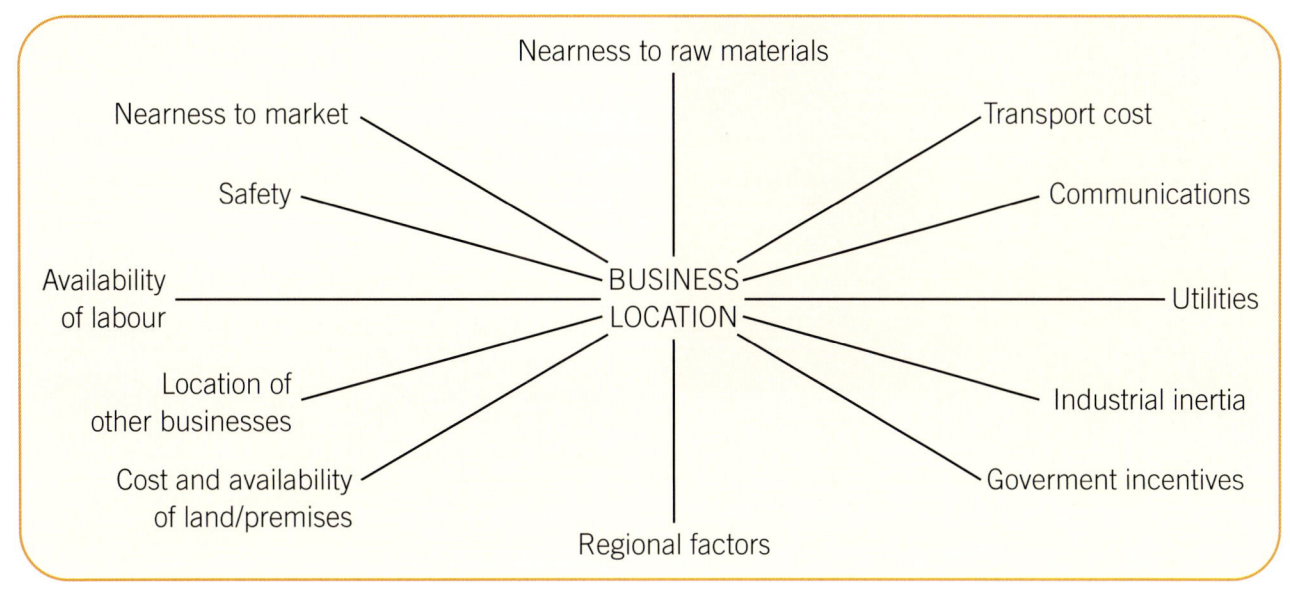

Figure 5.1 Factors affecting choice of location

materials. These are not expensive to transport, but when you add water and brew beer the finished product becomes expensive to transport, so it reduces the transport costs if breweries are located close to cities.

Nearness to raw materials
Some businesses use large amounts of heavy and bulky raw materials in making their products, which are expensive to transport. The finished products are often smaller and lighter than the raw materials used to make them, eg steelworks where it takes eight tonnes of coal, four tonnes of iron ore and one tonne of limestone to make one tonne of steel. These industries are known as bulk-decreasing industries because their output/finished product is cheaper to transport than their raw materials. These bulk-reducing industries locate near to their source of raw material or a port, to lower the cost of transporting the raw materials.

Figure 5.2 Steel works

Transport costs
The cost of transporting products can be as much as 25% of a product's total cost, so it is important that a business locates where its transport costs are at a minimum. However, many businesses sell their products in several markets and obtain their raw materials from several sources. The decision on the best location to minimise their transport costs can be more complicated.

Communications
Proximity to good roads, railways, ports and airports has become increasingly important in deciding where to locate a business. Many businesses today need to be able to distribute their products to their markets as quickly, cheaply and conveniently as possible, and for this reason they locate where the communication links are the best. These industries are said to be footloose, ie can set up anywhere and are not tied to one particular market or have to be near to their raw materials. Computer-making businesses, such as these along the M4 corridor between London and South Wales, are a typical example.

Cost and availability of land/premises
Some businesses need a large amount of space to produce their products (eg car manufacturing), so they will locate where they can find this amount of space at the right price. Retail businesses need to be located next to their customers. For many the best location would be in the main shopping area in a town centre, but rents here will be high so the business has to ensure that it will have sufficient revenue to pay high rents.

Availability of labour
Businesses which need skilled labour will locate where they can find it. This may result in a number of similar businesses being located next to each other, eg textile industry. Businesses which do not require skilled labour and wish to keep their labour costs down may locate in areas of high unemployment where labour is readily available.

Safety
Some industries have to locate away from heavily populated areas because their products may be dangerous to people, eg nuclear power stations and some chemical plants.

Utilities
All businesses need to have access to gas, electricity, water and waste disposal, so it is important that they locate where these are available and at a suitable price, eg paper mills need to have access to large amounts of water and cheap electricity.

Industrial inertia
Many businesses stay in their original location even though the original reasons for locating there no longer apply, eg textile industries in Lancashire.

Location of other businesses
Some businesses cluster together because customers like to shop around; any business not near the others will be at a disadvantage because potential customers will only visit the main cluster, eg travel agents and jewellers. Other businesses, such as newsagents, will want to locate away from their rivals, because if they are too close, they will split the market and lose sales.

Regional factors
Locating in an area with similar businesses, suppliers and markets could be an advantage and attract a business to that area. Businesses could share research facilities more easily, and local colleges may organise special training schemes. The quality of local schools, housing, environment, leisure and recreational facilities in an area may also influence where a business decides to locate.

Government incentives
Financial aid in the form of grants, subsidies and relief from taxes from local authorities, national government or the EU are a major factor in influencing the location of businesses. The main reason behind these incentives is to help regions which have high unemployment because their traditional industries have declined, eg shipbuilding in the north east of England. These areas receive investment aid from the government and EU to encourage new businesses to locate there and create new jobs.

> **Exam tip**
>
> To help you remember these factors, think about businesses near you and why they located there.

> **Task**
>
> Use the above information to help you decide which factors affect the location of the following businesses:
> - cement works
> - computer factory
> - bakery
> - car factory
> - newsagents.
>
> You could show these factors in the form of a star diagram. Under each diagram give a brief explanation of why you have chosen that factor.

> **Task**
>
> Many of the UK's new hi-tech industries are said to be 'footloose' and are located on industrial estates on the outskirts of towns and cities next to motorways.
> 1. What is meant by a 'footloose' industry?
> 2. Give three reasons why hi-tech industries are located on the outskirts of towns and cities next to motorways.

Task

Figure 5.3 An old factory and a modern factory

1. Look at the picture and match the phrases below to the correct factory. Do this in the form of a star diagram.
   - the factory is on a small site
   - the factory is a low building
   - the factory is on a large site
   - the factory site is clean and tidy
   - there is a lot of open space around the factory
   - the factory is a tall building
   - there is a motorway close to the factory
   - there are small roads close to the factory
   - the factory site is dirty and polluted
   - there are no houses close to the factory
   - there is little open space around the factory
   - there are many houses near the factory

2. Decide what are the advantages and disadvantages in each picture for locating a textile factory there. Highlight the advantages in green and the disadvantages in red.

3. Imagine that you are the manager of the textile factory which is currently located at the old site. You want to move to the new factory. Write a report to the directors of the company outlining the problems of the present site and the advantages of relocating to the new site.

Past Paper

Happy Ideas Ltd produces teddy bears. The factory is situated in Stoneybridge which is an area popular with tourists. The directors had been thinking of relocating the factory, but have now decided against this.

1. Apart from keeping the same workforce, identify three other benefits to the directors of Happy Ideas Ltd of staying in Stoneybridge. (3)

One factor which persuaded the directors to remain in Stoneybridge was the existing workforce.

2. Explain two reasons why this factor may have influenced their decision. (4)

3. Having decided not to re-locate, the directors of Happy Ideas Ltd are considering whether or not to expand on the present site. They are thinking of either demolishing the existing showroom/shop and building a new exhibition area with a shop extension, or keeping the existing showroom/shop and building six holiday flats. Which do you think they should do? Give reasons for your choice. (4)

(Edexcel, 2000, Foundation)

Happy Ideas Ltd is situated in Stoneybridge, an area popular with tourists. The directors have been thinking of relocating the factory, but have now decided against this. A local pressure group, SOS (Save Our Stoneybridge), helped influence the directors' decision to stay.

1. Outline the nature and purpose of a pressure group such as SOS. (3)

2. Give one reason why SOS wished to keep Happy Ideas Ltd in Stoneybridge. (3)

3. Describe and explain three reasons why Happy Ideas Ltd should remain in Stoneybridge rather than locating elsewhere. (9)

4. Overseas markets for Happy Ideas Ltd's products (teddy bears) include two European Union countries (Ireland and Germany), the USA and Japan. The directors wish to export more bears, and will select one of these countries for an 'export sales push'. Which country should the directors select? Explain the business reasons for your choice. (5)

(Edexcel, 2000, Higher)

Revision Questions

1. When Cutrite plc moved to its new site this was called:
   a) distribution   b) promotion
   c) relocation   d) refurbishment

2. A steelworks which uses large amounts of imported raw materials will have lower transport costs if it locates near:
   a) its market   b) a port
   c) a motorway   d) a large town

3. Which of the following is a bulk-increasing industry?
   a) steel works   b) brewery
   c) clothing manufacture
   d) newsagents

4. Which is the most important factor when deciding where to locate a small bakery?
   a) near to raw materials
   b) near to market
   c) a supply of skilled labour
   d) near to motorway

5. Which of the following is the best site for a nuclear power station?
   a) remote coastal area
   b) town centre
   c) industrial estate
   d) farming area

UNIT 5: LOCATION

Exam tip

Learn the factors that influence the location of businesses, and develop your ability to select and apply those which are relevant to the different types of businesses.

Summary

Businesses use location factors to help them decide on the best location for their business. Depending on the type of business, some factors are more important than others. If a business is to be successful, it has to make sure that it identifies the factors that are the most important to it and then find a site which has those factors.

Key terms

Bulk-increasing industry – an industry which is located near the market because the final product is bulky

Bulk-decreasing industry – an industry which is located near the natural resources because the raw material is bulky

Development area – area of high unemployment which receives UK government and EU funding in the form of grants and aid to encourage industries to locate there

Footloose industries – industries where costs of transport of raw materials and finished goods are low, so they can locate in a variety of sites

Greenfield site – rural land that is used for building

UNIT 6

TYPES OF BUSINESS ORGANISATION

> ### What you will learn
>
> **At the end of this unit you should understand:**
> - the differences between private and public sector enterprises
> - the differences between a sole trader, partnership, franchise, private and public limited company
> - the reasons why there are different types of ownership
> - the advantages and disadvantages of each type of ownership.

In most of the world's economies today, business ownership can be placed in one of two groups:

1. **Public sector** – owned by the public but controlled by the government or local authorities on our behalf. These enterprises include the army, police, hospitals, schools, fire service, leisure centres, retirement and care homes.
2. **Private sector** – businesses that are owned by private individuals. Each type of ownership has its own legal rights and responsibilities, so that individuals who wish to own and run a business can choose the type which suits their own financial and personal circumstances. Businesses in the private sector range from those which are owned and run by one person, to multinationals which are owned by many people and employ thousands of people in many countries.

SOLE TRADER

These are usually small businesses such as hairdressers, window cleaners, plumbers, local shopkeepers, electricians, freelance computer engineers.

Main features of sole trader
- owned – by one person
- controlled – by the owner
- managed – by the owner
- finance – raised by the owner through personal savings or borrowing from the bank or family and friends
- profit – goes to the owner

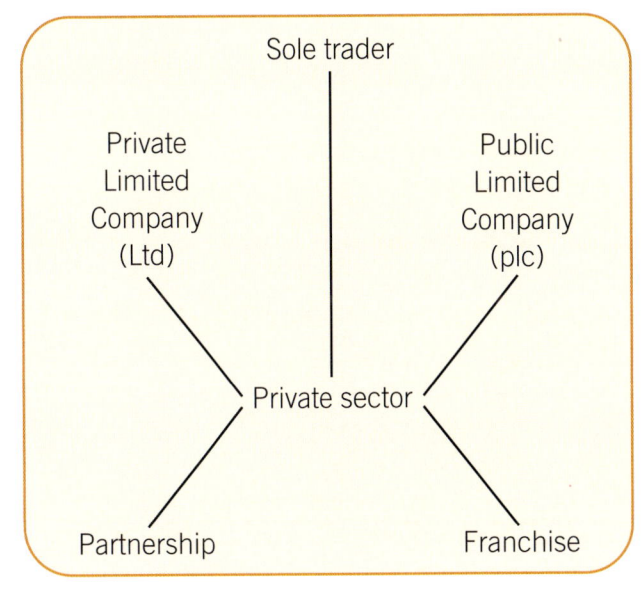

Figure 6.1 Different types of private sector businesses

Figure 6.2 Sole traders

These types of business are literally a one-person business. They may employ other people, but they are solely responsible for the success or failure of the business.

Task

Decide which of the following statements are advantages or disadvantages of a sole trader, and place them under the correct heading.

- are easy to set up – no complicated paperwork or solicitors needed
- cheap to set up – not much capital required
- unlimited liability – could lose everything they own if the business fails
- no one to share workload with – what do they do if they want to take a holiday or are sick?
- own boss – do not have to take orders from anyone, can make own decisions
- keep all of the profits – do not have to share them with anyone
- business affairs can be kept private
- finance can be difficult to raise – makes expansion difficult
- unincorporated – the owner and business are classed as legally the same so if anything goes wrong, it is the owner who is sued, not the business
- many responsibilities for one person – difficult to expect one person to be an expert in everything.

The main disadvantage of being a sole trader is unlimited liability. This means that if the business goes bust, the owner is legally obliged to pay all of his or her debts. In order to pay all of their debts, they may have to sell all of their possessions, ie house, car, furniture. Being a sole trader can therefore be a risky business, but many people are prepared to take the risk because the financial and personal rewards can be great.

PARTNERSHIP

These businesses can also be formed easily and include businesses such as solicitors, doctors, dentists, accountants and other professionals. There must be a minimum of two and a maximum of 20 partners.

Main features of a partnership
- owned – by the partners
- controlled – by the partners
- managed – by the partners
- finance – raised by the partners through personal savings or borrowing from the bank
- profits – go to the partners

Partners have an equal say in the running of the business and an equal share of the profits unless the deed of partnership states otherwise. A deed of partnership is a legal contract between the partners which sets out how profits and losses will be shared, the amount of capital invested by each partner and the responsibilities of each partner.

Figure 6.3 Partners

⚠ Exam tip

Examiners like to test your knowledge of unlimited liability so it is important to learn about it. They also like to ask you to discuss the relative advantages and disadvantages of changing from a sole trader to a partnership.

✎ Task

Imagine that you and two of your friends are going to start up a business cleaning wheelie bins. Draw up a deed of partnership for your business. Items to include are:

- names and addresses of partners and business
- amount of capital invested by each partner and how profits will be shared
- rules that will ensure the fair running of the business, ie working hours, holidays, responsibilities
- arrangements in case a partner falls ill or dies.

✎ Task

Decide which of the following statements are advantages or disadvantages of a partnership, and place them under the correct heading:

- more owners means more capital
- profits must be shared between partners
- more ideas
- work can be shared
- partners can specialise in what they do best
- can cover for each other during holidays
- all partners have unlimited liability (except sleeping partner – has limited liability but does not take part in the day-to-day running of the business)
- partners have to consult each other before decisions can be made
- decision-making can be slow
- partners may disagree about the running of the business
- each partner is legally responsible for the actions of the others
- financial details of the partnership are private.

❓ Past Paper

1. Leroy Green is a plumber in business as a sole trader. He has been thinking of forming a partnership.

   a) Explain three reasons why Leroy Green might want to form a partnership. (6)

   b) Explain one risk for Leroy Green in forming a partnership (2)

   (Edexcel, 1998, Foundation)

2. 'Teddies on the Circle' is situated close to Happy Ideas Ltd in Stoneybridge. It is a partnership run by Maggie Gray and Charles Bernard.

UNIT 6: TYPES OF BUSINESS ORGANISATION

The following are features of business organisations:

- between two and 20 owners
- unlimited liability
- shares bought and sold by the public
- have a separate legal existence
- shared responsibility.

a) From the list above, identify three features of a partnership. (3)
b) What do you think are the two most important advantages of a partnership? Give your reasons. (5)

(Edexcel, 2000, Foundation)

LIMITED COMPANIES

There are two types of limited company:

1. **Private** Limited Company which must have the letters Ltd after the company name.
2. **Public** Limited Company which must have plc after its name.

These types of business are more expensive to set up than a sole trader or partnership, but carry less financial risk for the owners because they have limited liability. Limited liability means that if the company goes bust they only lose the amount of money they invested in the company, and not their personal possessions. Limited companies are also incorporated, which means that the company has a separate legal identity from its owners. It is the company that can sue or be sued, not the owners. It also gives the company greater continuity because its existence is not ended by the death or retirement of its owners.

Main features of limited companies

- owned – by the shareholders
- controlled – by the board of directors
- managed – by appointed managers
- finance – by selling shares, borrowing from banks
- profits – go to shareholders in the form of dividends

Figure 6.4 Why invest in a company?

The people who invest money in a company by buying shares are called the **shareholders**, and they are the owners of the company. By buying shares in the company they are entitled to a share of the profits known as a **dividend**. How much dividend a shareholder receives depends on how well the company is doing, the numbers of shares they have and the type of share they own.

The shareholders elect people to the board of directors to represent their interests and be responsible for the long-term strategy of the company. The directors will appoint managers to be responsible for the day-to-day running of the company. Some managers may also be directors and are known as executive directors. In a private limited company the major shareholders, board of directors and managers may all be the same people.

Task

Using the Yellow Pages, find five examples of plcs and five examples of Ltds.

```
                Ltd                                                          plc
                   ↘                                                     ↙
                          Memorandum of Association
                          (Outlines the external relationship
                          of the company and includes the name
                       of the company, company aims, location of registered
                       office, the amount of capital and the number of shares
                                   the company has)
                                          ↓
                              Articles of Association
                       (Outlines the internal rules of the company.
                    Includes rights and duties of directors, rights of shareholders,
                       types of shares and method of electing directors)
                                          ↓
                                   Companies Act
                                (Registrar of Companies)
                                          ↓
              Start trading ← Certificate of incorporation → Prospectus
                                                                ↓
                                                            Issue shares
                                                                ↓
                                                          Trading Certificate
```

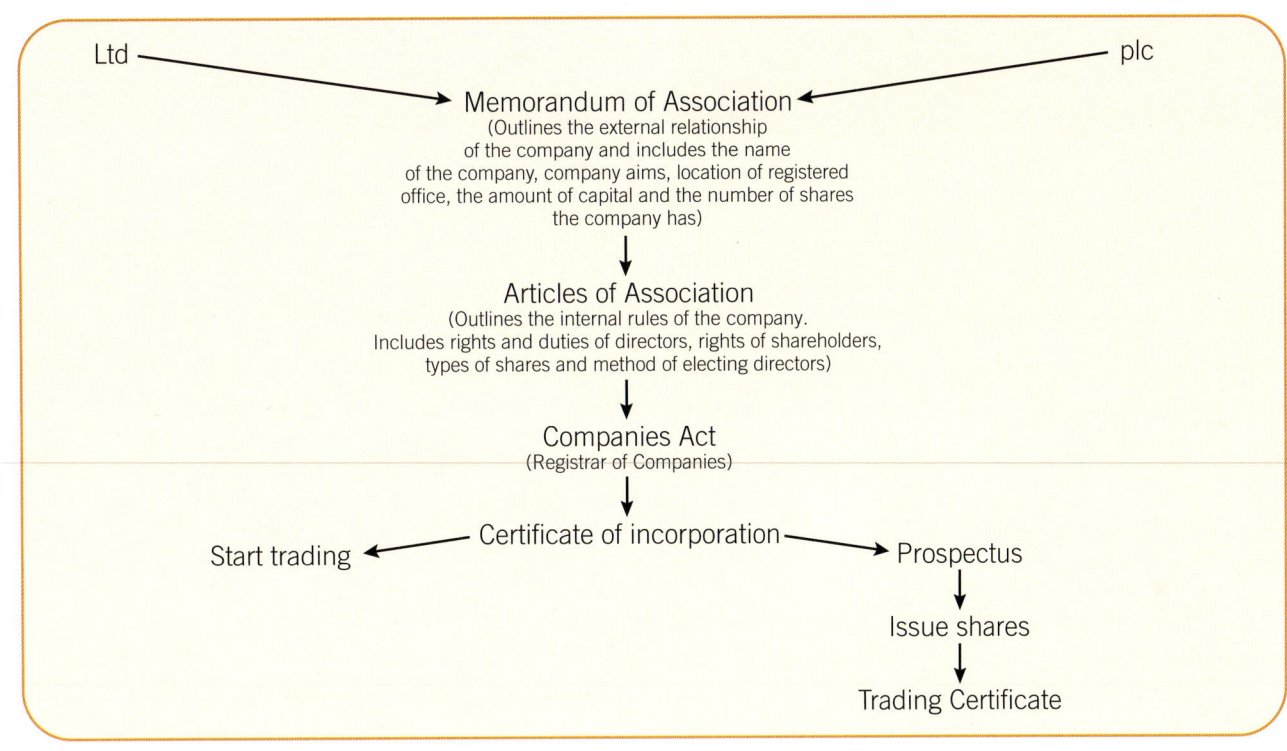

Figure 6.5 Setting up a limited company

Setting up a Limited Company

This is a similar process for both a Ltd and a plc and involves completing two documents: a Memorandum of Association, and Articles of Association. These must be registered with Registrar of Companies who grants a Certificate of Incorporation, allowing the company to conduct business.

All companies must produce a report and a set of accounts for the shareholders each year. The annual report and accounts must include a balance sheet, profit and loss account, a cashflow statement, a director's report and an auditor's report. This information allows the shareholders to see how well or badly the company has performed in the previous financial year.

All companies must also hold an Annual General Meeting (AGM). At this meeting shareholders are informed about the company's performance during the previous financial year. Shareholders can also ask questions to the directors about the company's performance and management. The shareholders can also vote on who should be elected to the board of directors.

Task

Decide which of the following are an advantage or disadvantage of a private limited company (Ltd) and place under the correct heading:
- shareholders have limited liability
- cannot sell shares on the stock market
- specialist managers can be employed
- money can be raised from selling shares to family and friends
- easier to expand the business
- annual reports have to be produced, by law
- expensive administrative work is required to set up company
- can only sell shares to family and friends
- no minimum investment needed before company can start trading
- transfer of shares must be agreed by directors.

UNIT 6: TYPES OF BUSINESS ORGANISATION

Past Paper

Hotspur & Sons (drapers) merged with Wren & Co (furnishings) in 1967 to form Hotspur & Wren Ltd (department store), a private limited company. Family members in each company became the original shareholders.

1. List two documents needed when forming a limited company. (2)

2. Discuss the reasons the original shareholders might have had for forming Hotspur & Wren Ltd. (6)

Hotspur & Wren Ltd decided to close and sell its high street site for redevelopment, close its out-of-town retail park store, and open a new store in a location closer to the town centre. It has been trading in its town centre store for a year.

3. Explain three factors which would determine whether the decision to relocate was a success or not. (12)

(Edexcel, 2003, Higher)

Task

Decide which of the following are advantages or disadvantages of a public limited company (plc) and place under the correct heading:

- shareholders have limited liability
- expensive administrative work is required to set up a company
- shares can be sold to the general public through the stock exchange
- annual reports have to be produced and published by law, which is an expensive process
- benefits from economies of scale (see Unit 25)
- specialist managers can be employed
- easier to expand company
- easy to raise finance from banks
- conflict of interest can arise between managers and owners
- diseconomies of scale because of size (see Unit 25)
- decision-making process can be slow
- minimum initial shares capital of £50 000 needed before company can start trading
- no restriction on the transfer of shares.

Figure 6.6 Buying and selling shares in public limited companies

Exam tip

A popular question the examiner asks you is to explain the benefits and drawbacks of a business becoming a limited company. They also test you on your understanding of the differences between a private limited company and a public limited company.

Task

Using the above information, identify the differences and similarities between a private limited company and a public limited company.

Past Paper

In 1989 Docdel Ltd became Docdel plc.

1. Explain two factors which might have influenced the decision to become a plc. (4)

2. Explain two disadvantages to the directors from changing ownership to a plc. (4)

3. The directors of Docdel plc must hold an Annual General Meeting and publish an Annual Report and Accounts. Explain what each of these is. (6)

(Edexcel, 1997, Foundation/Higher)

FRANCHISING

Franchising is a form of cooperation between two businesses. A company which has a well-known product or service allows an individual to buy the right to use their products or services and trade under their name.

Figure 6.7 Example of a franchise

The **franchiser** (the company which allows another person or persons to use their tried and tested product or service and to trade under their name for a fee), allows the **franchisee** (the person or persons who pay an initial fee and regular royalty payments for the privilege of trading under the franchiser's name), to set up their own business.

Main features of a franchise
- owned – by the franchisee
- controlled – by franchiser
- managed – by franchisee
- financed – by savings or borrowing from banks
- profits – kept by franchisee but the franchiser takes a percentage in the form of royalty payments

Task

Decide which of the following are advantages and disadvantages to the franchisee and place them under the correct heading:

- greater chance of success as the product has been tried and tested

UNIT 6: TYPES OF BUSINESS ORGANISATION

- not completely independent as they have to follow rules and regulations set by the franchiser
- product is advertised nationally
- can receive help and support from the franchiser
- cannot sell the franchise without the franchiser's agreement
- have to give franchiser a share of the profits (royalty payment)
- franchisee can decide the legal structure of the business
- easier to obtain loans from banks as they are seen as less of a risk
- franchise is not automatically renewed
- have to use materials supplied by the franchiser.

Task

Decide which of the following are advantages or disadvantages to the franchiser and place them under the correct heading:

- can expand their business without the need for large amounts of capital
- franchisee will be motivated to make a success of the business, which will make the whole business more successful
- the more successful the franchise, the more royalty payments they will receive
- would receive all of the profit if it had set up its own branches
- if franchisee does not maintain standards, it could damage their trade name and reputation.

There are currently over 500 franchises which include household names such as McDonald's, Kentucky Fried Chicken, Body Shop, Pronto Print. Franchises account for 20% of all retail trade, and are rapidly becoming one of the most popular forms of business organisation as they offer a ready-made business opportunity for those who have the capital and are willing to work hard.

Task

Buzz Cafe plc is a company which operates a chain of coffee shops throughout the UK. These are either company-owned or franchise-operated.

1. Give two examples of business that are run mainly as franchises.
2. State and explain two benefits of franchising to the franchiser.
3. State and explain two benefits to franchisees of this form of organisation.

PUBLIC SECTOR OWNERSHIP

The UK has a mixed economy, which means that businesses are not only owned by private individuals but also by the state. The public sector is made up of enterprises which are owned and controlled by central government or local authorities, on behalf of the people. These enterprises range from swimming pools to the Post Office. Some activities, such as defence, and law and order, need to be controlled by the government while others, such as health and education, are considered so important to the welfare of the people that they are also run by the state. Some industries are also considered to be so vital to the running of the country that they are controlled by the government and are known as **public corporations**.

Public sector enterprises do not necessarily aim to make a profit. They exist to provide a high quality service for the public, and to ensure that resources are used for the benefit of the community. Many of these services are financed by money the government obtains from taxes or borrowing.

Central government
Central government accounts for approximately 40% of all spending in the country. It raises this money through taxes and borrowing. It spends this money on a number of activities such as defence, health, education, transport and social security.

Local authority enterprises
Local authorities include county councils and district councils. Certain services such as refuse collection, swimming pools, leisure centres, libraries, housing and social services are the responsibility of the local authority. The local authority finances these services through council tax and/or grants from central government. They also receive revenue from services such as swimming pools and leisure centres.

Many of these services run at a loss, but because they benefit the local community, they are subsidised by the local authority from the council tax. During the 1980s and 90s, many of these services were privatised as it was believed that they would be run more efficiently by the private sector (eg public transport).

Figure 6.8 Example of a public service

Public corporations (nationalised industries)
These are similar to limited companies, but they are owned and controlled by the government on behalf of the people. The government appoint a Chairperson and Board of Directors to look after the day-to-day running of the company, who are responsible to a government minister. Examples of public corporations are the BBC, the Post Office and the Bank of England.

Reasons for public ownership
- To provide essential and important services, eg defence, health, education whether people can afford to pay for them or not.
- To stop the wasting or duplication of resources, eg railways.
- To stop the exploitation of consumers, eg water companies charging high prices for water.
- To protect industries and jobs which are vital to the country, eg nuclear power.
- To allow the government to control the economy, eg keep an iron and steel factory open in an area of high unemployment.

Reasons against public ownership
- Political influences and lack of business expertise may result in inefficiency and huge losses.
- Losses have to be paid for by the tax-payer.
- Lack of incentive to be efficient as making a profit may not be main aim.

Nationalisation versus privatisation
Before 1979, the number of public corporations was much larger than it is today:

- British Airways
- British Rail
- British Gas
- Electricity Board
- National Bus Company
- British Shipbuilders
- British Telecom

All of the above businesses were once public corporations, but since 1979 they have been privatised. Privatisation involves the selling of the

Figure 6.9 Nationalisation or privatisation?

state-owned companies to the private sector by selling shares to private individuals on the stock exchange. These companies then become public limited companies. However, many of these companies had originally been in the private sector but were taken into state ownership (nationalised) by the government of the time, for the reasons listed above. When nationalisation takes place, the original owners are paid compensation by the government. For example, in 1948 all of the regional railway companies which were in the private sector were nationalised and became British Rail. In 1995 British Rail was privatised; the rail network was broken up and sold to private companies such as Virgin and GNER.

Reasons for privatisation

There are a number of reasons why the government would return a state-owned business to the private sector:

- The industries will become more efficient because they need to make a profit to survive, as they will no longer have the state to support them if they make a loss.
- Consumers will benefit from lower prices and higher quality as the result of greater competition and efficiency.
- The government receives income from the sale of shares which it can use for other purposes, eg tax cuts/more hospitals.

Reasons against privatisation

- It is a one-off sale so the government loses any income it may have received from the profits made by these industries.
- Consumers may be exploited with lower quality and higher prices for the products and services they buy, eg water, gas and electricity are monopolies, which means they can charge a high price for a poor service because consumers have no alternatives.
- Loss of government control over important industries, eg as companies attempt to make greater profits, more workers may become

Task

BRITISH TELECOM

British Telecom is one of the UK's largest companies, with an annual turnover of £8 billion and a workforce of 200,000 people. It supplies a variety of services, many of which are based on the telephone system which the company runs.

Until 1984, British Telecom was a state-owned public corporation with a monopoly in the telecommunications field. In 1984 it was privatised and changed into a public limited company.

Using the above newspaper article to help you, answer the following questions:

1. What does the article mean when it says that British Telecom 'was a public corporation ... changed into a public limited company'?
2. Describe and explain how consumers may have gained or lost as result of British Telecom being privatised.

unemployed and there may be less regard shown for the environment.
- Important industries such as gas and electricity supplies should be owned by everyone in the country through an elected government and not by private shareholders.

It is important to remember that public limited companies are in the private sector and are owned by shareholders, while public corporations are in the public sector and are owned by the state on behalf of the people. When a public corporation is sold to the private sector, it is said to have been **privatised**. When a private company is taken into state ownership, it is said to have been **nationalised**.

Task

'Should the railways be a public corporation or a plc?'

Design a poster which puts forward the arguments for the railways being either state-owned or privately owned.

Task – Case Study

In the town centre below there are:

| three partnerships | three public limited companies | one private limited company |
| four sole traders | one public corporation | two privatised companies |

Figure 6.10

Using a colour code, identify which type of business organisations describes the following:

- Gas Board offices
- A. Stenton & D. Fairclough Doctors
- Boots plc
- Saunders Bakery
- Kirk & Tate Estate Agents
- Barclays Bank plc
- Huckle's Corner shop
- Tara's Hairdresser
- WH Smith plc
- Electricity Board showroom
- Hunt & Mills Solicitors
- Smiths Ltd
- Clems Fish & Chip Shop
- Post Office

Past Paper

1. Nocha Ltd makes and sells ice cream. In the 1950s, Nick Nocha remained a sole trader instead of forming a partnership with his family. To what extent was this a good business decision? (7)

2. When they opened a new factory in 1970, the business became a private limited company. What business reasons might Nick Nocha have had for this change? (6)

3. One of the first business decisions made by the directors of Nocha Ltd was to offer franchises to its ice-cream van drivers. Assess the benefits to Nocha Ltd of selling these franchises. (7)

(Edexcel, 1999, Higher/Foundation)

Revision Questions

1. Decisions about company policy are made by:
   a) workers
   b) students
   c) mechanics
   d) directors

2. As a private limited company, Gillens Ltd has to prepare each year:
   a) a memorandum
   b) an annual report
   c) a statement of account
   d) an invoice

3. The restaurant at an arts centre is owned by only one person, who is a:
   a) partner
   b) consumer
   c) sole trader
   d) employee

4. Which of the following applies only to a public limited company?
   a) dividends
   b) shares traded on the stock exchange
   c) two or more directors
   d) annual accounts

5. Cutrite plc is a ………… limited company.
   a) public
   b) private
   c) national
   d) package

6. Just Jeans Ltd is a private limited company and so its ………… cannot be traded on the stock exchange.
   a) dividends
   b) shares
   c) profits
   d) policies

7. When the shop Head First was first opened, it was owned by one person. This was a:
   a) sole trader
   b) partnership
   c) co-operative
   d) limited company

8. If the Directors of Just Jeans Ltd wanted its shares to be bought and sold on the stock exchange, the business would have to become a:
   a) partnership
   b) franchise
   c) public corporation
   d) public limited company

9. Cutrite plc has a contract with Vauxhall to sell new cars. This business arrangement involves:
   a) franchising
   b) privatisation

c) merger
d) nationalisation

10. When the founder of Cutrite plc started selling vans as a sole trader he had:
a) local liability
b) national liability
c) limited liability
d) unlimited liability

11. Cutrite plc is a:
a) public limited company
b) private limited company
c) public limited corporation
d) private limited corporation

12. Day-to-day control of Cutrite plc is by the:
a) agents
b) shareholders
c) managers
d) dealers

13. If Laura Designs became a plc, the company would be owned by:
a) employees
b) government
c) shareholders
d) consumers

14. Gemma set up as a sole trader. What would have been one of her reasons for doing this?
a) to sell shares
b) to share decision-making
c) to be independent
d) to have limited liability

15. A person employed by a franchisee is a:
a) director
b) franchisor
c) employee
d) employer

UNIT 6: TYPES OF BUSINESS ORGANISATION

Exam tip

This is a popular topic with the examiner, so it is important that you learn the structure and advantages and disadvantages of each type of business ownership. You will need to be able to compare and contrast the strengths and limitations of each type of ownership, and make a decision on which is the most suitable for a particular business. You will need to be able to explain why a business chose one type of ownership instead of another, and know the difference between unlimited liability and limited liability.

Summary

An individual or group of individuals wanting to set up a business has to decide on what legal form the business organisation should take. A number of factors will influence that decision:

- Ownership – How many people should own the business?
- Control – How much control do the owners want over the business? Does the owner want to be in complete control, or is he or she prepared to share it or give it to someone else?
- Profits – Does the owner want to keep all of the profits, or is he or she prepared to share them?
- Finance – How will the owners obtain the finance to start the business? How much finance will they need?
- Liability – Do the owners want limited liability, or are they prepared to accept the risk of unlimited liability?
- Administration – Do the owners want the extra cost and paperwork involved in becoming a company?
- Privacy – How much privacy do the owners want about the affairs of the business?

Depending on the answers to the above questions, the business will decide on whether to be a sole trader, partnership, limited company or a franchise.

Key terms

Annual Report – a report issued by a limited company which contains written and financial statements about the progress of the company

Articles of association – the document which gives details about the relationship between the company, its shareholders and its directors

Certificate of incorporation – a certificate issued by the UK Registrar of Companies to allow the company to do business

Company – a business which has limited liability and a legal identity separate from that of its owners

Deed of partnership – the legal contract that governs how a partnership will be owned and organised

Director – a person elected to the board of a company by the shareholders to represent their interests

Dividend – money payable to shareholders out of the profits of a business. It is a reward for taking the risk of investing in a business

Franchise – the right given by one business to another to use its name to sell its goods or services for a fee

Franchisee – the individual(s) who buy the right to use the product name

Franchiser – the business which gives the right to the franchisee to use its product name

Limited liability – when shareholders of a company are liable for the debts of the company only up to the value of their shares

Managers – individuals who are responsible for the day-to-day running of the company. They are answerable to the directors

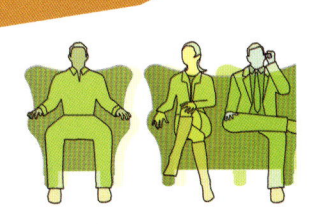

Memorandum of Association – a document which gives details of a company's purpose, shareholders address, name. Has to be placed with the Registrar of Companies before the company can start trading

Nationalised industries – industries which are owned and run by the government

Nationalisation – the purchase by the government of private sector businesses

Partnership – a business organisation which has between 2 and 20 owners who have unlimited liability

Private limited company – a company that has limited liability and cannot sell its shares on the stock exchange

Privatisation – the sale of state-owned businesses to the private sector

Private sector – part of the economy that is owned and controlled by private individuals

Public limited company – a company that has limited liability and can sell its shares to the public on the stock exchange

Public corporation – a business which is owned and controlled by the government

Public sector – part of the economy that is owned and controlled by the government on behalf of the people of that economy

Registrar of Companies – government official who is responsible for recording details of companies established in the UK

Sole trader – a business organisation where one person is the owner who has sole responsibility for the business. He or she has unlimited liability

Unlimited liability – a legal obligation on the owners of a business to pay all the debts of that business. In law there is no distinction between what the business owns and owes and what the owner owes and owns. The owner can therefore lose all of their possessions in order to pay the debts of the business

UNIT 6: TYPES OF BUSINESS ORGANISATION

GCSE BUSINESS STUDIES for Edexcel

Section 2
HUMAN RESOURCES

UNIT 7

INTERNAL ORGANISATIONS

> ## What you will learn
>
> **At the end of this unit you should understand:**
> - the relationship and inter-dependence of the following departments: production, marketing, personnel, and finance
> - the key terms in management of people
> - the roles and reponsibilities of employees in terms of compliance and accountability.

DEPARTMENTS OF BUSINESS

In all companies, no matter how large or how small they are, the various activities that take place within the company are broken down into sections, such as production, marketing, personnel, and finance. This is to help with the smooth running of the company. A smaller company may combine two of the areas together, such as personnel and finance, whereas a larger company may have various sections within personnel, such as people responsible for training, recruitment, etc.

Production department

The main function of this department is to produce or make an item, which is subsequently sold. In a larger company, the actual design of the product is carried out in a research and development department or product development department. In a smaller company this work will be done within the production department.

The person responsible for the department will have to ensure that it is working efficiently. Decisions to be made include the method of production and how the item is to be produced. Not all companies produce goods in the same quantity. Some companies may only produce one or two items a week (eg the Morgan Car Company); other companies, such as Ford, make hundreds of cars each week. However, in order to produce goods, the production department will need to have contact with other departments, to enable them to carry out their job efficiently and effectively. The materials and supply department will be in constant contact with the production department to ensure that there are sufficient parts to enable the cars to be made. The sales department will need to

Figure 7.1 Making products on a production line

know exactly how many cars have been completed so that they can deliver them to the appropriate car showrooms and ensure that they have enough vehicles. It is therefore imperative that departments make contact with each other to keep the company running smoothly.

Marketing department

The marketing department's responsibility is to carry out market research, to find out if there is a need for the product that is going to be made and then sold. Their job is to survey people and companies to identify what should or should not be in the product. An example is a survey on washing machines, in which members of the public are asked about what they most want in a washing machine, and what they do not like or do not use on the machine. Collecting opinions and thoughts and then putting these into practice by passing on this information to other departments is the chief role of this department.

Marketing is a very large department because they have to look at all of the aspects of the sale of the product: where, when and whom it is aimed at. They will have to also consider the four Ps (product, price, place and packaging). Again it is important that this department links very closely with all other departments to make sure that all details are correct and that the product will be ready to sell. It would be pointless to advertise a product stating that it will be on sale at a certain time, without having first consulted the production department to obtain up-to-date information on the availability (see Unit 27).

Personnel department

This department can also be known as human resources. They have to ensure that there are staff to work on the production line in the numbers sufficient to produce the product. Having insufficient staff to work the production line means that the business is not achieving its full potential. On the other hand, having too many staff, some of whom who are not doing any work at all, is very wasteful for the company.

This department therefore has to ensure that the correct people are employed at the correct time. Again, consultation with departments is essential to gather the information required so that they appoint the correct person or people that are needed. (This is dealt with in Unit 9.)

Human resources are also responsible for dismissing members of staff. They may need to make someone redundant, or deal with a worker has broken their contract; there are many other reasons for terminating the employment of a person at the company.

If a member of staff has a problem or grievance within the company then the personnel/human resources department will deal with the problem. However, they will have to communicate with other departments to ensure that they have all the facts and evidence needed to make the correct decision.

Finance department

The finance department is responsible for raising funds to purchase and pay for all expenses and bills received. This department plays a very important role within the company because all work undertaken has to be financed in one way or another, and therefore if the company does not have sufficient funds, then they are unable to continue with that project.

Another responsibility of the company is to ensure that staff are paid their wages/salaries and that they are paid on the correct day of the month.

One of the responsibilities of this department is to control the finances in and out of the company – the **cash flow**. This in turn means that they have to monitor and pay all the invoices that are received within the company, and balance all the accounts.

To ensure that the company survives, the finance department has to communicate with all departments within the company to plan and monitor the financial situation. If the company is not producing sufficient products and selling them to bring in revenue, then there is no point in taking on more staff or developing a new product, which could prove expensive (see Unit 9).

Figure 7.2 The finance department controls the cash flow

> **Exam tip**
>
> Try and visit a company that includes the departments discussed, so that you can talk to the people involved in each department to gain more insight to the work carried out. This will help in trying to remember the importance of each department.

ORGANISATIONAL STRUCTURE

For communication within the company to be successful, there must be people responsible for making decisions and taking control. Most companies have an organisational structure, which will take into account:

- who is in charge
- who has the authority to make decisions at each level
- who carries out the decisions
- how the information is passed to everyone involved.

It is important to have this structure so that everyone knows how the company works and how it is operated. It would be total chaos if no one took control – can you imagine school without the headteacher and heads of department?

> **Task**
>
> Draw up an organisational structure for your school. Start with the headteacher and end with classroom teachers.
>
> Were there any problems? Who did not seem to fit properly into the system?

Companies' structures are just as complex. A typical company structure could look like the diagram in Figure 7.3.

What is the purpose of having an organisational chart?

- Information can be passed down from one area/department to another, and if it is not being received then it can be traced.
- Employees can see where they are in the organisational chart, who has authority over them and over whom they have authority.
- It is very clear to see how the company is organised and which part of the business relates to another.

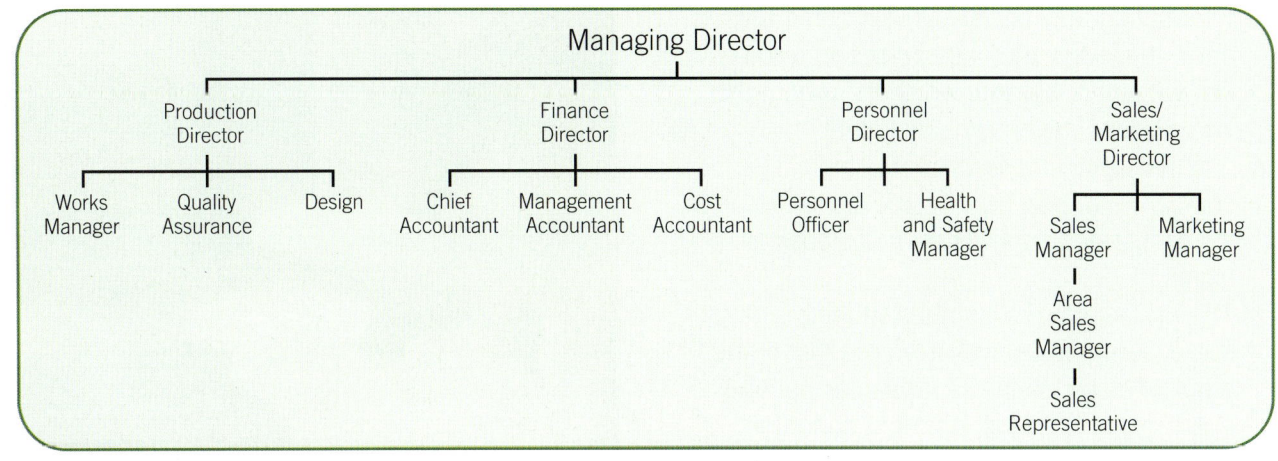

```
                        Managing Director
        ┌───────────────┬───────────────┬───────────────┐
   Production      Finance         Personnel       Sales/
   Director        Director        Director        Marketing
                                                   Director
   ┌───┬───┐      ┌───┬───┐       ┌───┐           ┌───┬───┐
Works Quality Design Chief Management Cost  Personnel Health    Sales   Marketing
Manager Assurance   Accountant Accountant Accountant Officer and Safety Manager Manager
                                                     Manager
                                                              Area
                                                              Sales
                                                              Manager
                                                               │
                                                              Sales
                                                              Representative
```

Figure 7.3 Organisational chart

Hierarchy

Smaller businesses will of course have smaller organisational charts. The fewer the employees, the less formal the chart will be. In a smaller company, people will see each other more often and therefore information can be passed on quickly and efficiently.

The **hierarchy** refers to the number of levels of responsibility or management within a company, from the lowest to the highest. In a small business there may only be two levels, the owner of the business and the employees. The owner is at the top of the chart because s/he is responsible for making all the decisions.

Most charts will have a smaller number at the top with a larger number at the bottom. It looks very much like a pyramid – narrow at the top and wide at the bottom.

Chain of command

The hierarchy also shows the chain of command, which is the way in which decisions are made and passed down the levels, and information is passed up.

The person at the top of the chain has the most control.

Drawbacks

Some of the main disadvantages of a hierarchical structure are as follows:

- Hierarchies usually have tall organisational charts, sometimes with seven or eight levels. This means that there is a long chain of command.
- Each employee is really only concerned with their own function or work, and therefore probably only has a limited amount of contact with other people within the business.
- There is a tendency for people to be very protective of their department or area and therefore to be more concerned about the 'office politics' than the interests of the whole company.

Figure 7.4 A hierarchical structure

UNIT 7: INTERNAL ORGANISATIONS

- Information may be very slow in being passed down the levels, and it could become something like the game 'Chinese whispers', where the information may become distorted.
- The managers or directors at the top of the company may seem or become too remote from the people working lower down the chain or hierarchy.
- The managers may emphasise their rank by segregating themselves from the rest of the employees by having separate car parking slots, longer holidays, different conditions of pay, etc.

However there are a number of companies which have introduced many features of the Japanese method of management. This type of system reduces the number of levels, and emphasises teamwork and performance rather than rank.

Flat structures

There are many disadvantages of a hierarchical structure, and in order to overcome this while still retaining the advantages, many large companies have reduced the number of levels of management, so that senior managers are closer to the workforce and support staff. Removing levels makes the structure much flatter.

A small company such as the local fish and chip shop will have a flat organisational structure because there are fewer people working there.

There are advantages to flat structures in that:

- the flow of information between the levels is much faster, enabling decisions to be made more quickly.
- as there are fewer levels, the workforce feels that they are more responsible for the job they are doing, which increases motivation and job satisfaction.

Making the structures flatter can reduce costs. An increase in the use of information technology has enabled flatter structures to be created.

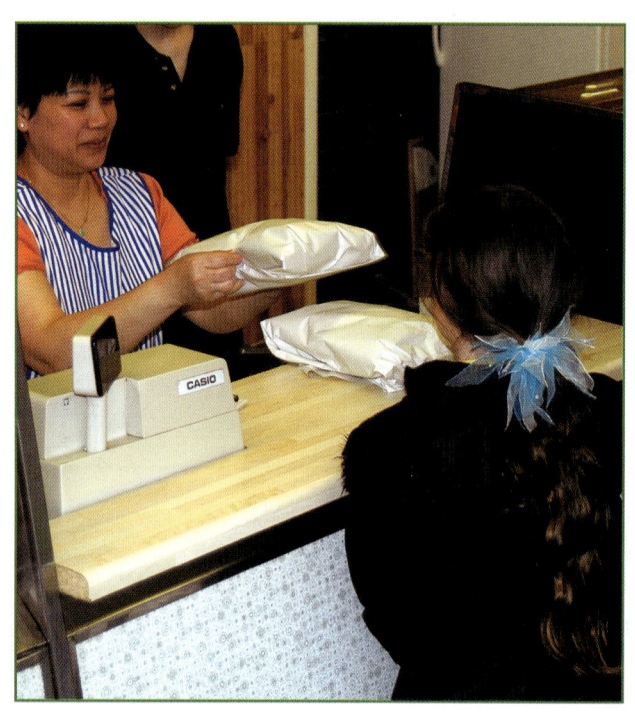

Figure 7.5 A fish and chip shop has a flat organisational structure

Span of control

The **span of control** refers to the number of people directly controlled by one person. In Figure 7.6 the area manager for the south has the span of control of three sales representatives. This means that s/he has responsibility or direct authority over three people.

A narrow span of control means that the person has authority or control over a small number of people, ie one or two. A wide span of control

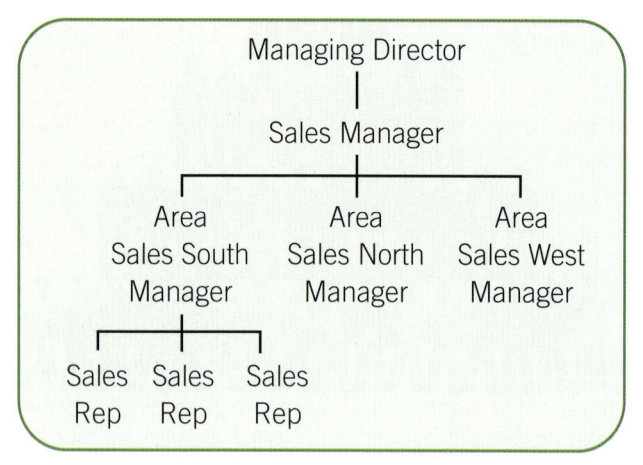

Figure 7.6 Chart showing spans of control

means that the person has authority over a larger number of people, ie seven or eight.

Having a narrow span of control means that managers are able to:

- have tighter control and closer supervision of staff
- have more time to plan and think rather than checking on a large number of employees and dealing with their day-to-day problems
- communicate more efficiently as there are fewer people to inform.

However, a disadvantage is that it may lead to too many levels of management. This kind of tall organisation can be difficult to organise.

A wider span of control means that managers have responsibility for more employees. If they have more people to manage, this means that:

- they may have to delegate more
- they will have to trust their staff to get on with their jobs as they will not have sufficient time to supervise them closely
- the staff may have the opportunity to make decisions
- the staff may be more motivated as they are trusted and given more responsibility.

A wider span means that fewer managers are required.

The manager who has control over staff or subordinates should:

- be good at their job and at least have a knowledge of the subordinates' jobs
- know the type of work which the subordinates carry out – does it require constant supervision, or little supervision?
- know how easy it is to communicate to all people, no matter where they are in the building
- know the type of decisions that need to be made.

Delegation

Delegation means giving the authority to carry out tasks and make decisions to people lower in the hierarchy.

The more a manager delegates, the wider the span of control that person could have, because the subordinates are doing the work for the manager as opposed to him/her doing it. However, the manager bears responsibility for the consequences if s/he has delegated a task and it is not done correctly.

The advantages of delegation to managers:

- Managers cannot do everything themselves, therefore it makes sense to delegate.
- Managers are therefore less likely to make mistakes as they can concentrate on the more important decisions that may need to be made.
- Managers are able to watch how their staff take on responsibility and how they are working. It is easier to determine who can cope with more responsibility.

The advantages to the subordinate:

- Delegation can make the job more rewarding, leading to increased job satisfaction.
- The employee feels more motivated and more valued.
- Delegation is a good way of training employees and giving them skills, which in turn improves job opportunities.

> ### ⚠ Exam tip
>
> *To help you remember some of the advantages and disadvantages of each section, try to make up silly or unusual words that will help you remember some of the important points; they then act as 'triggers'. For example, the advantages of delegation: CMW, Cannot do, less Mistakes, Watching staff.*

UNIT 7: INTERNAL ORGANISATIONS

Revision Questions

1. Each farm has two workers and a manager who reports to a director. This is a:
   a) hierarchy
   b) delegation
   c) dismissal
   d) job specification

2. The manager decides to give an employee a job to do. This is known as:
   a) productivity
   b) legislation
   c) delegation
   d) job share

3. The chain of command in a large company such as Harbon Estates Ltd is shown in:
   a) a business letter
   b) an organisational chart
   c) a balance sheet
   d) a break-even chart

4. Day-to-day control of Docdel plc is by the:
   a) agents
   b) shareholders
   c) managers
   d) dealers

5. Louisa's employees are directly responsible to her. What is this called?
   a) job satisfaction
   b) delegation
   c) chain of command
   d) organisational chart

Past Paper

1. After a merger of the company Flyaway plc, the company has the following employees:
   - a managing director
   - four departmental managers – personnel, finance, sales/marketing and operations
   - deputy managers for personnel, finance, sales/marketing
   - an operations department divided into two divisions – ground and flight – each with a deputy
   - a board of directors
   - two assistants for each deputy manager in operations.

   Draw up an organisational chart for the above company. (5)

   (Edexcel, 2001, Foundation)

Task

1. What is the importance of having an organisational chart within the company? How does it help the employees?

2. What do you understand by the term delegation? Why do you think it is important within a company or organisation to have someone who can delegate to? What are the advantages and disadvantages?

3. What are the problems with a large company which has many levels of hierarchy? What are the advantages of having a small number of levels?

4. Nocha Ltd is an ice-cream factory, which has recently opened a new site some 240 kilometres (150 miles), from the company's existing factory. Three of Nocha Ltd directors are listed below. Analyse the additional workload for each director when the new factory is opened.

   a) the production director
   b) the finance director
   c) the personnel director

Summary

At the end of this unit you should be able to:

- Understand the importance and function of the following departments within a company: production, marketing, personnel and finance
- Know the difference between span of control and hierarchical levels
- Identify and explain the importance of a simple organisational chart
- Understand why delegation is important within a company.

Key terms

Chain of command – the way in which orders and instructions are passed down through the organisation

Delegation – passing of work to someone else

Flat structure – a struture with very few levels, eg an owner and the workers

Span of control – the number of people working under one person or manager

Termination – to end a contract of employment. This can be either voluntarily, by moving to a new job or retiring, or forced, through being sacked or made redundant

UNIT 7: INTERNAL ORGANISATIONS

UNIT 8

COMMUNICATION

» What you will learn

At the end of this unit you should understand:
- what communication is
- the purpose of communication
- the communication process
- different types of communication
- the benefits of good communication
- reasons for poor communication
- the effects of poor communication.

WHAT IS COMMUNICATION?

Communication is the passing of information between people. In Figure 8.1 the person throwing the ball is like the person sending a message. The ball is the message itself. The person throwing the ball will know if the message has arrived because the person will have caught the ball and hopefully thrown it back. This is very much like communication: did the message reach the person correctly, (catching the ball), or did the message fail to arrive (not catch the ball)?

Figure 8.1 Communication

✎ Task

Try this out with a friend. Draw an object on a sheet of paper. Then try and describe the object so that your friend can draw it exactly the same as yours.

Check what you have done. Is it the same?

Can you answer the following questions honestly?

1. How long did it take?
2. Was the drawing exactly the same?
3. Did you communicate effectively and accurately?
4. How could you have improved?

In business it is very important that messages reach people correctly, otherwise it could have major repercussions for the company.

All organisations need to be able to communicate with people within the organisation and with other organisations in this country and throughout the world. We operate within a global economy where communication is vital. It is important that organisations overcome the problems of understanding communication: not every message sent is meaningful to those who receive it; poor wording and layout can create a bad impression. Any method of communication should be clear so all can understand the message or the information being sent.

The larger the organisation, the more difficult it is to ensure efficient communication. Methods and systems of communication have to be used that will keep everyone in touch and everyone informed.

We all communicate with people during the day, eg talking to teachers, friends, parents, shopping, etc. It is a very natural part of our life and one which we would find very difficult to cope without if we were unable to continue. Besides talking, there are many other different ways to communicate. These can include writing letters, using the telephone to speak to someone, and sending e-mails or faxes.

THE PURPOSE OF COMMUNICATION

The purpose of communication is:

- To give information – to let people know when is the next department meeting, or to notify the production manager of problems with the machinery, in order to enable production to continue.
- To collect information – gathering sales figures from the sales representatives, which will be needed by the production department to ensure that the correct quantity is produced.
- To clear up problems – misunderstandings within the company need to be sorted out, so that the customers are happy and keep returning.

Task

An urgent message has been received which needs to be passed on to a member of staff in another part of the building.

1. How many ways can you think of for getting the message to the member of staff?
2. Which one do you think is the most appropriate and why?
3. What could happen if the message is not passed on or is not correct?

- To keep the organisation running smoothly – everyone is kept informed and knows exactly what is going on.
- To give the organisation a positive public image by eliminating errors, managing problems and dealing efficiently with customers.

THE COMMUNICATION PROCESS

The process involves:

- the sender – the person who actually initiated the message. It is this person's responsibility to ensure that what they want to say is clear and straightforward
- the message itself – volunteers needed for overtime
- the medium – how the message is to be sent, eg memo, telephone
- the receiver – the person who is being sent the message has a responsibility to read or listen carefully so there is no misunderstanding
- feedback – this happens when the message is confirmed and acted upon, such as giving names of people wishing to volunteer for additional overtime.

See Figure 8.2.

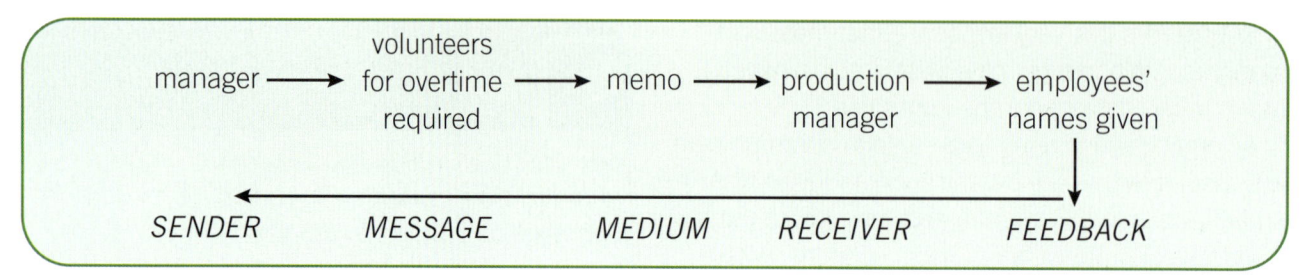

```
manager → volunteers    → memo → production → employees'
          for overtime           manager      names given
          required
  ←───────────────────────────────────────────────────┘
SENDER      MESSAGE      MEDIUM    RECEIVER     FEEDBACK
```

Figure 8.2 The communication process

INTERNAL COMMUNICATION

Internal communication takes place within an organisation, eg between a manager and a supervisor or between two employees. It can take place in various directions:

- upwards
- horizontally
- downwards
- diagonally.

Upward communication

```
        Manager
          ↑
        Employee
```

Upward communication is between employees and managers, or directors. It can provide useful information about problems and successes, and helps to keep managers in touch with employees. An example is an employee asking to complete the holiday sheet.

Downward Communication

```
        Manager
          ↓
        Employee
```

Downward communication is usually used to tell employees about decisions made, instructions or company policy. An example is a manager asking an employee for the hours of overtime s/he has worked this week.

Horizontal Communication

Employee ⟶ Employee ⟶ Employee

Horizontal communication occurs between employees at the same level in the organisation. It can be between managers or between employees. In smaller organisations it occurs frequently and tends to be informal because there are fewer employees. For example, one employee asking help from another employee on how to do a particular aspect of work.

Diagonal Communication

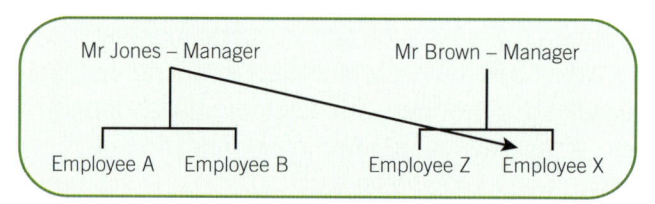

```
Mr Jones – Manager              Mr Brown – Manager
     ┌──────┴──────┐                 ┌──────┴──────┐
Employee A   Employee B         Employee Z   Employee X
```

Diagonal communication takes place across the hierarchy between people at different levels. Mr Jones may wish to introduce a new procedure, for which he needs the help of Employee X who works for Mr Brown.

Figure 8.3 Communication can happen at all levels and between different departments

Grapevine

There is also the **grapevine**. This is an unofficial or informal way of communicating and can be between people sharing a car, or those who sit together at break time, having a chat over coffee. Communication through the grapevine can sometimes be a problem because messages and information get muddled. On the other hand, it can be a useful way of collecting information or passing on information. Some companies use the grapevine to leak information to employees or the media to gauge their reaction before making decisions.

Task

Detailed below are various examples of communication. For each one state, the direction and your reasons for the choice.

1. The management team of a large nursery school meets each morning at 7.30 am before it opens to review the previous day and identify any changes needed for the coming day.
2. The manager of the sales department in Debenhams department store headquarters sends an e-mail to all the branch sales managers about the launch of the Christmas sale.
3. The management of Ford is in consultation with the union about the closing of Jaguar car production at the Browns Lane, Coventry site.
4. A presentation of a new product for sale is given by a sales representative to the board of directors in the company.

TYPES OF COMMUNICATION

There are five main types of communication:

1. written – letters, memoranda, reports, notices
2. oral – telephone, face-to-face, meetings
3. visual – charts, tables, posters, advertisements
4. electronic – facsimile, computer, e-mail, pager
5. non-verbal – body language

The information to be communicated dictates which method is used, depending upon:

- the nature of the information – Is it long or short? Is it confidential?
- the speed with which it needs to be sent – Does it need to arrive today?
- whether it is best in written or oral form – Would a telephone call be best?
- the cost – Would the cost be too much?

Written communication

Written communication uses words, numbers and images. A record is kept of the message, and it is possible to reach a large number of people at the same time.

Figure 8.4 Examples of written communication

Letters

This is a formal method of communication and is normally used to send messages outside of the company, ie externally. Each company will have their own special letter layout that everyone in the company should follow.

Letters can be used internally, in a formal context, such as the appointment, promotion or dismissal of an employee from the company. Advantages are:

- Letters provide a permanent record of the communication.
- Accurate, clear messages can be given.
- Letters can contain very detailed instructions.
- They can be confidential and targeted at the right person.

Disadvantages include:

- They are slower than other methods, eg telephone.
- They can be less personal because of the formal nature of the letter.
- There is no immediate feedback.
- There could be occasions when the person it is addressed to does not receive it – eg the secretary opens and deals with the post.
- The sender will only know of the impact once a response has been sent.

Memoranda

Memoranda, normally called memos, are usually an internal method of communication. They are normally a brief message and can be sent electronically as well as by internal post. Advantages include:

- They provide a permanent record for future reference.
- They are normally short and to the point.
- If sent electronically, then they can await the person if they are not in the office.
- They are useful when communicating from one branch of the company to another which may be in a different country.

Disadvantages are:

- There is no immediate feedback.
- Smaller pieces of paper can be lost or ignored.
- There is no guarantee of receipt.
- If too many are sent out, the importance of each one may be overlooked.

Reports

A report is a more formal written method of communication than a memo. It is usually used after someone has carried out some research or investigation, which is then presented to others. Most reports are very structured and formal, eg a report on the Health and Safety of the company, or future plans to install new computers. The language should be clear and concise. The report is normally word processed and will include recommendations, so that action can be taken. Advantages are:

- Reports can be copied and circulated to many people.
- Reports are normally for complicated matters that need consideration.
- Reports can contain detailed information including data, charts, graphs.

Disadvantages include:

- They can become very complicated.
- The language and detail can become confusing.
- Very time-consuming to prepare and present.
- Due to the length of reports, they may not be read fully and understood.

Notices

Notices are frequently used internally to communicate to employees within the organisation. They can be used to inform employees of forthcoming social events, meetings that will take place, job vacancies or fire drill procedures. Advantages include:

- They can easily be seen by a large number of people.
- They are cheap to produce.
- They are less time-consuming than trying to see everyone individually with the information.
- The information can be presented in a variety of different ways, such as graphics, charts, cartoons.
- They can encourage staff to participate.

Disadvantages are:

- Notices can be defaced very easily – ie torn down or drawn on.
- There is no guarantee that everyone will see the notice.
- They are a very impersonal method of communicating.
- Notices will lose their impact if they are not changed frequently.

> **⚠ Exam tip**
>
> Try to devise a chart showing the advantages and disadvantages of each method of communication. This makes it easier to learn and revise than just reading the text.

Oral communication

Oral communication is communication via the spoken word. No record is usually kept, although there are certain occasions when it is kept on tape.

Face-to-face

Face-to-face communication is usually in the form of a meeting, which can be with one person or many. Face-to-face communication can be a formal or an informal chat. Advantages are:

- Meetings ensure that everyone gets the same information.
- Everyone can look at any paperwork/charts/data and discuss freely any issues.
- Feedback can be given and received, immediately.
- Problems can be sorted out quickly.
- Body language can be effectively read by those at the meeting.

Disadvantages include:

- In large meetings there is no way of checking that everyone is listening.
- Also, there is no way of knowing if everyone has understood.
- Facial expressions/body language can act as a barrier to effective communication.
- Not everyone is always available for the meeting.
- Not everyone has confidence to speak at the meeting.
- People may have to travel to the meeting, which might not be cost effective.

Telephone

The telephone, in whatever format (mobile phones, standard phones), is an electronic form of oral communication. It provides a fast method of communication with people inside and outside of the company. It is probably the most widely used method of communication at present. Advantages include:

- It enables long-distance communication to take place.
- It saves time.
- Feedback is immediate.
- It is a two-way method of communication.
- Information and problems can be sorted out quickly.

Figure 8.5 A meeting: one example of oral communication

Disadvantages are:

- There is no written record of what has taken place.
- Verbal messages can be misunderstood.
- If the person is not available then it can be very time-consuming.
- Difference in time zones with people from other countries can be inconvenient.
- Mobile phones are not always clear, due to signal and reception.
- Some verbal communication can be misleading as the person communicating cannot see the reaction of the receiver.

Tannoy
Tannoys are used to make announcements via loudspeakers to many people, for example in a factory, or at an airport informing passengers about a flight. The advantage of using a tannoy is that a large number of people can be informed of simple instructions quickly and easily. Disadvantages are that there is no record of the message and no guarantee that everyone who should receive the message will hear it.

Visual communication
There are many different ways that information can be communicated visually, eg charts and diagrams, tables, films and videos, advertisements. Visual information can help in communicating because it is easy to see and can simplify points of information.

Charts and diagrams
These are a very simple way of displaying information, especially if it is a great deal of numbers or very technical work. They can make information much easier to understand.

Tables
Again, information presented in a table is much easier to understand and follow.

Films and Video
To watch something in a film or video is simple and gains the attention of the listener far more than listening to someone speak for a considerable time.

Advertisements
Advertisements are used by most companies to promote their business. They aim to be 'eye catching', to attract the attention of the person reading or watching. Companies spend a great deal of money on advertising. Advantages are:

- Information can be presented in a very clear manner.
- The information is much easier to read and looks better.
- Films and videos show actual size of product.

Disadvantages include:

- There is no feedback, unless the company checks that the message has been received and understood.

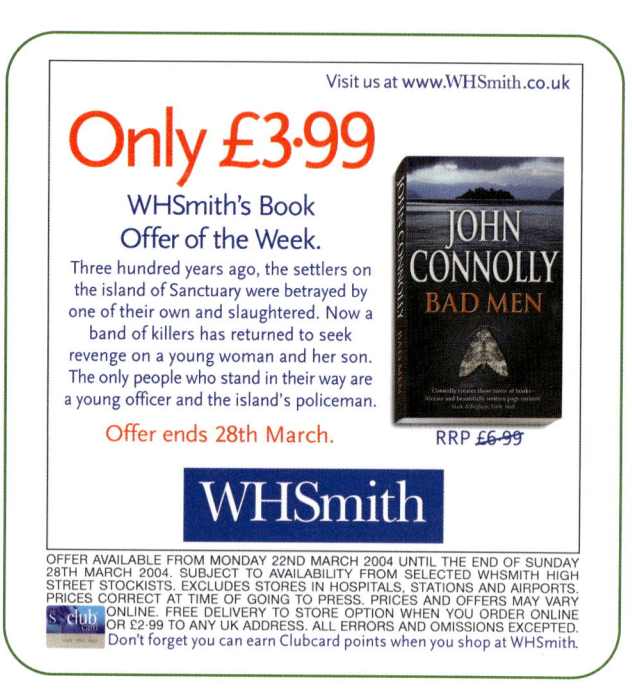

Figure 8.6 An advertisement

Electronic communication

Facsimile (fax)
The information is sent electronically between two fax machines using the telephone lines. The cost of sending the message depends on the distance between the two organisations and the length of time it takes to transmit the message (it is the same as a telephone cal of the same duration). Advantages include:

- Message can be sent quickly compared to letters.
- Exact copies of the message are sent.
- Quite easy to send and does not need someone at the other end to receive.

Disadvantages are:

- The hard copy received is occasionally of poor quality.
- The sender and receiver both need a fax machine.
- There can be problems with feeding individual sheets through; sometimes the machine can misfeed.
- The message is not always confidential.
- The fax machine can run out of paper in the middle of a transmission.

E-mail

Electronic mail, often shortened to e-mail, enables one computer to talk to another computer via a modem which accesses a telephone line. This has fast become a very popular method of communication between companies. Memos, reports, charts, diagrams are often sent by e-mail. Employees now check their e-mails instead of their in-trays for work. Some companies are totally paperless and rely on the computer. Eventually e-mail will possibly take over from the written form as we know it today.

Each person needs an e-mail address to communicate, such as j.jones@birmingham.sch.uk. Advantages are:

- Messages can be keyed-in and stored until needed.
- Allows communication easily over a number of different sites.
- People can keep in touch very easily – many messages can be sent.
- One message can be sent to a number of different people at the same time.
- Printout can be obtained if needed.
- E-mails can be sent and then await the receiver to read them.
- Attachments can be sent with the e-mail.
- Easier to refer back to rather than looking through different pieces of paper.

Disadvantages include:

- Users need a modem and computer.
- Connections can sometimes be lost.
- Users have to subscribe to a service provider, eg AOL, Blueyonder, etc.
- Problems with the service provider can mean not being able to send a message.
- Users have to check their mail regularly.
- Easy to delete a message by mistake.
- Users can forget to respond to messages.
- If the message needs to be printed out then it can be quite time-consuming.
- Messages can be intercepted, so it is not a good way of sending confidential material.

Pager

A pager is a small device that is carried around by the owner and enables contact to be made by the pager bleeping or vibrating. This is normally used in an emergency or for someone merely trying to pass on a message. For example, the school nurse may have a pager so that she can be contacted wherever she is in the building if there is an emergency. Some pagers are more sophisticated and allow messages to be relayed, others are there to let people know that they need to contact someone. Advantages include:

- They are light, very portable pieces of equipment.
- Not expensive to buy.
- There are no additional rental charges.

Disadvantages are:

- No two-way communication can take place.
- The pager has to be switched on.
- There is a charge for messages sent.
- They have to be in range of the base or switchboard.

Video conferencing

Video conferencing is becoming more and more popular with companies. It involves using computer links and closed-circuit television, allowing people to hear and see each other. Advantages are:

- Saves people travelling to meetings.
- Large savings can then be made in terms of time and cost.
- Face-to-face communication is possible rather than using telephone or letter.

Figure 8.7 Video conferencing

Disadvantages include:
- Links may not be very good.
- Hardware is still expensive to buy.
- Needs a dedicated telephone line.
- People still prefer 'live' meetings.
- Everyone needs to be available at the same time.

Non-verbal communication
Sometimes information is exchanged without speaking or writing. If no words are used, it is non-verbal. Body language is a way of communicating. A nod or frown will give an answer to a question. On some occasions, however, the message given by our body language is not the message we wish to portray. A forced smile might mean you agree on the surface, when really you do not.

Task
Present in a table the types of communication discussed, showing the advantages and disadvantages.

Exam tip
Talk to relatives to find out which methods of communication they use where they work. Which do they prefer? Which do they find is the easiest and most reliable method?

Practical discussion with people makes the topic more informative and realistic.

GOOD AND BAD COMMUNICATION
At the start of the unit, it was shown that for communication to be successful the message has to be received, and then acted upon. However, there are many occasions when things get in the way of good communication and therefore the communication is not effective. The things that get in the way can be termed 'barriers to communication', and they can occur at all stages of communication.

Good communication
Good communication is essential to any organisation:
- It ensures that action is consistent and coordinated.
- It ensures that information is accurate and up to date for customers and employees.
- It encourages motivation in employees, as they feel they have a say in the company.
- Clear instructions ensure that the job is completed correctly and on time.
- It can help clear up misunderstandings.
- It provides managers with information on which to base their decisions.
- It provides managers with feedback on previous decisions.

Poor communication
Poor communication can lead to dissatisfied employees and customers, a poor business image and problems with others outside the organisation.

Poor communication can mean that jobs are not carried out correctly because the employees do not understand. This could lead to poorly motivated employees.

Poor communication can lead to lost orders, loss of custom and increased workload.

The sender
The person may not be a good communicator, or may not have all the information that needs to be communicated. Or it could be that the person does not have sufficient influence to communicate the information, eg a production worker on the shop floor trying to persuade the management to listen to his or her idea.

The language used by the sender is not understood by the receiver, either it is too technical or is not using the words that the receiver understands.

The message
This may be far too complicated, either by being too long, or containing too much jargon for the receiver to understand. An example might be a tax accountant trying to explain the different methods of taxation and how a tax code is arrived at.

The medium
The sender may choose the wrong method to send the message. For example, sending out memos to staff rather than having a face-to-face discussion on a reduction in staff. Many staff could be unnecessarily extremely worried.

The receiver
The person receiving the message may not listen to or read it properly, or they do not wish to listen because it is something they may not like. An example of this is a memo being sent about a reduction in overtime; the person may not wish to read it because they rely on overtime to gain a better wage.

The feedback
The sender may not provide an opportunity for feedback to take place, eg the management deciding to close down the canteen without allowing the staff to comment on it.

The effects of poor communication
If good communication does not exist, actions will not be completed, and problems will develop.

- If the management do not keep in touch with their staff, it could lead to unrest within the workforce which could result in frustration, loss of motivation and eventually industrial action.
- If customers receive poor service, then they are unlikely to return to the company and will try to find someone else, thus damaging the company's reputation.
- Bad decisions could result in loss of business, which could consequently mean loss of jobs and money.

Rules for good communication
If the following points are followed, then communication should be efficient and effective, with fewer mistakes and less confusion.

- The message must be suitable for the people it is being given to. Different audiences require a different method of communication.
- Keep all information as simple as possible – the meaning of the message can be lost if it is too technical or too wordy.
- Keep the information as accurate and up to date as possible.

Revision Questions

1. To display information about a quiz night, a business might use a:
   a) memo
   b) questionnaire
   c) letter
   d) notice

2. Managers hold regular meetings. This form of communication is:
   a) e-mail
   b) face-to-face
   c) written
   d) vertical

3. How would you contact someone who is out of the office, but within the company?
   a) telephone
   b) pager
   c) video-conferencing
   d) swipe card

4. Information passed from a manager to an employee is:
   a) downward
   b) horizontal
   c) upward
   d) diagonal

5. When using e-mail to communicate, this means:
   a) using a report
   b) express post
   c) computer-to-computer
   d) using a fax

Past Paper

1. The National Farmers' Union also communicates with farmers and other interested people through its website, which has an e-mail facility.

   What are the advantages, to farmers, of communicating electronically via the website and e-mail? (5)

   (Edexcel, 2002, Foundation)

2. At the board meeting, decisions were made regarding airport security. The directors must communicate these decisions to their employees by holding a meeting, and to SafeBase (a specialist security firm) by letter. Explain why the directors chose these methods of communication. (6)

   (Edexcel, 2001, Higher)

3. The Directors of Happy Ideas Ltd are using the internet to advertise the Millennium Bear. Discuss whether this is an appropriate method. (4)

   (Edexcel, 2000, Foundation)

Task

Give examples of external communication.

Extension task

Good communication is often seen as vital to the efficient running of a firm. What factors might cause this communication to break down? Explain the implications of poor communication and suggest ways of improving these poor communication systems.

Summary

At the end of this unit you should:
- understand each method of verbal and non-verbal communication, and the various written methods
- be able to decide which method of communication is needed for a particular situation
- realise that communication is essential within a business
- understand the importance of good communication.

Key terms

Communication – the transferring of a message from the sender to the receiver

Communication barrier – something which prevents effective communication

Diagonal communication – messages can be passed between people in all directions, like a compass – North to South, East to West, North to East, etc

External communication – messages between people in different organisations

Face-to-face – speaking to someone personally, usually in a meeting

FAX – facsimile machine – a machine which can send a copy of a document via a telephone link

Grapevine – an unofficial channel of communication; how rumours are spread

Horizontal communication – messages between people on the same level

Internal communication – messages between people in the same organisation

Meeting – a coming together of people

Memorandum – or Memo – an internal method of communication

Message – information or instructions being passed between sender and receiver

Oral communication – spoken word

Video conferencing – people in different places can hold meetings where no one has to travel yet everyone can see each other.

UNIT 9

RECRUITMENT AND SELECTION

What you will learn

At the end of this unit you should understand:
- procedures involved in the recruitment of employees.
- legislation on employment.

All companies need to employ people. They may need to do this because someone has left the job or retired, or a new job has been created within the company. This is similar to school; when a teacher leaves then s/he is usually replaced.

Much discussion will probably take place between those involved in taking on the new person (**recruitment**) and the person who is in charge of the department they are going to work for. They need to decide exactly what they expect the person to do, as the job may have changed since the original person was appointed. For example, a person working in the finance department may now have to be familiar with a particular computer program in order to carry out the job. This was not required when the original person started because the program was not available then. Once agreement has been reached between all parties concerned, they will then start the process of recruitment.

There is normally a procedure that companies follow when trying to find the right person for the job. After initial discussions a list will be drawn up of jobs they expect the person to do and skills they expect the person to have. If the company is large enough they may even have a department especially dedicated to looking after recruitment and selection; this could be called the human resources department or personnel department. This department will carry out all the tasks of designing an advert, placing the advert in an appropriate place, selecting the people for interview and eventually appointing them. In a smaller company, such as a motor repair shop, the owner may well do all the work.

The more important the job within the company, the more time-consuming the process will be. They have to make sure that they have the right person for the job.

WHO TO RECRUIT?

When a company wants to take on a new recruit, there are two important documents that the company will need to draw up:

1. A **job description** – a description of the job that is being recruited for.
2. A **job specification** – a description of the sort of person who would be the ideal candidate for the job.

Job description

This allows the person applying to know exactly what is involved in the job. Also the company has a very clear idea of what they expect the person to do, if they secure the job.

Job descriptions should include the following:

- job title
- purpose of the job
- position within the organisation
- specific duties to be carried out

- any other responsibilities the job might have
- where the job will be based
- conditions of work and hours.

> **Task**
>
> You work in a human resources department and have been tasked by the manager to draw up a job description for one of the following:
>
> 1. a secretary
> 2. a cashier in a bank
> 3. a shop assistant
> 4. a labourer
>
> *Think about the types of jobs you would expect this person to do. Remember, there are main duties as well as occasional ones. Who would they be responsible to?*

The main function of a job description is to give the candidate applying an idea of what the job entails. They can be very detailed, including many different things such as the type of training, how long it will last, etc. Others can be quite brief, with only the minimum amount of detail given. If there is a dispute regarding what the employee should have done or not, they can refer back to the job description.

Once a job description has been drawn up the company can then draw up a **job specification** so that they can match the person correctly to the job.

Job specification

A job specification will be more prescriptive in what the company expects the person to be able to do. This will include the qualifications, training already undertaken, specialist skills and/or knowledge of the applicant, together with the type of personality or person the company would expect to employ. Some of these may be essential and some may be

Baverstock Foundation School and Specialist Sports College

Job title	Bursar
Department	Finance
Details of job	Senior member of the school, reporting directly to the Headteacher
Specific duties	To control financial spending of the school To negotiate all contracts within the school, eg school catering, minibuses, photocopiers To reduce spending wherever possible
Other responsibilities	To instigate the health and safety policy To maintain the fabric of the building To monitor staff directly responsible to the bursar
Location of work	In the main office of the school
Conditions of work and hours	30 days' holiday plus statutory holiday to be taken during school holidays 37 hours per week Local authority pension scheme

Figure 9.1 A typical job description

desirable. It is then up to the company which candidates they decide to interview.

The following are generally the main headings of a job specification, but companies will probably decide their own headings suitable for their company and the type of job.

- title of the job
- department where they are going to work
- description of the job
- qualifications that are required for the job
- experience required
- skills
- personal attributes or qualities.

> **Task**
>
> Now draw up a job specification for one of the following:
> 1. a teacher
> 2. a shop assistant
> 3. a cashier at a bank
> 4. a labourer

> **Task**
>
> Research two possible vacancies you would like to apply for when you leave school. Draw up their job description and job specification.

> **Exam tip**
>
> Remember, a job description is about the job, whereas the job specification is about the person.

ADVERTISING THE VACANCY

Many companies have a policy or a procedure that has been agreed, which states that any vacancy must be advertised **internally** within the company before it is advertised **externally** outside the company.

Baverstock Foundation School and Specialist Sports College

Job title	Bursar
Department	Finance
Details of job	Responsible to the Headteacher. Main aim to maintain all contracts within the school and to ensure value for money. Responsible for two general clerical assistants. To join Leadership Group to input where appropriate. Responsible for all health and safety within the building.
Qualifications	Essential: 5 GCSEs including English and Mathematics HND or similar Desirable: Degree in Finance
Experience	Minimum of 5 years' working within the financial sector
Skills	Ability to communicate effectively with people Good negotiator Ability to manage people
Personal attributes	Able to work under pressure Honest and reliable Good sense of humour

Figure 9.2 A typical job specification

Internal recruitment

If the vacancy is to be advertised internally then the person responsible will produce an advert, which is then displayed within the company. Some companies have a noticeboard where vacancies are advertised; others have a general newsletter, which is distributed. Some companies may even use e-mail or have a web page as a method of making staff aware of a job opportunity. It mainly depends on the size of the company as to which method they use; each company will have their own method.

The notice could be similar to this one:

> **REQUIRED**
>
> **COMPUTER PROGRAMMER**
>
> **WORK IN FINANCE DEPARTMENT**
>
> Scale II
>
> May be required to work shifts and weekends
>
> Letter of application to
> Mr Jones, Human Resources
> By Friday 30 November 2004

Figure 9.3 An example of an internal advertisement

An internal vacancy advert does not need to contain a great deal of detail, as the person applying will know what the company is like. The terms and conditions of employment remain basically the same. They will be interested in which department they could be working for and with whom, together with anything that may be different from their present job.

People applying for an internal job may have many reasons for doing so: they feel that they would like promotion; the job that they are presently doing may not be sufficiently interesting for them and they wish to have a change without moving company; their job may be about to disappear because of reorganisation within the company, etc.

Figure 9.4 An employee looking at an internal vacancy

There are many advantages and disadvantages to appointing someone internally, however, it depends entirely upon the company and what is best for them.

Task

You have been asked by the human resources manager to look into internal recruitment. Draft a report giving your reasons for and against appointing someone internally.

Exam tip

When writing a report, do not just list the points but write them in full sentences. This will help you gain the higher levels in your coursework.

External recruitment

It can take an extremely long time to organise external recruitment, and eventually to gain the right person for the job.

After deciding what the details of the job are going to be, an advertisement will have to be drawn up. In this advertisement much more detail is needed than for internal recruitment, or instructions on how the applicant can gain more information.

> **Task**
>
> Research your local paper and gather together different advertisements for job vacancies. Make a list of all the main points that are supplied about each job.
>
> Now draw up three advertisements of your own, making sure you include all the points you found out above.

Where to advertise
There are many different places that a company can advertise a vacancy. Here are some of them:
- job centres
- careers service
- recruitment agencies
- learning skills council
- local radio
- local and national newspapers
- specialist job magazines.

The vacancy could also be filled from a personal recommendation.

Job centres
These are run by the government through the Department for Education and Skills. The main aim of a job centre is to find local work for local people. This can be an inexpensive way of finding a person. However, finding a specialist for a particular job or someone with special skills may be more difficult.

Careers service
Connexions was set up in 2001 and is the amalgamation of the Careers Service and the Youth Service. The aim of the service is to provide as much information as possible to help school leavers in deciding what careers or training programmes are available to them.

Figure 9.5 Looking for vacancies at the job centre

Recruitment agencies
These are specialist agencies who help people find a job, and also help companies find employees where internal applicants are not available. The larger known agencies are those such as MSX International, Manpower and Pertemps, to name a few. There will probably be a number of smaller local agencies, which can be found in the telephone directories. Some agencies specialise in the type of work they offer, or they may have one or

> **Task**
>
> Find out who is in charge of careers in your school. What is the name of your adviser, the person who comes into school and helps you with advice? Try to find copies of some of the jobs they have available on offer for you.

two employees who look after one particular aspect of work, eg engineering, selling, secretarial, construction work.

A company will employ an agency to find suitable candidates for a job. The agency will carry out all the advertising, checking/screening of curriculum vitaes (CVs) and will only put forward to the company a small selection of people who they think will be suitable for the job. This will save the company a great deal of time and effort in advertising, looking through CVs and interviewing. The company has to pay a fee for this service, which can either be a percentage of the person's salary for a period of time or a fixed rate.

Learning Skills Council (LSC)
This organisation is similar to Connexions but more for adults who wish to return to work or change their particular career. The service also provides funding for various courses and for people to gain qualifications such as National Vocational Qualifications (NVQ) levels 2 and 3. However, they do not guarantee employment after the training. Part of their work is to promote the Modern Apprenticeships – this is where people can gain recognised work and qualifications through a larger well-known organisation.

Local radio
Local radios often have certain slots within the day when they advertise jobs. This is a useful opportunity to advertise the company on the radio.

Local newspapers
Local papers normally have one night in the week when they focus on recruitment and advertise any vacancies. For example, the *Birmingham Evening Mail* advertises that they have on average 50 pages of job vacancies in the paper on a Thursday evening; they do, however, run small numbers of job advertisements during the other days of the week.

Sometimes there are papers which advertise in a specific district, and therefore the jobs offered will be local to that area.

National Newspapers
These are very similar to the local newspapers in that they will advertise jobs when any company

---

OFFICE JUNIOR
£7000 PA

To check invoices and calculate costs for the company.
Experience preferred, but school leaver will be considered, if they have studied business-related subjects.
Neat handwriting and aptitude for figure work essential. Minimum of 4 GCSEs including English and Maths
- Flexible hours
- Subsidised canteen
- Bus route nearby

Applications in writing to:
Mr G White, Human Resources
Riddlers Limited, 64 Grosvenor Road,
Newtown, Derbyshire DB4 6XZ

Figure 9.6 An example of an external job advertisement

---

wishes to pay. The difference is that the jobs are more likely to be specialist, and salaries will be higher than you see in local newspapers. Papers also advertise jobs to suit its readers, eg the *Times* may look for directors and senior executives of companies, whereas the *Daily Mirror* and the *Sun* may be looking for sales representatives.

Specialist magazines
Some specialist jobs have their own magazines in which vacancies are advertised, eg *Supply Management* specialises in purchasing and supply opportunities for buyers, managers and directors.

Personal recommendation
For a smaller company this is one way to obtain a new employee. Someone who works for the company recommends a friend or acquaintance or someone they know for the job. This word-of-mouth recommendation is often used by companies and can save a great deal of time and money. Frequently the person is selected after an interview, so the process from start to finish is rather short.

> **Task**
>
> Draw up a chart showing the advantages and disadvantages of each method of advertising. If possible, try to find the price for an advert for each method.

LETTERS OF APPLICATION/ CURRICULUM VITAES

Once you have seen a particular job you would like to apply for, you will need to write a letter of application or carry out the instructions given in the advertisement. Most will require a letter of some form. The advertisement will give you a very clear idea of what is required in the letter, with clues and important information about the company. Also, if the company has forwarded to you further details about the position, this will help you compose your letter. Follow the instructions given – if it asks for a handwritten letter, do not word process it.

In your letter of application you should include the following:

- your home address, including postcode
- any telephone numbers to contact you
- e-mail address if you have one
- name and address of the person to whom the letter is addressed
- which job you are applying for
- qualifications or examinations to be taken
- personal interests
- any experience relevant to the job
- most importantly, why you want the job and what makes you think you are suitable.

Quite often companies will ask you to include a curriculum vitae.

Curriculum vitae

A curriculum vitae is a brief history of the applicant's career, including details of the schools attended, qualifications gained, relevant experience and interests, plus the names of two people willing to comment on how you work, who are known as referees.

Figure 9.7 Someone typing up their CV

If a CV is included, then the letter accompanying it should be briefer.

> **Task**
>
> Make a list of all the headings you should have in a CV.
>
> Have you written your CV yet? Gather a variety of different layouts and choose the one that suits you.

References

From the many applicants for the job advertised, human resources will short-list a few of the most promising applicants and invite them to attend an interview. For this reason, the written application is very important if the applicant is to reach the next stage. Once the applicants have been short-listed, the company will contact their referees so that a reference can be given. A reference will normally contain information on the person, such as their personality, time-keeping, honesty, reliability and any other information that has been requested. It is important that the person giving the reference gives an honest opinion of the person. All references are confidential, but the referee should not make derogatory remarks. Quite often if something is not very complimentary then they will not mention it, eg if timekeeping has been poor then this will not be mentioned. It is then up to the receiver to decide on the points not mentioned; are they important?

Alternatively, references can be sought after the person has been appointed but before they start at the company. It is up to the company and the policy or routine that they follow.

Sometimes one can submit an 'open testimonial' – this is where a reference is given from a company to no one in particular which can be used by the applicant to show prospective employers.

If you are a school-leaver then you would normally list the school as a referee; if already employed then you would list your employer.

THE INTERVIEW PROCEDURE

Interviews are the most common method of obtaining a new employee, but they are not always the most reliable method. It is difficult to check what the applicant is actually like, whether they are capable of doing the job, and whether they will fit in with the rest of the employees. These are some of the points raised with regard to the interview process.

Preparation before the interview

Here are some pointers when preparing yourself for an interview.

- Do some homework/research on the company you have applied for – Do they have a website? Background information may be very useful to you.
- Dress carefully – be well presented and look clean and tidy.
- Remember the name of the person you have to see.
- Know exactly where and when the interview is to take place.
- Plan your route beforehand – practise the route if time permits.
- Arrive in plenty of time for the interview.

At the interview

- Take the letter of invitation with you.
- Do not arrive too early but certainly not late.
- Wait to be told what to do – ie where to sit and when.
- Do not chew during an interview.
- Try to be relaxed and confident.
- Concentrate fully on the person or persons interviewing.
- Answer all questions.

Figure 9.8 An interview

- Try to ask some questions when invited to – it shows interest.
- Do not be flippant and over-familiar with the interviewer.

Questions you could be asked
- Why do you want the job?
- What qualities do you have that will help in the job/company?
- What is your future ambition?
- Do you have any hobbies/interests?

Questions you could ask
- What does the job actually involve?
- What are the hours?
- What opportunities are there for training and promotion?
- What are the holiday arrangements?

Additional tasks that could be carried out on interview

Nowadays it is becoming more popular for companies to ask interviewees to carry out other exercises additional to an interview. The purpose of these exercises is to check whether the company has selected the right person for the job, and whether the information stated in the CV and letter of application is correct.

Skills tests
The candidate is asked to carry out certain procedures, eg teachers attending interviews are expected to teach a class.

Aptitude tests
These show whether the candidate is capable of carrying out additional tasks or training in the future.

Personality tests
These attempt to discover whether the candidate matches the needs of the job. Can they work under pressure and stress? Will they fit in with the existing team.

Role-play situations
Applicants are watched as they perform various tasks to assess their strengths and weaknesses. Can they work as a team member? Are they leader or a follower? Are they shy and quiet or outspoken and brash?

Making the decision
Once all the prospective candidates have been interviewed then a decision is made as to which one is successful.

Some companies inform the unsuccessful candidates in person on the day, others by telephone or by letter. It all depends on whether all candidates were present on the day of the decision.

When the successful candidate has accepted the job offer and agreed the starting date, they may have to receive training for the job; this is discussed in the next chapter.

> **Task**
>
> Draw up a flow chart showing the process of recruiting a member of staff.

PROTECTION OF THE WORKFORCE

Legislation affects all companies which employ people in ensuring that employees are protected in the following areas:

- employment protection
- discrimination.

Employment protection
Companies must follow the set procedures laid down by the government. Some of them are detailed below:

- As soon as a person accepts an offer of a job, there is a contract between the employer and the employee even though they may not have exchanged any written details.
- If an employee works more than eight hours a week, they are entitled to a written statement of terms and conditions of employment within their first two months of work.
- Once you have worked for a company for at least a month, and you decide you do not wish to work there anymore, then you must give at least one week's notice (unless something different is written in the contract).

- The length of notice that an employer has to give an employee may differ depending upon the length of service the employee has given. The basic notice is after one month of work then at least one week, after two years' service then at least two weeks, three years', three weeks, etc. Again this depends on what was agreed in the contract.
- An employee is entitled to written notification if they are dismissed from their job and have been employed for longer than two years.

Figure 9.9 The Equal Opportunities Commission covers issues on sexual discrimination and equal pay

- If an employee is dismissed after two years of working, they can appeal to an industrial tribunal.
- If an employee has worked for a company for more than two years then they are entitled to redundancy pay. The amount depends on service to the company and what is written in the contract.

Discrimination
Discrimination of any kind is not allowed, and legislation exists to protect employees in their work (regardless of whether they are full-time or part-time).

The Sex Discrimination Act, 1975
Nobody should receive less favourable treatment on the grounds of their sex. Sex discrimination legislation makes it unlawful to discriminate against a person, either directly or indirectly, in the field of employment. The legislation imposes responsibility on the individual as well as the employers to ensure that the law is upheld. Promotion should also not be affected on the grounds of gender.

The Equal Pay Act
People doing the same work must have equal pay. A man should not earn more than a women, and vice versa, for the same job.

The Disability Persons (Employment) Act, 1944
Employees with disabilities should not be treated less favourably than able-bodied employees with regard to job applications, promotions, career development and training. Companies may need to make reasonable adjustments to working conditions, working hours and parking facilities close to the place of work, etc, to accommodate disabled employees.

Figure 9.10 The BBC – an example of an equal opportunities employer

The Race Discrimination Act, 1976
Employees should not be discriminated against at work because of their race or ethnic origins. This also applies to recruitment and pay.

It is easier for a larger company to ensure that all procedures are followed in accordance with the relevant legislation. However, smaller companies may find it more difficult. For example, a small company may not be able to afford all the alterations that are needed to accommodate a disabled person. However, they should try wherever possible to accommodate them.

Revision Questions

1. People applying for a job at a company would have to complete
   a) a job description
   b) a memorandum
   c) an order form
   d) an application form

2. The personnel department in a company could also be called the .... department.
   a) production
   b) marketing
   c) human resources
   d) finance

3. Jobs for new workers at a company are usually .... in local papers.
   a) promoted
   b) advertised
   c) selected
   d) interviewed

4. The personnel department of a company will always try to promote existing staff. This is called .... promotion.
   a) internal
   b) induction
   c) recruitment
   d) external

5. People chosen for interview would be on:
   a) an induction
   b) a short list
   c) a programme
   d) an agenda

Past Paper

1. Apart from recruitment, list three other responsibilities of the personnel department. (3)

2. Explain one advantage and one disadvantage of internal recruitment to a company. (4)

3. Some specialist jobs could not be filled internally, so the personnel department had to look outside the company.

   List two ways, other than a letter of application, that the personnel department might use to find out details of applicants. (2)

4. After details of applications have been received, the personnel department can draw up a short list. They then invite suitable applicants to attend an interview.

   Why do you think the personnel department decides to use an interview? Explain your reasons. (4)

5. The recruitment and selection process takes time to complete.

   Explain why the directors of a company think the time spent recruiting and selecting staff is worthwhile. (2)

   (Edexcel, 2001, Foundation)

Summary

At the end of this unit you should be able to:
- understand the purpose of the human resource department
- draw up a job description
- draw up a job specification
- draw up an advertisement for a job.

Key terms

Contract of employment – a legal agreement between a company and an employee

Curriculum vitae – details of a person, eg schools, work experience, interests

External recruitment – position filled from outside of the company

Industrial tribunal – a legal meeting where complaints are heard and discussed

Internal recruitment – vacancy which is filled within the company

Job analysis – details of the job are recorded and identified

Job description – list of duties and responsibilities of a job to be carried out

Redundancy – when someone loses their job, as it is no longer required (not that the person is not very good at their job)

Salary – the amount earned within a year, normally paid each month

Short list – when a small number of applicants is selected from a larger number

UNIT 9: RECRUITMENT AND SELECTION

UNIT 10

TRAINING

>> What you will learn

At the end of this unit you should understand:
- the different types of training
- the main purposes of training
- the benefits of induction, on-the-job and off-the-job training
- government training schemes
- and be able to analyse the costs/benefits to the management and the employee of training.

There are many reasons companies need to train their employees. In every type of job there is always training of some kind or another.

Training may be needed for several reasons:
- to explain how to use new machinery
- to improve the efficiency of the company
- to improve the productivity of the company
- to increase employees' skills
- to reduce the risk of accidents in the workplace
- to introduce someone to the company and the way they should work.

Training should be worthwhile to both the company and the employee. If the employee is clear about the purpose and the reason for training, then it is likely that they will learn the new skills quickly and effectively.

There are various ways in which training can be carried out, such as **induction**, which is the training before the person starts their actual job. This can be similar to having a mentor, someone who helps you through the first few days or weeks. Training while the person is actually learning the job, taught by someone who already works for the company is often referred to as **on-the-job**, and the other main method of training is **off-the-job**. This is away from the workplace when someone goes to another establishment to be taught, eg college.

Training can be anything from a short half-day course to several years, depending on the skills that need to be acquired and the person themselves.

INDUCTION TRAINING

The purpose of induction training is to introduce a new employee to the company, the way the company works and how they expect their work to be carried out. Often it is used to acquaint the new person with the people in the company and how the company works, before they start work.

An induction programme may last for anything from half a day to several weeks. It all depends upon the company and what they expect the new employee to do. A person working on the shop floor may only have a half-day induction, whereas someone who is going to be a manager may have a week or more to understand how the company works.

Most new school pupils will have an 'induction day'. This is where you are introduced to the school and some of the staff that will teach you. You may meet your form tutor, Head of Year, as well as certain staff, eg the PE department. Part of the induction process may be to introduce you to the school building itself, helping you find your way around, as

ON-THE-JOB TRAINING

This type of training is where the employee will watch and work with someone who already has the skills and knowledge. They are then trained in the way the company wants them to work. This is probably the best method for those jobs which are not highly skilled, but the unskilled or semi-skilled worker can gain tremendously from this experience.

Many jobs in industry and employment have relied on this method of training, eg student teachers who take over the class are training while on-the-job. A number of years ago, apprentices would work alongside a skilled worker who would teach or show them how to complete a job. In the manufacturing industry this was the traditional method of training. Although this type of training has declined in recent years due to the decline in the manufacturing industry in the UK, there are now Modern Apprenticeships (MAs) which are designed to provide today's young workforce with specific skills.

Figure 10.1 Introducing a new employee to the company

well as the routine of school, break-time, lunch-time, etc. Joining a new company is exactly the same, you would want to know where you can go for breaks, and what the routine is for using the canteen.

Task

Plan a typical induction day for pupils at your school. Draw up a timetable of what you would expect them to do, and then give your reasons why.

Exam tip

Relate your own experience of training – What training did you receive before you attended secondary school? Have you taken part in any training for work experience? Thinking about practical situations which you have experienced can help in the understanding of this topic.

Figure 10.2 On-the-job training

Advantages to the employee
- They do not have to travel for training.
- They are familiar with the workforce and the staff.
- They are not responsible for the errors made.
- They are learning relevant and practical skills, which will help them in their job.

Disadvantages to the employee
- They do not gain any external qualifications.
- The skills learnt may only be relevant to that company.
- Training is normally short.
- The trainer may not be trained in how to teach other people, and therefore the transfer of skills and knowledge may be poor.

Advantages to the employer
- They know where their employees are.
- Employees are trained in the methods they want, not what someone else thinks.
- Employees are more productive, working while training.
- Not as expensive as sending them on a course.
- The employee is less likely to move companies as skills may not be transferable.

Disadvantages to the employer
- The trainer will not be as productive while they are training the trainee.
- Mistakes made by the trainee can be expensive and damaging.

OFF-THE-JOB TRAINING

This is where the trainee receives training away from the company. They will normally attend a local college or training centre, or even another part of the building to gain the skills and knowledge required.

The trainee will gain more skills and knowledge because they are being trained by a professional trainer, someone who has learnt how to train others. The methods of training may be more varied, eg from practical skills gained, to working in a classroom situation, thus enabling a broad range of skills to be taught.

Advantages to the employee
- Employees are able to gain external qualifications, eg NVQs, GNVQs.
- Qualifications and skills will enhance employee's chances of promotion or new job.
- Opportunity to spend time out of the normal routine of work.
- Gain new acquaintances and friends.
- Company pays for the training.

Disadvantages to the employee
- May involve travelling.
- Courses may be outside of the normal working day – eg evening courses.
- Skills may not be readily transferable to the company.

Advantages to the employer
- Employee is gaining useful skills.
- Mistakes made do not impinge on the company.
- If courses are held during the evening then it is more cost effective, as the employee is not having time off work.

Disadvantage to the employer
- Expensive to send employee on the course, ie course fees.

Figure 10.3 Off-the-job training – at a vocational college

- Employee not working while at college.
- Employee gains skills which could mean that once trained they might leave.
- Checking on the employee is harder when they are off-site.

Most companies will probably use a mixture of the two methods of training, on-the-job and off-the-job.

OTHER TYPES OF TRAINING

Recently, more companies are becoming involved in training and taking a more active and committed part in ensuring that their staff are trained with the necessary skills and knowledge. The Confederation of British Industry has promoted the idea of training targets for all companies, and recent government initiatives have backed the idea.

Exam tip

Which training do you think is most successful, and why? Training is an important part of any organisation and should be considered very carefully.

Learning Skills Council (LSC)

As mentioned on page 95, this is an organisation to help find jobs and training schemes for adults. The LSC promotes the Modern Apprenticeship and many other schemes.

Connexions

This organisation helps school-leavers find jobs and training to enable them to find permanent employment (see page 94).

Task

There are many website addresses that offer training schemes. Make a list of the ones you can find – it may come in useful later. Make a list of the training you might like to undertake.

Revision Questions

1. Workers who go to college receive .... training.
   a) off-the-job
   b) induction
   c) permanent
   b) on-the-job

2. The skills of employees at Happy Ideas Ltd are improved by ....
   a) pay
   b) training
   c) recruitment
   d) selection

3. Specialist off-the-job training is most likely to be provided by which one of the following?
   a) a job centre
   b) a further education college
   c) a trade union
   d) Connexions

4. The first training that a newly recruited motor mechanic will receive is:
   a) induction
   b) promotion
   c) delegation
   d) off-the-job

Past Paper

1. The company's aircraft maintenance staff need re-training, so that they will be able to service and repair the three new long-haul aircraft. Either 'on-the-job' or 'off-the-job' training could be used. Discuss which method of training the maintenance staff might prefer. (4)

    (Edexcel, 2001, Foundation)

2. Explain two problems, other than cost, that the directors of Flyaway plc may face as a result of needing to re-train their maintenance staff. (5)

    (Edexcel, 2001, Higher)

3. The directors need a new sales force, which will sell directly to major UK supermarkets and freezer centres. Outline and evaluate suitable approaches to training the new sales force. (4)

    (Edexcel, 1999, Higher)

Key terms

Connexions – an organisation involved in helping people gain training as well as giving careers advice

GNVQs – General National Vocational Qualifications

Induction – initial training for a new employee

NVQs – National Vocational Qualifications

Off-the-job – being trained away from where you work

On-the-job – being trained by watching an experienced worker work

Training – providing employees with new skills and knowledge

Summary

At the end of this unit you should:

- understand the different methods of training used by companies
- be able to explain the difference between each method of training
- understand that there are now many other agencies or organisations becoming involved in training of staff.

UNIT 11

MOTIVATION AND REWARDS

What you will learn

At the end of this unit you should be able to:
- understand how employees are motivated and rewarded
- understand the motivational theories of Maslow and Herzberg
- understand the various reward systems
- analyse the effectiveness of financial and non-financial incentives.

MOTIVATION

Motivation is best described as an internal force or a set of forces that pushes people to do something. What makes us get up and go? Some people are motivated purely by money, others are motivated by the satisfaction a job brings. Every person is very different; the way we think, the way we were brought up, where we live all has an effect on how we look at life. We are born with different amounts of intelligence, our personalities are different, the build of our bodies is different and our daily lifestyle also affects us. Some people strive or want to do certain things – to become the Prime Minister, or to be a professional footballer, to travel around the world, or to be self-employed and to manage their own business.

Abraham Maslow

Each person has different wants and needs, which they can gain at work. Abraham Maslow studied employee motivation and, in 1954, published his findings. He decided to put all these wants and needs under a number of different headings in a chart. This has since been known as Maslow's hierarchy of needs.

Only once one need is fulfilled does the next need (above in the chart) become important to an individual. Someone may be prepared to work just

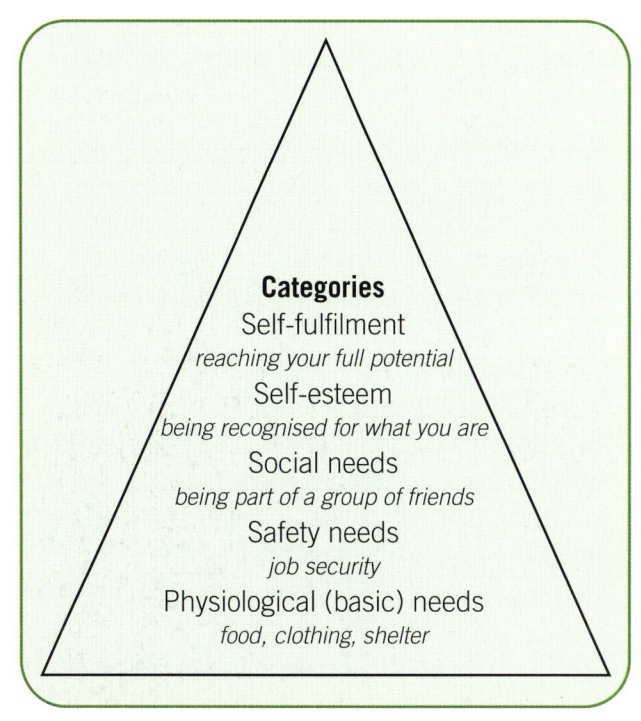

Categories
Self-fulfilment
reaching your full potential
Self-esteem
being recognised for what you are
Social needs
being part of a group of friends
Safety needs
job security
Physiological (basic) needs
food, clothing, shelter

Figure 11.1 Maslow's hierarchy of needs

for sufficient money to cover their basic wants. Others may be more motivated and wish to gain promotion, to give them extra funds to buy luxury items. Others may be pleased to have a job that gives them security. Others may enjoy going to work because of the friends they have made and the enjoyment they feel from meeting with them and socialising. Others like gaining promotion and the satisfaction and recognition that this brings. Hence there are a variety of things that motivate people.

> **Task**
>
> What motivates you? Write down a list of points that are motivating you at the moment while studying this GCSE course. Compare these with the factors that would motivate a person working on the shop floor of a production line.

Conclusions

Maslow was thus able to draw certain conclusions from his studies:

- If a lower need is not met then the higher ones are forgotten. For example, if some staff are threatened with redundancy then any other schemes the company has for improving productivity will be ignored. Staff will be more concerned with the fact that they may be made redundant.
- If one of the needs is not met then the staff can become very frustrated. For example, a member of staff has been overlooked for promotion. This will make that person feel rejected and this will have an adverse affect on their work/performance. They may not be putting the same amount of effort into the job.
- Once one need is met then it will no longer motivate the person. If a member of staff has received promotion, then they will no longer be working to attain that increase in status and recognition. Another form of motivation will now be needed for that person.

The world of work has changed considerably from the very industrialised country of the early 1900s. Many people years ago were employed in factories producing different items. Companies realised that they needed to keep their staff motivated while working on the production lines. This is probably where the productivity pay and piece rate phrases and methods of payment became common, in an effort to motivate employees. This is dealt with later on in the chapter.

Frederick Herzberg

In the 1960s Frederick Herzberg conducted research into the way people worked. His study asked people what they liked about their job. His findings identified the following factors which determine whether or not employees like their work:

- salary and job security
- relationships with other people in the company
- supervision by the immediate person in charge of them
- working conditions – what the building is like
- company rules and policies.

Herzberg decided to call the above the 'hygiene factors'. He felt that if the staff do not have these factors addressed then it is unlikely that they will feel satisfied and happy in their work. The factors do not make people work better, but they are there to remove some problems that could make them unhappy.

Another group of factors include:

- gaining promotion
- being given responsibility
- doing something well and being recognised by the company for the achievement
- the job itself
- personal achievement.

To this group he gave the name 'motivators'. These are the things that drive people to work and what they aim to achieve.

It is therefore important that directors, managers, supervisors and team leaders who are responsible for employees are aware of these theories, to ensure that they achieve the best from their staff and take into account all their needs and wants.

> **Exam tip**
>
> It is not essential to memorise all the factors of each of the theorists, but you will need to understand the basic important points of each one.

Task

Figure 11.2 Ahmed and Katie May at work

Ahmed Wagstaff works for the local baker. His responsibilities are to open the bakery every morning, switch on the ovens and prepare the mixture for the items to be baked that day. He left school with two GCSEs, working at the bakery part-time while he finished his studies. He then continued working for the company full-time once he gained his qualifications. He works a 40-hour week and earns £7000 per annum. In the bakery there are ten other people controlled by one manager.

Katie May works in a school science department where she is a senior laboratory technician. She is responsible for three other members of staff who help the science department. Her work includes ensuring that all the equipment the staff need is prepared and ready for use each lesson. She has worked for the school for four years, having worked in a previous school for two years as a laboratory assistant. She completed her HND in Science and earns £21 000 per annum. Her hours vary depending on the work needed – there are no fixed hours.

1. What areas of dissatisfaction might exist for
   a) Ahmed
   b) Katie May?

2. What opportunities for motivation might exist in
   a) Ahmed's job
   b) Katie May's job?

3. What are the differences between the two answers for Ahmed's job and Katie May's job?

REWARD SYSTEMS

Having a happy and well-motivated workforce can provide an enormous benefit to a company. These gains could be a workforce that takes very little time off through ill health, which is motivated to see the company succeed and so productivity will be increased, and reluctant to take industrial action if there is a grievance of any kind. These are all benefits to the company. However, the staff or workforce will need to be motivated. Their motivation can be:

- job satisfaction
- monetary rewards (how much they are paid)
- non-monetary rewards (other payments which are not money, eg health care, company car, free meals in restaurant, health club)

Job satisfaction

Job satisfaction is important for every employee and they can gain this satisfaction in many ways. If the management of the company does not respect employees and praise them for their work, this can lead to a disgruntled staff. No amount of pay and other benefits would make the staff feel satisfied about what they are doing. If certain staff feel that their pay is not as high as others, this might lead them to believe that their work is not valued.

Job satisfaction can be offered by many factors:

- the working environment – facilities, décor, lighting, desk space, rest areas
- the type of work they have to do – manual, repetitive, or up to the individual to manage their own tasks
- colleagues
- working hours – fixed or flexi time
- fringe benefits.

Task

Make a list of anything else you think affects job satisfaction.

There are several ways in which a company can improve the job satisfaction of an employee. Examples of this are **job rotation** and **job enrichment**.

Job rotation

There are a number of jobs which need to be carried out within an organisation that can sometimes be very boring or monotonous. Therefore, if you were employed to carry out one of these jobs, you may decide that your skills and knowledge are not being utilised and this may make you leave the company. Some companies realise this, and to avoid people leaving they will ensure that after a certain period of

Figure 11.3 Repetitive jobs – a watch factory

time they are moved to another job. Thus the employee learns a new skill or job and should gain a better understanding of the company. Sometimes the jobs are so monotonous that they move or rotate people after a couple of hours.

Job enrichment

This can be similar to job rotation. A company will try to make the employee more interested in the job that they are doing by giving them additional tasks to carry out. This enables the employee to demonstrate more skills and abilities.

> **Exam tip**
>
> Learn all the phrases and words you are not familiar with – it helps when answering examination questions.

Monetary rewards

Money is probably the most rewarding motivation factor. However, there are many different types of monetary rewards that an employee may receive.

Wage

Wages are the reward or payment for work carried out, normally each week. Payment can be made in a variety of forms such as cash in a pay packet, cheque, or paid directly into the person's bank account.

The type of jobs that are paid by this method are those in small companies, or manual works, such as bricklaying and carpentry.

Normally someone within the company is paid to calculate the wages each week; a person may have worked more hours in the week than actually required and would therefore be entitled to overtime pay. Overtime pay rates can vary, depending upon when the person actually did the work. For example, a firm may pay someone for a basic 35-hour week at £5 per hour. If the worker works more hours, say 40, they are paid overtime for the five extra hours. Overtime rates are usually paid at premium rates – time and a half, time and a quarter, double time or Saturday and Sunday working. With overtime paid at time and a half, this means the employee would receive £5 plus another £2.50 per hour, making a total of £7.50 per hour or £37.50 for the extra five hours.

For overtime at double time, the employee would receive £10 per hour, thereby making a total of £50 extra for the five hours. There are even occasions when people are paid 'triple time' for the hours worked. Often this is when they are working on a bank holiday or special time, eg Christmas. The employee would be receiving £15 per hour. For five hours this would be equal to £75.

In a number of firms, people work overtime and then have 'time off in lieu'. This means that they can choose when to take as holiday the additional hours worked. This saves a company money, firstly by not paying premium rates and secondly by allowing the employees to take the time owed when work is low; MG Rover has a 'banked hours scheme' which runs on this basis.

> **Exam tip**
>
> Talk to members of your family and ask them what motivates them in their job. What are the important aspects?

FP Tours

NAME:	Megan Osborne
PAYROLL NO:	76/234
NATIONAL INSURANCE NO:	YY 76 43 24 D
TAX CODE:	470L
WEEK NO:	17
BASIC PAY:	£270.00
OVERTIME PAY:	£ 75.00
GROSS PAY:	**£345.00**
NI CONTRIBUTION:	£ 56.25
UNION FEES:	£ 12.00
INCOME TAX:	£ 83.40
TOTAL DEDUCTIONS:	£151.65
NET PAY:	**£193.35**

Figure 11.4 A wage slip

Time rate

Businesses that pay their workers by a time rate system must have a method of recording the hours worked by their employees. Companies may use a 'clocking on' and 'clocking off' system. This means that the person has their name on a card and when they arrive at work they ensure that their card has been punched with the time they start; when they leave work they have the card punched again. The company can then calculate the hours which they have worked.

It also means that if the person is late, it is recorded, and further action may be taken by the company if this happens on a regular basis.

Many companies have now moved away from the traditional system of 'clocking on and off' and have changed to electronic time recording with the use of swipe cards. The method is still the same, but the computer calculates the hours rather than a wages clerk or the human resources department.

This is a very effective way of calculating the person's hours, but it does not really provide the employee with any incentive to work harder and be a better employee. The worker is paid the same amount regardless of the speed or the quality of work produced – they are just paid for the hours they work.

Figure 11.5 'Clocking on' using a swipe card

Piece rate

This is a payment system where the worker is paid for each piece of work they complete that meets a given standard. It is a very common method of payment in the textile and electronic industries. For example, a worker in the electronics industry will

Task

Copy out Table 11.1 and calculate how much overtime payment each worker has earned.

TABLE 11.1

Name	Hourly rate	Hours of overtime	Overtime rate	Total overtime payment
Megan Osborne	£5.00	5	double time	
Paul Russell	£4.50	5	time and a half	
Charlotte Cosnett	£6.00	7	time and quarter	
Owen Russell	£5.50	4	time and a half	
Vera Twigg	£6.50	8	double time	
Ben Hampson	£7.00	4	time and a half	

be paid for each circuit board they complete to an acceptable standard.

This system encourages workers to produce as many items as possible in the time available, thus overcoming the problems of time rate system. However, to ensure that poor quality goods are not produced, each worker's output has to be monitored closely, so careful inspection is required.

Task

Figure 11.6 Siân at work

Siân Osborne works in a clothing factory making dresses. She is paid £2.00 for each dress she makes. Once she has produced more than 200 dresses per week, the piece rate goes up to £3.00 a dress.

1. In a good week Siân can produce 300 dresses. Calculate her pay for that week.
2. Some weeks Siân does not produce as many dresses. Suggest reasons why this might happen.
3. What problems might there be if Siân tries to make up her lost production?

Salaries

Salaries tend to be associated with white collar workers – this means people who are not involved in manual work, eg office clerks, managers of shops, computer operators, teachers. They are paid an annual salary. This salary is then divided into twelve equal parts and paid each month into the employee's bank account. For example, an office worker earning £12 000 per annum will receive £1000 a month less reductions for tax and national insurance.

A salary is paid either by cheque or electronically. The amount paid each month rarely varies as these workers are not usually paid for any overtime or extra work they do over and above their normal working hours. However, their pay may be increased through many other incentives for the employee, such as commission, bonuses, or profit-sharing schemes as detailed later.

A person receiving a salary may also be on an incremental pay scale. This means that each year until a certain figure has been reached they receive additional money, on top of their salary. There is a minimum and a maximum rate of pay for the job. For example, a nurse's incremental pay scale may be based on a nine-point scale, which ranges from £10–21 000. This means that a new nurse will receive £10 000 per annum and will get an automatic progression/pay rise each year until they reach the top of the pay scale.

Many public sector workers are on this type of pay scale.

In the private sector some employees' pay is decided between managers, unions or staff associations. Some of these jobs may be on an incremental basis also. The disadvantage of this system for employers is that employees get a pay increase each year irrespective of how good they are at their job. In addition, when an employee reaches the top of the scale, they may become less motivated.

To overcome this problem many businesses have introduced performance-related pay – PRP. In this system, employees only receive a pay increase if they achieve targets that have been previously agreed between themselves and their line manager. For example, a buyer for Jaguar Cars must make a 10% saving on his annual commodity spending if he is to be considered for the performance-related pay.

Additional payments
Both wage earners and salaried earners can earn additional money through various incentives that the company may offer in addition to their basic pay.

Commission
Commission is a payment to people who are employed in selling the products or services of a business. This system ensures that employees have to work hard to earn their pay, but if they are successful their earnings can be unlimited. Conversely, if they fail to meet the required turnover or sales figures, they receive no commission.

Salespeople tend to be paid a smaller basic salary and then earn more money by selling more units and being paid commission for the number sold. For example, a car salesperson may have a basic salary of £10 000 a year but for each car he sells he could earn £50. If he sells 15 cars a month, his commission could be £9000 for the year.

Commission can also be earned when selling goods through catalogues.

Bonus
A bonus can be paid within both the time rate and piece rate systems. In the piece rate system, once a worker has produced more than their target levels, they will receive a payment greater than the basic piece rate for any items they produce. This encourages the worker to produce more.

Under the time rate system, a bonus is paid if the workers reach their production targets, which could be hourly, daily or weekly targets. This is to encourage workers to work at their maximum output and so overcome the problem of lack of incentive.

Bonuses can also be paid to employees who have nothing to do with the production of the company but are involved in the administration of the company. If a company reaches certain targets then all employees may receive a lump sum payment. This could be paid at the end of a financial year or during the year at certain intervals.

Profit-sharing
Profit-sharing is a system where businesses set aside a portion of their profits which are then shared between their employees. It is similar to a bonus and is paid in addition to a person's wage or salary.

This profit-sharing scheme will help to motivate the workers because if the business is doing well then everyone shares in the success of the company. The employees feel that their efforts are being rewarded.

Share ownership
Some companies offer their employees shares within the company as a means of rewarding them for their efforts. Some of the larger companies, such as John Lewis Partnership, have run such a scheme since the company was set up. These shares have the potential to increase in value in the

Figure 11.7 A car salesman having just made a sale to earn commission

future. However, everyone must be aware that shares can dencrease in value as well as increase; there is no guarantee as to which way they will go.

Non-monetary rewards

In addition to giving an employee monetary rewards, there are also many ways in which a company rewards its employees with benefits other than actual money in their hands. These are sometimes known as 'fringe benefits' or 'perks'. A company car is classed in this category because you are not actually paying for the car, but you have the use of it.

The more senior you are within the company then the more perks you will probably have. A director of a company could be given the following:

- company car for himself and his wife
- children's school fees paid
- healthcare paid for the family
- discounts on company products
- share option
- pension
- expense account
- membership of health clubs
- subsidised canteen.

Figure 11.8 Membership of a health club – an example of a non-monetary reward

There are a number of people who totally disagree with all these additional benefits paid to an employee. However, it is a matter of opinion, and the benefits and disadvantages of having non-monetary rewards can be a discussion point.

Some people would not remain in their job unless they had the non-monetary rewards, as these account for a great deal of additional expense that the employee would otherwise have to pay out. If you had to purchase lunch every day at work, it could be quite expensive, whereas if the company can provide you with a meal at a fraction of the cost, this could also save you having to cook a meal in the evening.

The government in recent years has become more aware of these benefits and is beginning to realise that it is possible to begin taxing people on them, to the extent that they no longer become a benefit. An example of this is the company car. The government has introduced taxation bands based on annual mileage. Therefore, if you were given a company car but only use it for pleasure you will be taxed highly, thus making the car an expensive benefit and one which could make you decide not to take it.

Companies which are very keen to keep their workforce have to introduce different methods of keeping their staff motivated, especially when companies are more competitive and finances are kept under tight control. Some of these methods are listed below.

Team working

Groups of workers gather together and share their ideas on how best to work. This can be useful as the actual workers can bring their firsthand practical experience and can perhaps see the best way forward. This can be very productive, although there are occasions when the team does not gel very well, and this can cause conflict.

Consultative committees

This can be where the management invite employees at all different levels to put forward ideas and suggestions for improving the company.

The committee then discusses the ideas and gives feedback on the suggestions. The management does not always follow the comments made by employees, but they should take into account their points of view.

Under recent European Union (EU) legislation, all companies with over 1000 employees and which exist in two or more EU countries, must set up a European Works Council to give information and consult with employees on important company decisions.

Single status company

A number of Japanese companies operate this system, whereby all employees wear exactly the same uniform or overall. One cannot distinguish between a manager walking around the company and a person working on the production line. All working conditions are exactly the same – there is no difference in where people eat or park, and there is no clocking on or off. The only difference is the pay; all benefits are the same.

Investors in People

This kitemark is awarded to companies which have met certain criteria that allow them to use the sign below on their paperwork. It may mean that they have encouraged training and development of staff, and that there is good communication between management and staff. It shows that the company is offering and developing good practice for its workforce.

Problems encountered with non-monetary rewards

While such methods have helped companies to motivate their workforce, there are a number of problems that they have encountered:

- Setting up training schemes takes time and effort from the company.
- Job enrichment also takes time and the benefits might take a long time to come into effect.
- When companies try to reorganise and change things, there can often be a great deal of resistance from the workforce, thus making the changes difficult to introduce.
- A number of the jobs in any company may be difficult to enrich or allow rotation, eg a shelf stacker in a supermarket. Those with higher skills and ability are able to change direction, but those with fewer skills are not able to do so.
- Quite often managers are seen as trying to change things too much and staff become wary of their reasons for doing it – Is redundancy on the cards?
- According to Maslow's hierarchy of needs, job security is essential to the workforce. If there is doubt here then the other levels of the hierarchy will not be met.

Figure 11.9

Revision Questions

1. To a farm worker, a tied cottage is a:
   a) financial benefit
   b) non-financial benefit
   c) financial cost
   d) non-financial cost

2. Commission paid to travel agents by Flyaway plc depends upon the number of:
   a) people employed
   b) enquiries received
   c) holidays sold
   d) complaints made

3. When Nocha has a profitable year, the employees are rewarded with a:
   a) mark up
   b) wage
   c) salary
   d) bonus

4. Employees of Nocha Ltd are provided with protective clothing. This is a .... benefit.
   a) non-financial
   b) public
   c) financial
   d) social

5. Some employees are paid equal monthly payments. This is a:
   a) piece rate
   b) bonus
   c) discount
   d) salary

Past Paper

1. The Personnel Director at Hotspur & Wren Ltd, Danny McDearmid, is keen to maintain motivation amongst staff. He believes in Herzberg's two-factor theory of:
   - hygiene factors
   - motivating factors.

   Explain the difference between the two factors and how they help to motivate employees. (8)

   (Edexcel, 2003, Higher)

2. Airport security is provided by the employees of Flyaway plc. The directors must now decide whether to continue using their own staff for airport security, or whether to employ SafeBase, a large national specialist security firm.

   One director said at the board meeting: 'If we employ SafeBase, we have to consider three issues. These are the effects on:
   - staff morale
   - our costs, and
   - our customers.'

   a) Select one issue that could be in favour of Flyaway plc continuing to use its own staff for airport security and explain your choice. (4)

   b) Select one other issue that could be used against Flyaway plc keeping its own staff for airport security and explain your choice. (4)

   (Edexcel, 2001, Higher)

3. The directors need a new sales force, which will sell directly to major UK supermarkets and freezer centres. Outline and evaluate suitable approaches to motivating the new sales force. (4)

   (Edexcel, 1999, Higher)

Summary

At the end of this unit you should:

- have an understanding of the different motivational theorists
- understand the different methods of rewarding staff for their work
- realise the importance of ensuring that employees are satisfied with their job
- understand the difference between financial and non-financial rewards.

Key terms

Fringe benefits – benefits additional to your actual pay; extras

Hierarchy – the order and structure of something

Hygiene factors – conditions in which staff work

Job enrichment – additional tasks carried out to make the job more interesting

Job satisfaction – feeling that you have done a good job

Job rotation – moving from one job to another

Monetary rewards – the pay you receive for your job

Motivation – something that makes someone want to work

Motivators – things you like about your job

Non-monetary rewards – rewards additional to your pay that make your job more pleasant

Overtime – extra pay over normal payment

Salary – a payment made to an employee for a year, which is divided into 12 equal payments

Time off in lieu – paid time off work given to a worker who has worked extra hours

Wage – payment received each week for work

UNIT 12

NEGOTIATION AND CONSULTATION

What you will learn

At the end of this unit you should have an understanding of:

- the role of trade unions
- their impact on relationships and management of people
- collective bargaining
- industrial action
- protection of employees.

WHAT ARE TRADE UNIONS?

Trade unions exist to represent the interests of employees in a particular organisation. They will negotiate on their members' behalf with the management of a company in respect of wage claims, hours of work and conditions. The joining together of people makes the group more powerful when trying to come to an agreement, as opposed to one person trying to talk to the management of a company on their own. This joining together of workers to negotiate is known as **collective bargaining**.

There are many different types of unions, such as:

- NUT – National Union of Teachers
- ATL – Association of Teachers and Lecturers

There are some unions that represent a group of workers in several industries, such as:

- TGWU – Transport and General Workers Union
- AEEU – Amalgamated Engineering and Electrical Union

Figure 12.1 A vote being taken at the TUC Conference

Exam tip

It is not essential to learn all the names of the different unions, perhaps only one or two.

Task

Try and find out as many different unions as you can. Note who they represent, ie what type of industry or worker.

Most of the unions belong to the Trades Union Congress, known as the TUC founded in 1868. This represents approximately 70 trade unions in national discussions with the government and employers' organisations, such as the Confederation of British Industries (CBI).

During the last century, unions took a very active role. During the 1970s and early 1980s there was a tremendous amount of industrial action by different unions, such as the coal miners' strike in the 1970s and 80s, when all coal miners came out on strike for a better deal in their pay. This caused many problems for the country; no coal was mined, which had a knock-on effect on coal supplies, and the miners endured long periods without pay.

Some companies do not have any unions representing their workers because the company is too small. If a person has a problem regarding hours or conditions, they are more likely to speak to the owner directly rather than through someone else. The problem or disagreement could be sorted out quite quickly by simply discussing the issue. However, the larger the company, the more likely it is that members will belong to some form of union because it would be very difficult for each person to go to the employers and discuss a problem.

Companies are more likely to deal with a representative of a group of people than individuals. The reason for this is the amount of time which the company can save. The union can negotiate on behalf of a group of people quite quickly, as opposed to a number of individuals negotiating separately. The representatives from the union are probably trained or have experience in negotiation, and will of course have knowledge of the rules and regulations.

Unions are also there to support their members in times of trouble. A union can be classed as a pressure group; they aim to change the way in which the company is operating at the present moment in time.

WHY JOIN A UNION?

Why do people join a union? Often it is for the security of knowing that there is someone who is willing to help you if you find yourself in a situation that may require negotiation with the company. It is known as 'peace of mind'. Unions can:

- negotiate rates of pay, working conditions and safety
- give legal advice on matters pertaining to work and life outside
- provide lawyers to help you and represent you in court if needed
- support members in times of crisis, eg strikes, lock-outs accidents
- provide a range of services for its members, eg mortgages, insurance, loans discounts on holidays.

Figure 12.2 Attempting to negotiate directly with employers

Most people will understand that unions negotiate for pay, but do not realise that they can help in a wide variety of other ways.

Unions can also support workers in trying to improve all working conditions. Examples of this could be having a rest room, gaining sufficient training, ensuring that the employer complies with the Health and Safety regulations. As the TUC represents a large number of members, they can negotiate with the companies and government to improve conditions such as sick pay, maternity pay, training and pensions by having a national perspective on what the requirements are for the whole country. This applies to the public sector where salary scales are set and conditions of working are laid down, eg teachers and nurses.

Task

You are employed as a shop steward for J Buns Ltd and you have been informed that there is a new recruit to the company who is 17 years old. Give your advice to the new recruit as to why you think s/he should join the union.

Local bargaining

This is where the union will negotiate for their members on items that affect them locally, where the work base is. It might be that they agree that people working the night shift should receive an additional payment per hour than those people working in the day. If the company is in London, they may agree that employees should be paid a cost-of-living allowance of a certain amount.

Other items that may be negotiated are things such as the redundancy policy for the company, or an appraisal system.

There are many advantages and disadvantages to being represented by a union who can negotiate on your behalf:

Advantages
- one person speaks for many people
- creates a better working relationship between companies
- negotiators are highly skilled in their job.

Disadvantages
- gives greater power to the union
- may reduce workers' motivation
- can increase labour costs
- reduces the choice of managers to negotiate with.

Many companies are now moving over to an appraisal system, whereby employees receive additional pay increases for achieving certain targets provided by the company. This means that a valuable worker can receive additional pay, as opposed to everyone receiving exactly the same, no matter how hard they work.

Changes in 'new style' agreements

As many companies are now opening branches in different parts of the world, the trade unions have had to introduce 'new style' agreements. The reason for this is that the unions and managers have to work more closely together because of globalisation; many companies now have branches in other parts of the world, and are often dealing with people who will be working for them but are not employed by them.

They may agree on the following:

- no-strike agreement – employees will not go on strike
- team work – working together
- labour flexibility – people changing jobs
- single-status employment – everyone is treated the same, managers and shop floor.

The Employment Relations Act of 1999

This applies to all employees whether they are members of a union or not. This means:

- Maternity leave has been considerably increased.
- Fathers as well as mothers can have unpaid leave for up to three months on the birth of their baby in the first five years.
- Parents are given reasonable time off for family emergencies.

- Maximum payment for unfair dismissal increased from £4000 to £50 000.

Works Council

This was introduced in 2000 under European Law. If a company employs more than 1000 workers in two different countries within Europe then they must set up a European 'Works Council'. This means that the council must be consulted on anything that affects the workers in both countries.

INDUSTRIAL ACTION

In recent years the numbers of strikes in the UK has been considerably lower than in the late 1970s. During this time millions of days were lost due to strike action, whereas nowadays it is estimated to be about a couple of hundred thousand days per year.

Going on strike, which means that the staff do not work, is probably the most powerful method of making the employers take notice of the employees. A strike is normally the last thing that the employees will do.

When staff strike, the company is affected in many ways:

- production is halted
- revenue is lost but fixed costs will still have to be paid – eg rent
- orders may be lost
- reputation of the company could be damaged by bad publicity
- relationship between staff and employers is damaged.

The staff are also affected because:

- they will not receive any pay
- the company may lose money and therefore have to lose staff through redundancy
- the company could close, whereby all staff lose their jobs.

There are different types of strike action that employees can take:

- A token strike – a short period of time, eg a morning, afternoon or whole day.
- Selective strike – certain workers may go on strike, probably the ones most affected and the ones that will cause the most disruption.
- All out strike – everyone stops work.

Figure 12.3 Industrial action

The employees may be paid a small sum of money from the union if the union is backing the strike. There are some occasions when the employees decide to strike without backing from the union. This is called a 'wild cat strike' and no payment is made from the union funds.

Most unions will ballot their members before taking strike action to ensure that there is a majority agreement. Some union members may not agree with the action taken and will therefore take no part in the decisions made. These people are sometimes called 'black legs'.

Picketing

This is a method of demonstrating that people are not happy with the company decisions. The members will probably be on strike and instead of sitting at home doing nothing, they will stand outside the company to try to prevent other people from entering the company and working. These people will often be seen carrying banners with slogans.

Picketing often gains publicity from the press, which in turns gives the company bad publicity. Usually the company is very keen to resolve the situation so that the employees can carry on working and reduce the amount of damage to the company.

Overtime ban

Another method taken by employees which is not as drastic as actually striking is to refuse to work any overtime requested by the company. A number of companies rely on their employees working overtime to ensure that the work is carried out. If employees only work the hours they are paid for, then the company could suffer considerably as the employees will not take on any extra work. The company may lose orders because they cannot complete on time. The employees receive their pay but are unable to earn any extra money.

Work to rule

Employees when 'working to rule' will only do exactly what is written in their contract. They will carry out no other duties. If a certain person is absent or is very busy, no one will do their job or help out. They will wait until the person is available. 'Working to rule' tends to slow down everyone's work and can take much longer for everything to be carried out. Most people are willing to help someone out if they are very busy or have too much work on at the moment in time, knowing that they will receive help when they are busy. 'Working to rule' does not allow for that.

Employees are not doing anything wrong when carrying out this type of action, and they still receive their pay for the work done.

> **Exam tip**
>
> Have any members of your family or friends experienced industrial action? What was the reason for the action? How was it resolved?

Non-cooperation

This is when employees refuse to cooperate with their employers on principle. It may mean that if something new is introduced, then the employees do not have to agree with it, as it is not in their contract. This could be something simple like changing their lunch hour.

Go slow

As the name suggests, this means that the employees do not work as quickly as they could. This is very similar to working to rule. Employees deliberately take longer to complete a task than they should.

EMPLOYER'S ACTION

Employers can also take action against their employees.

Closer supervision

Employers can check on their employees more regularly to see if they are doing their job correctly. It can be extremely annoying for staff to have their work checked regularly.

Pay freeze
The employers do not have to increase the employees' pay. They can state that there is a pay freeze which means that the employees will not receive any more money than at present, regardless of the inflation rate.

Lock-outs
The company can take drastic action and not allow the employees into the company. However, this can, have a very negative effect upon the company. It will lose out as well as the employees: the good image of the company can be lost, together with the fact that the company still has to pay its overheads even though it does not have to pay its employees.

Figure 12.4 A lock-out

Closure of the company
The final thing that the employees can do is to close the company. This is an extremely drastic measure, and will have a dramatic effect on the employees, surrounding area and the employers/owners.

> **Task**
>
> It has been agreed with the workers at your company to take some form of action against the management. What would you recommend, and why? Also mention which method you would not use and why.

ACAS
In order to avoid industrial action of any kind when companies and employees cannot agree they may take their dispute to ACAS (Advisory, Conciliation and Arbitration Service). ACAS aims to create better employment relations between employer and employee through providing information, advice, training and workplace services. It can help with everything from advice on employment law to settling disputes for organisations if relations begin to break down. It is an independent, publicly-funded organisation and many of its services are free.

More recently ACAS has had to deal with fewer and fewer complaints as there is less union action taking place. Most companies can resolve their differences with the employees fairly easily.

Figure 12.5

EMPLOYEES' RIGHTS

The Employment Relations Act of 1999 has made it much easier for trade unions to gain recognition, and has also increased the individual's rights at work.

The following are some of the benefits:
- Employees cannot be dismissed for taking industrial action.
- A trade union representative can accompany employees to any disciplinary hearing.
- Consultation must take place between unions and employers if there are to be any redundancies, take-over bids or mergers, which could consequently incur job losses.

Other legislation

There are many laws, which affect the employees and protect them from their employers abusing them. These are dealt with more thoroughly in Unit 5.

- Race Relations Act 1976
- Equal Pay Act 1970
- Health and Safety at Work Act 1974
- Employment Protection Act 1978 – all employees should receive a written contract of employment
- Trade Union Reform and Employment Rights Act 1993 – employees have the right to join a union or not
- Disability Discrimination Act 1995 – applies if the company has more than 20 employees
- Employment Relations Act 1999 – employers must recognise unions with regard to any disputes.

In 2000 the government brought in legislation that allowed all part-time workers the same rights as full-time workers. This means that they are entitled to pensions and annual leave.

DISCIPLINE

The Human Resources department should inform every new employee of the procedure for any grievance or discipline situation, so that if a problem arises the employee knows exactly what they have to do.

All employees have to be treated fairly. If an employer is dissatisfied with an employee they should follow the code stated in their terms and conditions of employment. The code should also inform the employee how to make a complaint. The disciplinary procedure should include the following, although the company's code may differ slightly:

- how the first offence is dealt with
- the number of warnings to be given for offences that follow
- which warnings will be oral and which written
- who has the authority to dismiss the employee
- how the employee appeals and to whom.

Dismissal

There are normally only one or two offences for which the employee can be dismissed instantly. One is that the employee has stolen from the company. Other offences are normally with given notice. The employee is given time to rectify the situation and if s/he does not then they can be dismissed. Persistent misconduct or the inability to do the job are some reasons for being dismissed.

Figure 12.6 Dismissal of an employee

If an employee is dismissed for misconduct then it must be proved that the company has followed the correct procedure. If the reason for dismissal is the inability to do the job then the company should be able to prove that they have provided the employee with the opportunity to be trained and carry out the work asked of them.

Redundancy is slightly different. It is classed as dismissal but instead of being on the grounds of the employee not being capable of doing the job, it is because the job itself is no longer required at the company. Quite often large companies will make several people redundant at one time, as opposed to one or two. The employer must give the employee as much notice as possible and must ensure that the selection of people chosen was fair. If not then the employee can take the company to an employment tribunal.

These tribunals are composed of legally qualified people, members from the trade union and a representative from the employer's organisation, who will then discuss the case and make a decision. If they decide that the company was in the wrong, then the employee can receive quite a large sum of compensation.

Most companies will discuss with union representatives when they are going to make some of their staff redundant, thus hoping to avoid situations where the employee will have a case to take them to a tribunal.

Revision Questions

1. What is a trade union?
2. The National Farmers' Union acts for farmers as a:
   a) co-operative
   b) pressure group
   c) chain of command
   d) span of control
3. A .... sometimes negotiates for farm workers in dispute with their employer.
   a) bank
   b) trade union
   c) college
   d) building society
3. People who object to the building work at the airport could form a
   a) pressure group
   b) trade union
   c) franchise
   d) co-operative
4. If no agreement is reached with employers, the members of a trade union may need to take:
   a) industrial action
   b) profit sharing
   c) unlimited liability
   d) contracts of employment

Summary

At the end of this unit you should:
- understand the importance of unions within a workforce
- understand the many different benefits that a union can offer
- realise the importance of a trade union when negotiating with a company
- know the different types of industrial action that members can take.

Past Paper

1. Before reorganisation and the move to the town centre, Hotspur & Wren Ltd had negotiations with the trade union, USDAW (Union of Shop, Distributive and Allied Workers).

   Explain why Hotspur & Wren Ltd negotiated with the trade union. (5)

   (Edexcel; 2003, Higher)

2. Delta Homes plc provides written contracts of employment for employees. State three problems which an employee might have without a contract of employment. (3)

   (Edexcel, 2001, Higher)

Key terms

Collective bargaining – joining of workers together to negotiate

Employment tribunal – organisation to help employees who have been dismissed

Go slow – staff do not work at a fast pace

Non-cooperation – staff refuse to do exactly what the management wants them to do

Pressure group – group of people who try and change something

Strike – employees not working

TUC – Trades Union Congress

Wild-cat strike – employees going on strike without the support of the trade union

Working to rule – staff only do the work they are contracted to do

Works Council – employees in two countries working together

UNIT 12: NEGOTIATION AND CONSULTATION

GCSE BUSINESS STUDIES for Edexcel

Section 3
ACCOUNTING AND FINANCE

UNIT 13

BUDGETS

> ## What you will learn
>
> At the end of this unit you should understand:
> - the use and interpretation of a budget
> - how budgets can be an aid to decision-making in business.

WHAT IS A BUDGET?

A budget is a financial plan for the future. It contains the planned revenue or **income** (money coming into the business) and expected **costs** (money going out of the business) over a particular period, usually a year. The difference between the revenue and the costs will be the projected or expected **profit** for the year. Of course, if the revenue falls and the costs increase then the business will make a loss, not a profit.

The revenue or income will come from anticipated or expected sales of products or services. The costs will be items such as raw materials, power, staff or labour costs, advertising and rent. Past experience and previous budgets are used to draw up the budget or plan of action, which is what the business hopes to achieve.

The budget is agreed in advance and based on the objectives of the business. For example, if an objective of the business is growth, then an increase in revenue or income will be seen in the budget.

> ### ⚠ Exam tip
>
> A budget is another financial tool used in business to help planning.

Budgets force departmental managers to think ahead and ensure that each manager takes responsibility for his or her decisions. For example, the sales budget will contain the target level of sales for the coming year. The sales manager may set the budget 5% higher than the previous year in order to motivate sales staff to work harder, to achieve this higher target. If they do this, bonuses may be available.

The budget can be compared with actual figures and any difference between the two – called a **variance** – can be identified. Appropriate action can then be taken if the planned profit is not going to be achieved. This might mean having to increase sales or reduce costs in order to achieve the planned profit.

Figure 13.1 The Chancellor of the Exchequer with the Budget – the Government's income and expenditure plans

TABLE 13.1 Sales Budget

	January Budgeted	Actual	Variance	F/A
Product A	5000	7000	2000	F
Product B	6000	6500	500	F
Product C	5500	4500	(1000)	A
Raw material costs	2500	2700	(200)	A
Labour costs	2000	1800	200	F

(All figures in tables are sterling)

In the table above, the budgeted or projected figures and the actual figures are given for January. The variance between the budgeted and actual figures is said to be either **favourable** (F) or **adverse** (A). A **favourable variance** is one which has higher than expected results, eg profits/sales up or costs down. An **adverse variance** is one which reduces profit, eg lower than expected profits/sales or when costs are higher than the budgeted figure. Negative figures are shown in brackets.

Advantages of using budgets

- Budgets provide targets for managers and staff to aim for.
- Managers and staff involved in budget setting are more likely to be motivated towards achieving targets.
- By comparing the budget with actual results, managers can highlight weak areas in the business and do something about them.

Task

	Budgeted	Actual	Variance	F/A
Sales	500	600	100	?
Selling price	10	9	(1)	?
Sales revenue	?	5400	400	?
Total costs	4000	?	?	?
Profit	?	1300	?	?

(Profit = sales revenue − total costs)

1. Fill in the missing figures.
2. Fill in the F/A column.
3. Using examples, explain what favourable and adverse mean.

- Once the budget is set, coordination between departments should be improved because each department's activity fits in with the business's overall objectives.
- Spending and costs are controlled.
- Problems can be anticipated in advance and something done about them.

Disadvantages of budgets
- If budgets are set too high and are seen as unachievable, then employees can be demotivated. For example, if the sales budget is set too high, then sales staff will lose interest as they know they will not reach their budgeted sales figure.
- If employees are not involved in preparing budgets and they are imposed by managers, employees could become resentful and motivation could suffer.
- If budgets are not flexible then the business could suffer. For example, a member of staff cannot attend an important training event because the training budget has been spent for the year.

Figure 13.2 Set too high perhaps!

Exam tip
Remember, you need to know what the causes of variances might be and whether they are favourable or adverse.

Task

	November B	A	V	December B	A	V	F/A
Sales revenue	10 000	9800	(200)	12 000	13 000	1000	F
Raw materials	4000	4200	(200)	4500	?	100	?
Labour costs	3500	3600	?	3600	3700	?	?
Other costs	2000	1900	100	2500	2400	100	?
Profit	500	?	?	1400	?	1100	?

(Profit = sales revenue − (raw materials + labour costs + other costs))

1. What are the six missing figures.
2. Complete the F/A column.
3. What strengths and weaknesses can a manager deduce from the figures?

Task

The following data shows the March budgeted and actual figures for Krancioch's Carpets Ltd:

	Budgeted	Actual	Variance	F/A
Carpets sold	1000	1100	100	?
Price per carpet	60	50	(10)	?
Sales revenue	?	?	?	?
Fixed costs	8000	?	–	–
Variable costs	16 000	?	(2000)	?
Total costs	24 000	26 000	(2000)	?
Profit	?	?	?	?

(Profit = sales revenue − total costs)

1. Fill in the missing figures.
2. Fill in the F/A column.
3. Comment on the variances.

Extension task

A budget system is about to be introduced into Frosty Frozen Foods Ltd. Steve McAdam needs to persuade his colleagues that using budgets will benefit the company.

1. Explain two arguments he could use to persuade his colleagues.
2. Explain two disadvantages of using budgets at Frosty Frozen Foods Ltd.

Key terms

Adverse variance – when the difference between actual and budgeted figures results in lower profits

Budget – a financial plan

Favourable variance – when the difference between actual and budgeted figures results in higher profits

Variance – the difference between forecast and actual figures

Summary

- Budgets are a tool for managers.
- Budgets are set for the future.
- Variances can show poor performance which can lead to appropriate action.

UNIT 14

CASH FLOW FORECASTING

» What you will learn

At the end of this unit you should understand:
- the use and interpretation of a cash flow forecast
- how cash flow forecasts can be an aid to decision-making in business.

WHAT IS CASH FLOW?

When a business is operating it will need to make sure that it has enough cash to pay its debts. The business might appear profitable, but if it has not enough cash to pay all of its bills or staff wages, it could fail because it is suffering from a shortage of cash or a cash flow problem. **Cash flow** simply means the flow of cash into and out of the business, usually calculated over a year.

A business will find that inflows and outflows of cash do not balance and this is when problems can occur. To stop this happening, businesses prepare a plan that helps them predict future flows of cash into and out of the business. This is usually known as a **cash flow forecast**. After the business has traded for a while, the actual flow of cash can be checked against this forecast so that the business can take action before it suffers any problems.

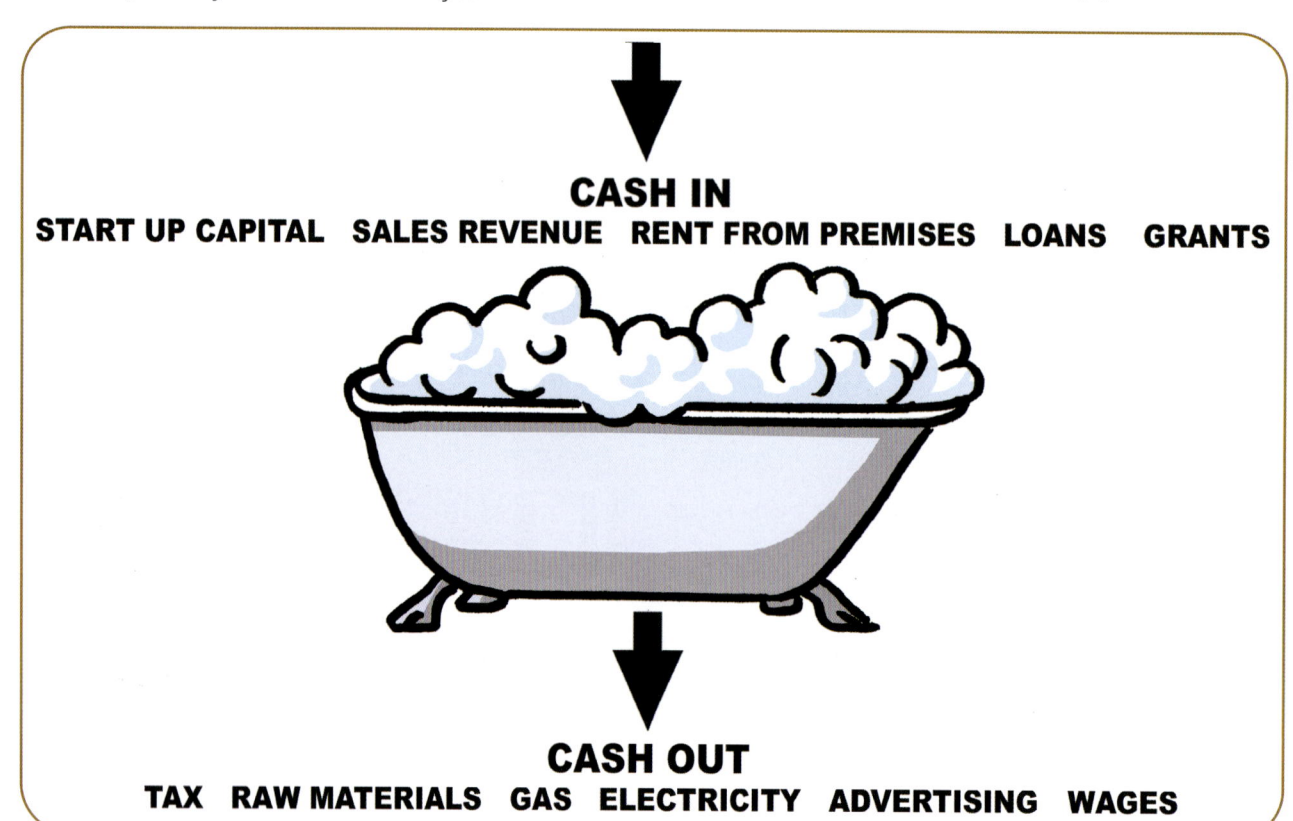

CASH IN
START UP CAPITAL   SALES REVENUE   RENT FROM PREMISES   LOANS   GRANTS

CASH OUT
TAX   RAW MATERIALS   GAS   ELECTRICITY   ADVERTISING   WAGES

Figure 14.1 The flow of cash through a business

TABLE 14.1 Cash flow forecast

	January	February	March	April	May	June
Cash in						
Cash sales	1000	900	1050	1200	1100	1250
Credit sales	1200	500	400	350	1370	1460
Total in (A)	2200	1400	1450	1550	2470	2710
Cash out						
Raw materials	600	500	450	600	550	650
Wages	700	700	700	800	800	800
Heat and light	0	0	200	0	0	200
Advertising	120	120	110	140	135	120
Other overheads	300	320	400	340	450	500
Total out (B)	1720	1640	1860	1880	1935	2270
Net cash flow (A–B)	480	−240	−410	−330	535	440
Opening balance	450	930	690	280	−50	485
Closing balance	930	690	280	−50	485	925

Causes of cash flow problems
- Customers of the business may be slow in paying for goods and/or services.
- Sales may not be as high as expected.
- A new competitor may be taking sales away from the business.
- The price of raw materials may increase.
- Interest rates or other overheads may have increased.

> **Exam tip**
>
> Cash flow forecasting is necessary to predict what is likely to happen in the future.

Forecasting cash flow
The cash flow forecast in the table above consists of:
- cash in
- cash out
- net cash flow
- opening balance
- closing balance.

Cash in consists of revenue from cash and credit sales as well as income from other sources (eg if the business rented out some premises).

Cash out consists of cash spent on raw materials and overheads.

The difference between cash in and cash out is known as the **net cash flow**. If cash out is more than cash in, then there is a negative cash flow, which means the business will be short of cash in April. For example, the business knows in advance that it needs approximately £1880 to pay bills and it can now do something about it.

Opening balance is the business's cash position at the beginning of the month (it was the closing balance of the previous month).

Closing balance is the net cash flow + the opening balance. This now becomes the opening balance for the next month.

UNIT 14: CASH FLOW FORECASTING

Task

You might like to do this task using a spreadsheet.

	September	October	November	December
Cash in				
Cash sales	6000	6500	8000	11 000
Credit sales	2000	3000	?	4000
Total in	8000	?	11 500	15 000
Cash out				
Materials	2500	3400	3600	5600
Wages	4000	?	4000	4500
Other overheads	1400	1500	1500	?
Total out	7900	8900	9100	12 200
Net cash flow	100	?	2400	2800
Opening balance	800	900	?	3900
Closing balance	900	1500	3900	?

1. Fill in the missing figures.
2. What would be the new closing balance if cash sales in December were £2000?
3. What implications will this have for the business?

Why prepare a cash flow forecast?

Monitoring cash is vital to all businesses, both large and small. If a business is not good at managing and controlling its cash then this can have damaging effects.

- If it is a production or manufacturing company, poor cash flow can slow down or stop production because it may not be able to pay for raw materials or pay wages.
- If the business borrows money from the bank, it will have to pay interest charges and this can affect profits.
- If profits are reduced because extra costs have to be paid, future investment plans may have to be put on hold.

Figure 14.2 Poor cash flow means this manager cannot pay his workers

- Businesses are more likely to experience cash flow problems in their first few years of trading. It is for this reason that banks like to see evidence of planning in the form of a cash flow forecast before they will grant loans and overdrafts. Banks are more likely to grant loans if they can see the business has planned the management of cash throughout the year.
- By identifying times in the year when it will not have enough cash to pay its debts, a business is demonstrating good planning. It can then make the necessary arrangements.

A business can survive without making a profit for a short time, but if it has no cash to pay wages and suppliers, it will not survive for very long. It is important therefore that a business manages the timings of cash in and cash out carefully because it may have to wait for payment from its own debtors/customers while having to continue to pay creditors/suppliers and other debts it owes.

Exam tip

Do not confuse cash flow with profit – make sure you know the difference.

Task

Stadium Electrics plc is a manufacturer of microchips used in computers. Next year it predicts that:

- It will receive a VAT repayment of £20 000.
- Vehicle/machinery maintenance will cost £40 000.
- It will have to pay £120 000 for raw materials and components.
- Sales of microchips will be £230 000.
- The sale of land it does not use will bring £80 000.
- Other expenses will be £150 000.

1. List those items which are receipts or income for Stadium Electrics plc.
2. List those items which are payments or outgoings for Stadium Electrics plc.
3. Using the above figures, prepare a cash flow forecast showing their closing balance. Stadium Electrics plc had £50 000 at the beginning of the year.

Past Paper

Peggy Turnbull is responsible for keeping all the financial records for Wheatfields Ltd. One of her jobs is to make sure that Wheatfields Ltd has enough cash. She does this by using a cash flow forecast.

The following is an extract from Wheatfields Ltd's cash flow forecast for the first six months of 2002.

	Jan	Feb	Mar	Apr	May	June
Opening bank balance	32	44	40	−11	−6	1
Cash inflow	25	26	32	27	25	18
Cash outflow	13	30	83	22	18	14
Net cash flow	12	−4	−51	5	7	5
Closing bank balance	44	40	−11	−6	1	5

1. What do you notice about the closing bank balances in March and April? (1)
2. What could Peggy do about this? (2)
3. Explain how a cash flow forecast can help an existing business such as Wheatfields Ltd. (6)

(Edexcel, 2002, Foundation)

Not to be confused with profit

Cash flow and profit are not the same. Cash flow is concerned with the movement of cash in and cash out of the business on a month-by-month basis. Profit is the difference between revenue and costs, and is usually calculated at the end of the financial year in the profit and loss account.

HOW TO IMPROVE CASH FLOW

The cash available for the day-to-day running of the business is called **working capital**. It comes from the payments made by customers for goods and services and is used to pay for raw materials and other bills. When a business identifies a cash flow or working capital problem, it needs to decide how it is going to solve the problem. The business needs to speed up cash coming into the business and slow down cash going out. It can do this as follows:

1. By arranging extra funding when it is required – an overdraft is an arrangement with the bank to draw out of a bank account more than there is in the account. High interest rates are paid but businesses consider it is worth it for the flexibility of being able to overdraw when necessary. Another disadvantage is that the bank can demand instant repayment of the overdraft, which might not always be convenient for the business. A short-term loan could also be arranged with the bank; the interest repayable is less than an overdraft, although it is not as flexible.
2. Lease rather than purchase expensive fixed assets like vehicles or computers.
3. Encourage customers to pay more promptly by offering discounts – usually customers are given anything from 30 to 90 days to pay for goods bought on credit. If customers pay for goods quickly cash is received earlier, so some businesses offer discounts to customers to encourage them to pay quickly, say in 30 days rather than 60 days. The business could also ask for cash with sales.
4. Arrange trade credit with suppliers, or if the business has trade credit, try to agree a longer credit period. This means payment for goods can be delayed until the goods are sold or made into other goods for re-sale.
5. To allow capital to stay in the business, it could rent rather than buy premises. It could also postpone purchasing expensive fixed assets like machinery, and purchase only essential items.
6. Storing stock costs money, so the business can reduce these costs by trying to reduce their stock levels.
7. The owners could reduce the number of withdrawals they make from the business or they could put more capital into the business.

All of the above measures should help the business survive a cash flow crisis. Whatever action the business does take, it must be taken quickly and it is also important to identify why it happened and make sure it does not happen again. Comparing the actual cash flow with the projected cash flow should help the business do this.

Figure 14.3

> **Exam tip**
>
> Cash flow and sources of finance are closely linked. Remember, you need to know where the money might come from to improve cash flow.

Task

You are asked to explain cash flow forecasting to a new member of staff.

1. What is cash flow?
2. What is a cash flow forecast?
3. Why is it important to use cash flow forecasting?
4. Why might a bank manager want to see a cash flow forecast?
5. Explain the difference between cash flow and profit.

Extension task

Jenny Cooper has just opened a business manufacturing homemade wedding and speciality cakes. She has the following figures and has asked you to help her prepare a cash flow forecast:

She expects her sales to be £3000 per month. She also expects to sell candles and other decorative items for the cakes which she hopes will bring in £500 per month.

Her raw materials are estimated at £1200 per month and she is expecting to have labour costs of £800 per month. Rent is £120 per week, and she expects other overheads to be £900 per month. She will be paying £1200 insurance payable in two instalments – one in March and one in September. Her opening balance is £200.

1. Using the above information, draw up a cash flow forecast for March, April and May.
2. Comment on the closing balance for March.
3. If Jenny experiences any cash flow problems, suggest three ways she might solve them.

Exam tip

You will not be asked to draw up a cash flow forecast, but you may be asked to fill in missing figures. You will be expected to know what has caused the cash flow problem if there is one.

Summary

- Monitoring cash flow is very important in business.
- Remember, cash flow forecasts are based on estimates, and actual figures can differ considerably.

Key terms

Cash flow – money in and out of the business

Cash flow forecast – a plan of expected money in and out of the business

Net cash flow – difference between total cash in and total cash out each month

UNIT 15

SOURCES OF FINANCE

What you will learn

At the end of this unit you should understand:
- why businesses need to raise finance
- the main types of internal and external sources of finance for businesses
- the difference between short-term and long-term finance
- the factors which influence the decision to use a particular source of finance.

WHY IS FINANCE NEEDED?

Any business, large or small, needs money, but where can it find this money or finance? It can raise this finance from inside the business, known as **internal finance**, or from outside the business, known as **external finance**. Large businesses will find they have several sources of finance available to them, while small firms may find only a limited number available. In addition, as businesses grow they will find that their financial needs change.

There are three main reasons a business will need money:

1. When the business begins, it needs **start-up capital** which is provided by the owners of a business. This capital is used for premises, machinery, raw materials and perhaps initial advertising. A sole trader might put his or her own savings into the business, but this may not be enough for all the start-up costs, so the business may have to take out a loan. Another source of finance might be friends or family who can see a good business opportunity and are willing to put money into the business.

2. Once the business is up and running it will need finance for day-to-day expenses like wages, rent, power and for when the business may run short of cash. This is called **revenue expenditure** or **working capital**.

Figure 15.1 A sole trader

Exam tip

Cash flow and sources of finance are linked and you will need to remember this in the exam.

3. If and when the business expands or grows, it may need money in order to acquire more premises or larger premises, employ more staff and purchase additional equipment. The purchase of fixed assets either at start-up or for expansion is called **capital expenditure**.

How finance is used

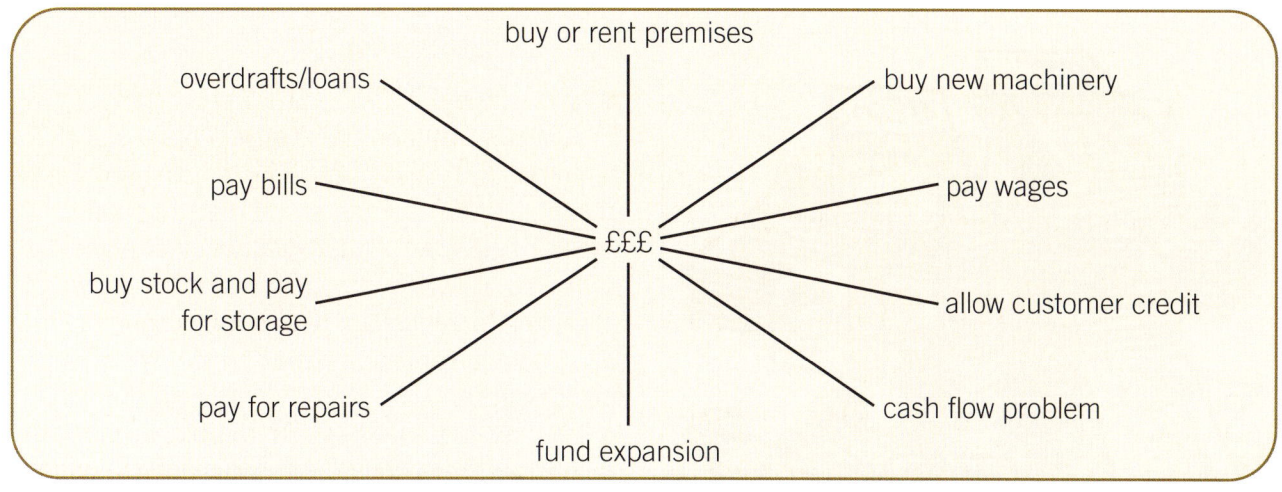

Figure 15.2 How finance is spent

Labels around £££:
- buy or rent premises
- overdrafts/loans
- buy new machinery
- pay bills
- pay wages
- buy stock and pay for storage
- allow customer credit
- pay for repairs
- cash flow problem
- fund expansion

Task

1. What is meant by internal finance? Give an example.
2. What is meant by external finance? Give an example.
3. Explain the three main reasons a business will need money.
4. Explain the difference between capital expenditure and revenue expenditure.

Short-term finance	Long-term finance
trade credit – external	loans – external
overdraft – external	mortgages – external
factoring – external	capital – external
lease – external	government grants – external
hire purchase – external	retained profit – internal
loans – external	debentures – external

SHORT- AND LONG-TERM FINANCE

Once the business is up and running, it needs money for day-to-day expenses. This money is called **short-term** or **long-term finance**:

- **Short-term finance** is finance which will be paid back quickly, usually in less than one year.
- There is also **medium-term finance** which will be paid back in one to five years.
- **Long-term finance** may be paid back over many years, at least over five years.

Short-term finance

Trade credit
This is finance received from suppliers. It means buying goods but not paying for them for perhaps thirty days, if the business has received one month's trade credit. It may also receive a cash discount if payment is made within the agreed time. However, if payments are not made on time and this is repeated, the supplier may stop the trade credit and insist on cash with goods.

Overdraft
An **overdraft** is when a business draws more money from its bank account than it currently has in the account. It has permission from the bank, which sets an agreed limit called an **overdraft limit**. Interest is payable on the overdraft and this is calculated on a daily basis. An advantage of an overdraft is that money is only borrowed when needed; this means that interest is only paid when the bank account is overdrawn.

A disadvantage of an overdraft is that the bank can insist that it is repaid immediately. However, because of its flexibility an overdraft is probably the most frequently used way to solve a cash flow problem.

UNIT 15: SOURCES OF FINANCE

Figure 15.3

Factoring

A business which has debtors (people who owe money to the business) may have to wait quite some time for its money. If this is a problem and the business needs cash quickly, it can use a **factor**. A factor is a specialist company, usually a bank, which will provide immediate payment of part of the debts owed, normally around 80%. The other 20%, minus a fee of maybe 5–10%, will be paid when the debts are settled.

The advantages of factoring are that the business gets cash immediately, the factor collects the debts and if any customers do not pay, the factor suffers the loss.

Leasing

This allows businesses to have expensive assets like machinery, equipment and computers without having to pay out large sums of money for their purchase. The advantages of leasing are:

- maintenance and repairs are done by the leasing company
- businesses are usually offered the most up-to-date equipment.

The disadvantages are that the business never owns the asset, therefore it cannot sell the asset if it needs to raise money.

Hire purchase

This means that a business buys a piece of equipment but does not pay for it in one payment (though it does have the use of the equipment). The business pays a fixed number of monthly payments. However, the business does not own the equipment until the last payment has been made to the company providing the finance, known as a **finance house**.

The main disadvantage of hire purchase is that if the business falls behind with payments then the equipment is repossessed, which means that the finance house takes the equipment back.

Loans

A loan is a sum of money borrowed from a bank. It can be classed as a short-, medium- or long-term loan. The loan has to be repaid in fixed monthly instalments. The business also has to pay **interest** on the loan. The interest payable can be fixed or variable. Fixed interest means the same interest is paid for the duration of the loan; this would be preferred if interest rates are rising. Variable interest varies in line with current interest rates.

Figure 15.4

In addition the business may be required to provide security or collateral against the loan. This means the bank will sell something the business owns if the business does not make the loan repayments.

Task

1. Explain one advantage and one disadvantage of using overdrafts.
2. Why might a business use leasing when it needs new vehicles?
3. What are the advantages of factoring?

Past Paper

Leroy Green is a self-employed plumber who is sub-contracted by Delta Homes plc (a house building company). He wishes to purchase new tools and equipment to use for his work at the 'Sleepy Hollow' development. He has approached the bank for a loan.

1. Explain why the bank may be unwilling to grant Leroy Green a loan. (3)

2. As the sale of properties in 'Sleepy Hollow' goes ahead, interest rates rise. Assess two effects on Harbon Estates Ltd (a property development company) of a rise in interest rates. (6)

(Edexcel, 1999, Foundation and Higher)

Long-term finance
Mortgages
These are long-term loans usually offered by banks or building societies. They are usually used for the purchase of buildings, and the buildings are used as security for the mortgage. This means that if the mortgage payments are not kept up, the bank or building society will require the building be sold to repay the mortgage.

Figure 15.5

Capital
As we saw above, the money put into a new business is called start-up capital. When a business wants to raise more money or capital it can sell shares, called **share** or **equity capital**. A share is a certificate which shows that the holder owns part of the company. The people who buy these shares are called **shareholders**. If the business sells lots of shares it can raise large sums of money.

The reasons for shareholders to invest in companies are:

- to receive a return on their investment in the form of **dividends** (a proportion of the profits the company makes each year)
- to see their investment grow if the company is successful and the price of the shares increases.

Both private and public limited companies raise capital by selling shares. However, you will have seen in Unit 6 that only public limited companies can trade their shares on the Stock Exchange, which gives them access to an unlimited number of shareholders. This enables them to raise very large amounts of capital.

Grants
These are another form of external finance available to businesses from the government and the European Union. However, some grants are

only available in certain areas of the UK. The grants are given to encourage:

- firms to move or locate to one of these areas
- firms with few employees to create more jobs
- firms located in certain inner city and enterprise zones to create employment and regeneration.

These grants might take the form of:

- tax allowances to purchase equipment
- assistance with start-up costs
- a reduction in rent or rates.

They are all designed to encourage businesses to operate in certain areas. These grants and loans can be important sources of finance for companies in the UK.

Debenture

This is a special type of loan which is: long-term with a fixed rate of interest and an agreed repayment date. Debentures are often mentioned along with shares but unlike a shareholder, the debenture holder is not a part-owner of the business, and s/he does not receive dividends but interest on the loan.

Retained profit

This is the only internal source of finance which we study. This is profit which is not distributed to the owners of the business but which is ploughed back into the business from one year to the next. Retained profit is the main source of long-term finance available for smaller businesses in particular. Using its own profits means a business has no interest or dividends to pay.

A business plan

Before granting a loan, the bank will nearly always insist on seeing a **business plan**. If a business has no idea of where it is going because it has not planned properly, then a bank will be very unlikely to grant it a loan. A business plan is a concise report which explains how a business works – what it is, where it is going and how it will get there. It will show how finance will be obtained and the likely sales, costs and profits of the business. If the bank can see that a business has produced a well-considered plan, it is more likely to lend money.

Your business plan

This form has been produced for you to use as the basis for your business plan, and has been specially designed to work in conjunction with **'Guide 2 – Setting up and running your business'**. The sections on the form relate to the sections throughout the Guide – so you'll be able to refer to the Guide, if you need to, as you fill in the form. We've tried to make it suitable for most businesses, but if there are parts which you feel are not relevant to you or you can't complete, don't worry. We will be pleased to offer you any help or assistance you might require.

Name of business ______

Address ______

Post Code ______

Telephone number ______

☐ Sole Trader ☐ Partnership

☐ Franchise ☐ Limited Company

Start-up target date or date business began trading ______

Type of business ______

Planning

My ultimate goal is ______

I expect to achieve the following over the next few years

Year 1 ______

Year 2 ______

Year 3 ______

Knowing the market

My market may be described as (eg type, size, location) ______

My customers may be described as ______

My product/service is special because ______

Product/service comparison table

	My product/service	Competitor A	Competitor B
Price			
Quality			
Availability			
Customers			
Staff skills			
Reputation			
Advertising			
Delivery			
Location			
Special offers			
After sales service			

The main advantages of my product/service over my competitors' are

Competitor A ______

Competitor B ______

Figure 15.6 An extract from a business plan

A business plan is vital in the financial planning of any business. The major high street banks provide assistance on completing business plans to new start-up businesses as well as businesses seeking finance. The plan should include:

- name of company – what it does, type of ownership, size (number of employees), aims and objectives
- the product or service – price of products, services, quantities to be produced, what makes the product or service different from those of competitors
- market research or proposed market – results of research, market size, potential customers, competition, proposed promotion and advertising
- personnel – experience and skills of the people involved in the business
- costs – fixed and variable costs, purchasing costs (what suppliers charge)
- premises or equipment – where it is located, type of premises, details of equipment (what equipment is there, its age and its cost)
- financial details – where the capital comes from, a cash flow forecast, a predicted profit, what the business wants to borrow.

Task

Try to find some material on business start-ups from banks. Have a go at completing a business plan for a business of your own choice.

Exam tip

As well as being able to describe the main sources of finance, you need to apply your knowledge of them. You need to know which source of finance would be appropriate in a given situation and why. You will need to consider the advantages and disadvantages and then give a sensible choice.

Task

1. Why would a bank want to see a business plan before it lent money?
2. Explain two benefits to a business of preparing a business plan.
3. What should be included in a business plan?
4. A business plan is a forecast. Explain why a business might draw up a range of possible forecasts.

Extension task

Tim Laws started his own joinery business with £8000 inherited from his grandmother. He had worked for ten years for a well-known local business and had managed to build up a reputation for himself as being reliable and capable of doing a good job. Quite a few people had asked him to do jobs for them, so with these guarantees of work he was able to negotiate a bank loan to cover the rest of his start-up costs. He offered his house as security for the loan.

Initially Tim found he had under-estimated how long it would take for his invoices to be paid, while he still needed to pay wages and buy raw materials.

After a couple of years Tim was doing well. He employed 15 men and he had expanded to building work as well as joinery. He realised the time had come to decide whether to expand further or stay as he was.

1. Other than from his grandmother and the bank loan, where else could Tim have found money from to start-up his business?
2. What is meant by security?
3. Why did the bank need this security?
4. How might Tim have solved his cash flow problem of:
    a) having to wait for payment
    b) having to pay wages
    c) buying raw materials?
5. If Tim decided to expand further, how might he finance this?

Revision Questions

1. If a bank provided a large loan to Gillens Ltd it might request:
   a) incentives
   b) tax relief
   c) costs
   d) security

2. Gillens Ltd could ask the bank for a .... to buy a new tractor.
   a) mortgage
   b) commission
   c) revenue
   d) loan

3. The purchase of fixed assets is called c............ e..........

4. Short-term finance will usually be paid back within how long?

5. Long-term finance will be paid back over how long?

6. Is selling shares an internal or external source of finance?

7. State one advantage of using retained profits for finance.

8. Where would a business receive an overdraft facility from?

9. When a business takes out a loan, it pays i............ on the loan.

10. The money paid to shareholders out of profits is called a d............

Summary

By the end of this unit you should:
- know the difference between internal and external sources of finance
- understand the three main reasons a business will need money
- know the difference between short-term, medium-term and long-term finance
- know the main sources of finance and their respective advantages and disadvantages.

Key terms

Business plan – a document which contains the aims of a business and how it will achieve them
Capital – funds invested in the company
Capital expenditure – money spent on fixed assets
Debentures – long-term loans which have a fixed rate of interest
External finance – finance received from outside the business
Factoring – immediate payment of invoices from a specialist company
Grants – finance available from the government or the EU
Hire purchase – paying for something by instalments. The item does not belong to the business until the last payment has been made
Internal finance – finance from within the business
Leasing – paying a monthly fee for the use of an asset, eg a van
Loans – a sum of money, borrowed usually from a bank
Long-term finance – money borrowed for over five years
Medium-term finance – borrowed money which will be paid back in one to five years
Mortgage – a form of loan secured against property
Overdraft – where a business takes more money from its bank account than it owns
Retained profit – profit left after tax and dividends have been paid
Revenue expenditure – money spent on day-to-day expenses
Short-term finance – borrowed money which will be paid back in less than one year
Start-up capital – money provided by the owners of a business when it is set up
Trade credit – the time between getting goods from suppliers and paying for them

UNIT 16

REVENUE, COSTS AND BREAK-EVEN ANALYSIS

>> What you will learn

At the end of this unit you should understand:
- the different types of costs involved in business
- the difference between direct and indirect costs
- the difference between fixed and variable costs
- that a business receives revenue from selling its products/services
- how break-even analysis is used in business.

REVENUE

Any money received from selling goods or providing a service is called **sales revenue**. Businesses calculate sales revenue using the following formula

sales revenue
= total number of goods sold × selling price

Figure 16.1

As long as the revenue is more than costs then the business will make a **profit** – if not, and the costs are more than the revenue then the firm will make a **loss**. A business can, to some extent, control how many products it sells by reducing the selling price in the hope it will sell more. However, this does not always happen because competitors may also reduce their prices, and the revenue will hardly change.

A business may also increase its selling price, but this may result in a reduction in sales. However, the reduction in sales will depend upon the loyalty of customers and whether the product is one which customers will still buy regardless of cost. Think about the trainers you wear – does the price make any difference to whether you buy them or not?

Higher prices mean:

- more sales revenue is gained from each product sold, but
- fewer products may be sold so some sales revenue may be lost.

Lower prices mean:

- less sales revenue is received from each product sold, but

- more goods may be sold so sales revenue may be increased.

COSTS

Whatever a business does, whether making products, selling goods or providing a service, it uses a wide range of resources. These resources have to be paid for and we call these payments **costs**. A business will have to pay many costs, which can include premises costs, raw material costs and wages costs.

We can divide the costs of business up into:

- fixed costs
- variable costs.

Fixed costs

These are costs which do not change whether the business produces lots of goods or produces no goods at all. These costs still have to be paid, regardless of output. For example, the rent on a shop will still have to be paid whether or not the shop has any customers. Sometimes fixed costs are also called **indirect costs** or **overheads**. Other examples of fixed costs are:

- interest payments on loans
- managers' salaries
- rates payable to the local council

Figure 16.2 Making a profit

- rent
- loan repayments.

Variable costs

These increase directly with the level of output. This means that if the business increases what it produces, then its variable costs will rise. For example, if a business manufacturing children's clothes increases production, then it will use more raw materials, which in this case would be fabric. Sometimes variable costs are also called **direct costs**. Other examples of variable costs are:

- wages of machinists
- gas and electricity
- parts and components.

Fixed or variable costs

For some businesses costs cannot always be easily classified into fixed and variable. For one business some costs will be fixed, but for another business they will be variable. For example, all businesses use the telephone; for the majority these will be a fixed cost as the same charge will be made each quarter for line rental, but they will still be making varying numbers of calls, so call charges will vary. For a call centre where they make thousands of telephone calls each day, their telephone costs will be variable because the more calls they make, the more their telephone bill will be. We can say that these costs are **semi-variable** – part fixed and part variable. Can you think of any other examples of semi-variable costs?

Total costs

Total costs are all of the costs of a business added together and are calculated as follows:

total costs = fixed costs + variable costs

> ⚠️ **Exam tip**
>
> It is very likely that you will be asked to explain revenue and costs in your exam. Make sure you know the definitions.

Task

1. For each of the costs below, indicate whether it is fixed or variable.

Cost	Fixed	Variable
Machinist's wages		
Rent		
Rates		
Loan repayments		
Salaries		
Insurance payments		
Components		
Raw materials		

2. Explain what a semi-variable cost is.
3. Explain two consequences to a business of raising its prices.

Figure 16.3 Break even: total revenue = total costs

BREAK-EVEN ANALYSIS

Businesses have to decide how much to produce. The business will also want to know whether the products are making a profit or not, and how many products need to be sold in order to **break even**.

- Break even is the point where **total revenue = total costs**.
- The business is making a **profit** when sales revenue is **more** than total costs.
- The business is making a **loss** when sales revenue is **less** than total costs.

Businesses use break-even analysis to:

- help them to decide, when setting up, what level of output and sales are needed
- support an application to a bank for a loan so that the bank can see the business has good planning
- see the results of 'what if' changes – what if the selling price is increased or costs increase.

Break even can be calculated using a formula, or it can be shown on a graph or chart. A break-even chart is shown below for a product which has a selling price of £5, a variable cost of £2.50 and fixed costs of £200. It is easier to prepare a table of all the figures first.

Plot these figures on the graph as follows:

- draw the horizontal or x axis from 0 to 100 and label this axis 'Output'

Output	0	20	40	60	80	100	120	140
Revenue	0	100	200	300	400	500	600	700
Fixed costs	200	200	200	200	200	200	200	200
Variable costs – £2.50	0	50	100	150	200	250	300	350
Total costs	200	250	300	350	400	450	500	550

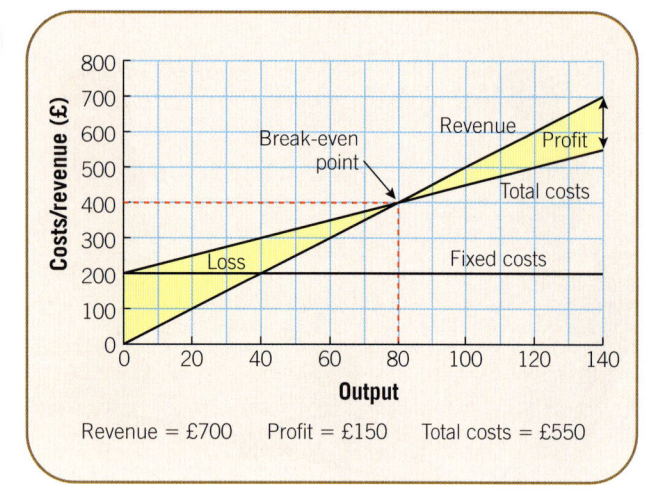

Figure 16.4 Break even graph

- draw the vertical or *y* axis from 0 to 500 and label this axis 'Costs/revenue'
- plot the fixed costs line and label it 'Fixed costs'
- plot the total costs line starting at the fixed costs line and label this 'Total costs'
- plot the revenue line starting at 0 and label it 'Revenue'
- the break-even point is where the total costs and revenue lines cross – mark this
- you can now draw two lines from the break even point going down to the *x* (output) axis and across to the *y* (costs/revenue) axis – these show the number of items that need to be sold to break-even and the revenue which would be received at this break-even point.

The point at which the revenue line = the total costs line is **break-even**.

Exam tip

In the exam you will not be asked to draw a chart from scratch but marks are usually given for labelling lines and axis – so don't forget to do this for extra marks!

When drawing a break-even chart, it is not always necessary to plot all costs and revenue for all levels of output. You can save time by just plotting the highest and lowest figures for total costs and revenue and then joining the two points together. In the example above, you need only plot from 0 to £700 for revenue and from 0 to £550 for total costs.

Analysing the break-even chart

You can see from the break-even chart that the break-even point is 80 products. This means that the business must make and sell 80 products to cover its costs. Anything below this, say 79 products, would mean that the business was making a loss. Anything over 80, say 81, would mean that the business was making a profit.

Task

Carden Coats Ltd manufacture wax jackets in a small factory on the outskirts of Hartlepool. Their sole customer is a major UK chain store, which purchases 1000 jackets each month. The factory's capacity is 1250 jackets per month. The company charges the chain store £40 per jacket.

Fixed costs per month:

	£
Rent	1400
Rates	800
Salaries	9000
Other costs	800

The manufacture of each jacket costs:

	£
Materials	12.00
Labour	13.00

1. Draw up a table of costs and revenue.
2. Construct a break-even chart from your figures.
3. What is the break-even point?

Task

Philly O'Keefe is opening a burger bar in the centre of town on Friday and Saturday evenings only. He thinks he can sell 120 burgers for £2 each. His fixed costs are estimated to be £100 per week and the burgers, bread buns and mustard/ketchup will cost 80p per burger.

Figure 16.5

1. Draw up a table of costs and revenue.
2. Construct a break-even chart from your figures.
3. How many burgers will Philly have to sell each week in order to break even?
4. What will the revenue be if 100 burgers are sold each week?
5. What will the profit be if 100 burgers are sold each week?

Margin of safety

This is the difference between the break-even point and the current level of output. If, in the example in Figure 16.6, output is 120, then the margin of safety would be:

120 − 80 = 40 products

This means that production would have to drop by 20 products before the business was making a loss. The higher the margin of safety the better.

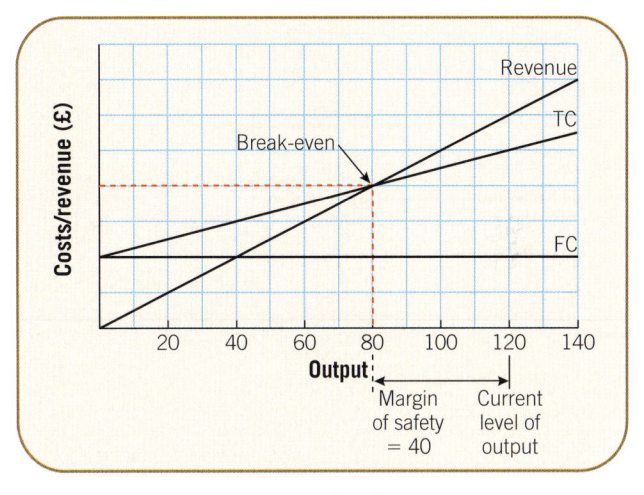

Figure 16.6 The margin of safety

Task

On the break-even charts which you completed in the two previous tasks, indicate the margin of safety.

Calculating break-even without using a graph

Break-even can also be calculated without using a graph. A formula is used as follows:

$$\frac{\text{fixed costs}}{\text{selling price} - \text{variable costs}}$$

Using our example earlier, break-even can be calculated as follows:

$$\frac{200}{5 - 2.50} = \frac{200}{2.50} = 80$$

This means that the business would have to sell 80 products in order to break even.

UNIT 16: REVENUE, COSTS AND BREAK-EVEN ANALYSIS

Task

Calculate the following break-even points using the formula.

1. fixed costs   £4000
   selling price   £400
   variable cost   £200

2. A business has the following costs:
   rent   £200 per month
   rates   £30 per month
   salaries   £450 per month
   selling price £9
   raw materials £7

3. A business making t-shirts has the following costs:
   fixed costs   £50 000 per year
   variable costs   £3.70 per t-shirt
   selling price   £12.00 each
   a) Calculate the break-even point.
   b) What would the revenue be at break-even?

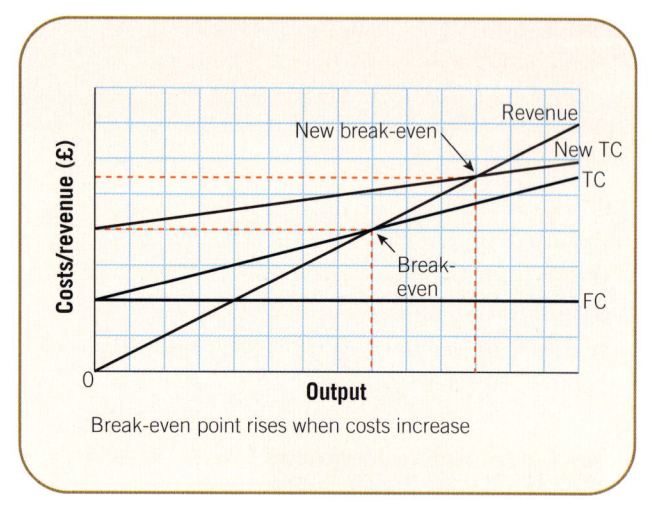

Figure 16.7 Increased costs

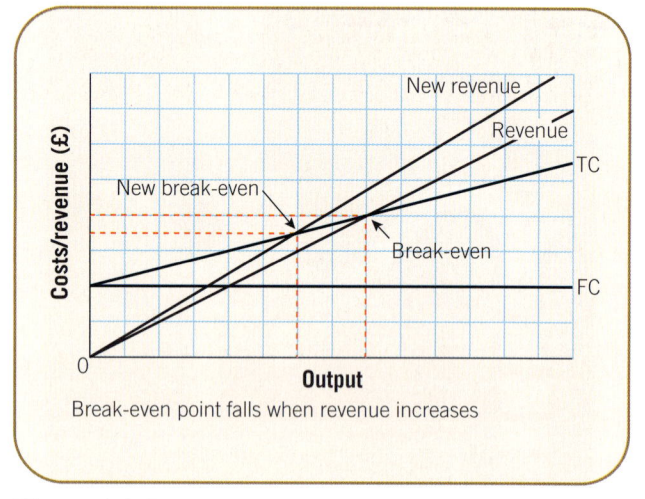

Figure 16.8 Increased revenue

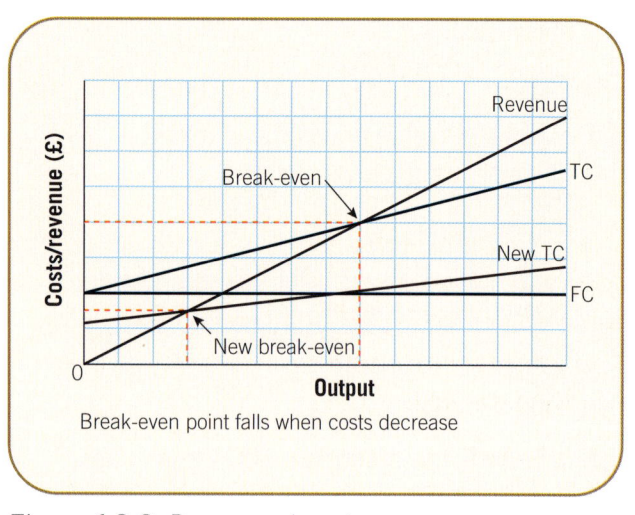

Figure 16.9 Decreased costs

What happens when costs or revenue change?

It was stated earlier that break-even analysis is good in 'what-if' situations. For example, what if:

- costs increase because the rent goes up?
- revenue increases because the selling price is increased?
- costs decrease because a new supplier can supply raw materials at a cheaper price?
- revenue decreases because the selling price has been reduced?

What will happen to the break-even point? It is very useful for businesses to know this so that they can take action accordingly.

If costs increase or revenue falls, the break-even point will **rise**, so the business will need to sell more products to make a profit.

If costs decrease or revenue increases, the break-even point will **fall**, so the company will not need to sell as many products to make a profit.

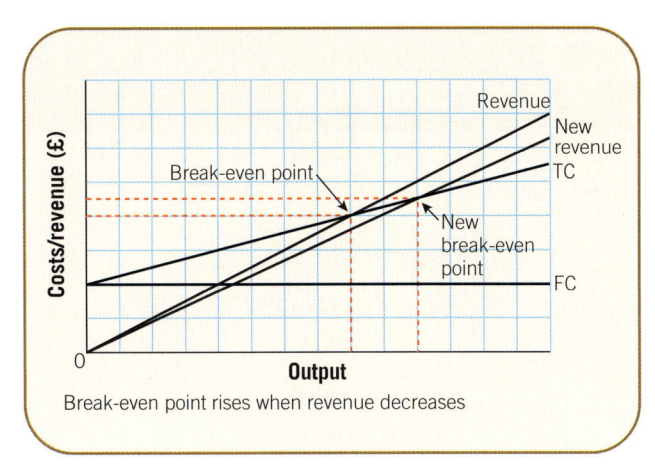

Figure 16.10 Decreased revenue

Task

Use the break-even chart you used for Philly's burger bar and make the following changes:

1. If the landlord puts the rent up by £10 per week, how many burgers will Philly have to sell now to break even?
2. If Philly puts the price of his burgers up by 10p, what will happen to the break-even point?
3. Philly's burger bar is having problems and he finds he is only selling 70 burgers a week. What problems would this create for the business?
4. Explain how Philly could overcome these problems.

Advantages and disadvantages of using break-even analysis

Break-even analysis can be vital in planning, forecasting and decision-making, but it does have limitations as well.

Advantages
- Break-even analysis is a simple technique to use and it gives quick results.
- No specialist training or financial consultants are required (managers can easily read them), so it is particularly suitable for small businesses.
- It can help a business to spot problems and do something about these problems.
- The margin of safety will allow businesses to work out by how much output and sales can fall before they face a loss.
- As already mentioned, it can assist when applying for a loan.

Disadvantages
- Break-even assumes that all goods are sold when in fact this is not always the case for a number of reasons – seasonal demand, goods going out of fashion.
- Break-even also assumes all goods are sold at the same price, which again is not always the case.
- Figures could change – there might be a wage increase or the rent goes up.
- The chart is only a forecast based on current figures – How accurate are the figures?
- A break-even chart is not as useful for businesses providing a service, because the charge for services can vary so much from customer to customer.

Task

A business making clocks sells and makes 80 000 each month. Its break-even chart is below. Study the chart and answer the questions.

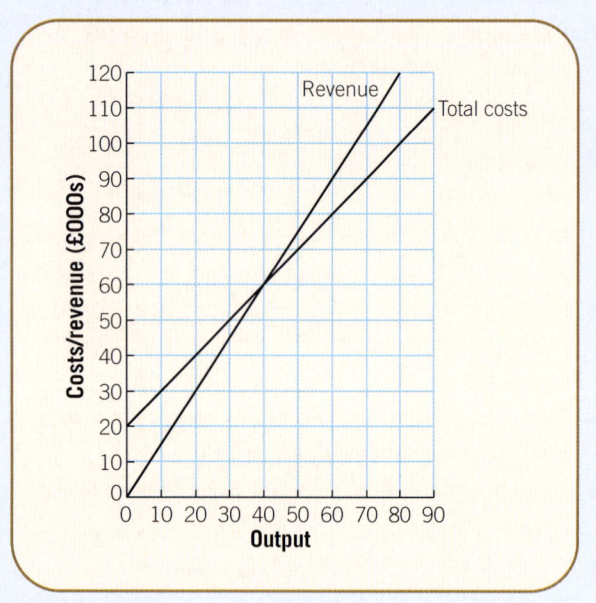

Figure 16.11

1. What is the break-even point?
2. What are the fixed costs?
3. What is the selling price of each clock?
4. What is the profit or loss if:
   a) 30 000 clocks are sold
   b) 60 000 clocks are sold
   c) 90 000 clocks are sold?
5. What is the margin of safety?
6. Explain why total costs rise as the production of clocks increases.

Extension task

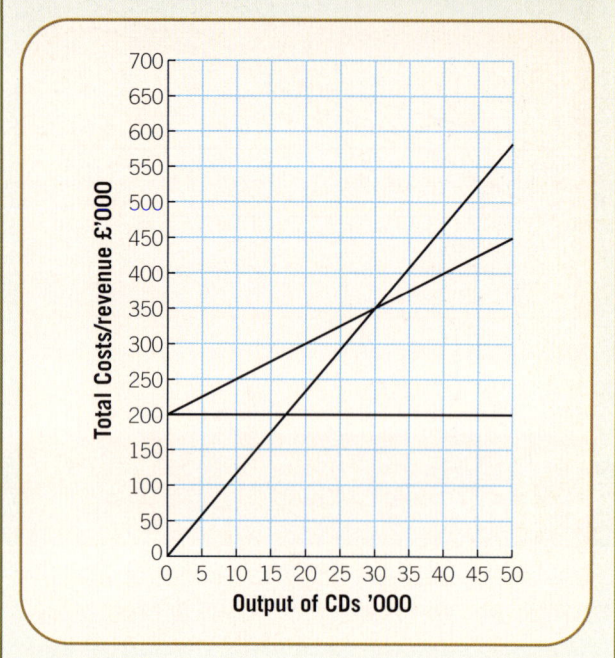

Figure 16.12

Ceedisc plc uses the break-even chart above.

1. Explain what is meant by the term 'break even'.
2. Copy out the break-even chart and label the:
   - revenue
   - fixed costs
   - total costs.
3. Label the break-even point on the chart.
4. How many CDs have to be sold to break even?
5. Explain what is meant by variable costs and fixed costs. Give examples of both associated with the production of CDs.
6. Explain the relationship between revenue, costs, output and break-even.

Revision Questions

1. Which one of the following would be used in Gillens Ltd when producing a break-even chart?
   a) cash flow forecast
   b) units of production
   c) Articles of Association
   d) profit and loss account

2. Raw materials bought by Gillens Ltd to make bears are ………… costs.
   a) fixed
   b) total
   c) capital
   d) variable

3. Costs that stay the same are known as:
   a) variable costs
   b) profit
   c) fixed costs
   d) loss

4. Which one of these is a fixed cost?
   a) production workers' wages
   b) travel costs
   c) raw materials
   d) rent

5. Why is the fixed cost line on a break-even chart horizontal?

6. How much profit does a business make at its break-even point? Explain your answer.

7. Explain the importance of break-even for a business.

8. Explain two weaknesses of break-even charts.

Summary

- Break-even analysis is an important, useful decision-making tool used in business.
- The break-even point shows when total costs = total revenue, and indicates when the business will make a profit or loss.
- Break-even can be calculated using a graph or using a formula.
- Break-even is useful in 'what if' situations.

Key terms

Break-even – the level of output where total costs = total revenue

Break-even chart – a line graph showing costs, revenue and break-even

Fixed costs – costs which do not alter

Margin of safety – the difference between break-even and current output

Revenue – income which comes from selling goods and/or services

Semi-variable costs – part fixed and part variable costs

Total costs – fixed costs + variable costs

Variable costs – costs which change according to output

UNIT 17

FINAL ACCOUNTS

What you will learn

At the end of this unit you should understand:

- what accounts are
- why accounts are prepared
- how accounts are used in financial decision-making
- the purpose and content of final accounts – profit and loss account and balance sheet
- how the accounts can be used to assess business performance.

WHAT ARE ACCOUNTS?

All businesses keep some record of their finances. They do this in order to know their financial position. These records are called the **accounts**. These accounts are a way of recording how the business has done during a given period of time, usually a year. The person responsible for the accounts is usually the **accountant**.

Figure 17.1 Accountants

However, there are other users of the accounts:

Shareholders
If the business is a limited company, the shareholders will want to know whether a profit has been made, what the dividends will be and what the business is worth.

Potential shareholders
If the business is a public limited company, the accounts are published so any potential shareholders will be able to see how well the business is doing. This will affect a decision of whether or not to buy shares in the business via the Stock Exchange.

Managers
Managers will look at the accounts to see whether the business has improved its performance from the previous year.

Employees
Employees would be anxious to see whether the business is performing well and therefore their jobs are secure. They would also want to know whether profits are sufficient to give them a wage increase.

Creditors
Suppliers and the bank would be interested in seeing the accounts to see whether the business is able to pay back its debts.

The government
Taxes are calculated on the profits made by businesses both large and small.

Customers
Customers would be interested to see whether the business is performing well and likely to survive, otherwise guarantees on products and replacement parts would be affected.

Competitors
Other similar businesses will look at the accounts to compare performance.

Accounting documents
In order to understand why keeping accounts is important in business we should look at what businesses do. All businesses, whether they produce a product or provide a service, trade to make a profit. In order to measure whether profits have been made, records of all transactions have to be kept.

These records of transactions are recorded in the **book-keeping system** of the business which, will consist of journals and ledgers. Bear in mind that most businesses nowadays keep their book-keeping records on computer. A large number of documents will be created as a business buys and sells its goods and services. These documents deal mainly with **credit transactions** – where a business buys goods but pays for them at a later date. It is therefore vital to keep records of what is happening, in order to:

- see who owes money to the business – the customers
- see who has paid
- see who the business owes money to – probably suppliers
- provide data to the Inland Revenue and Customs & Excise so these government agencies can calculate how much tax the business owes
- inform owners and managers and assist in planning.

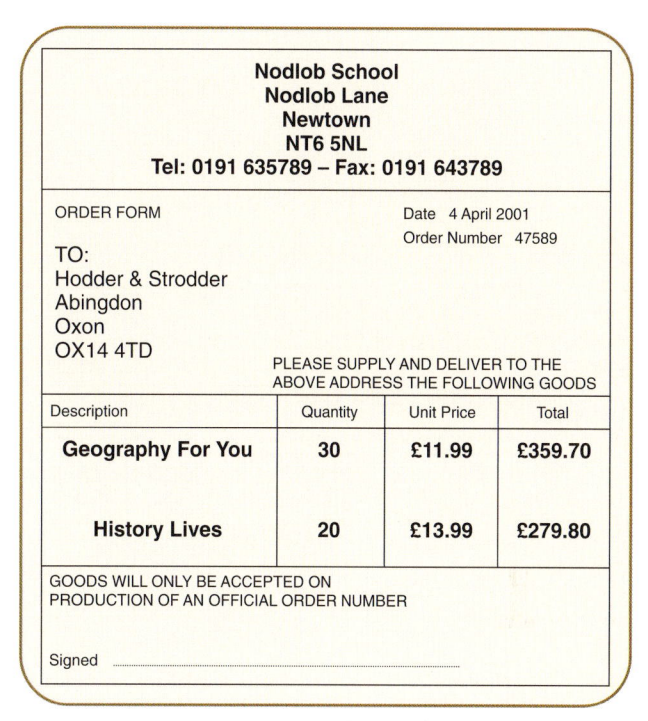

Figure 17.2 An order

The main documents used in business for sales and purchases on credit are as follows:

The order
This shows the goods to be bought, the quantity, a product reference number or description, how much each product costs and the total cost.

The delivery note
This is sent with the goods by the seller. Details of the goods are given so that the buyer can check that the correct goods have been delivered.

The invoice
This is the main business document and shows all the details of the transaction. It is sent by the seller, and shows which goods have been purchased, the quantity, the price of each item, the total price with any discounts and VAT.

A credit note
This is issued by the seller to the purchaser if for some reason goods have been returned (eg some of the goods were damaged). The credit note reduces the total amount owed on the invoice.

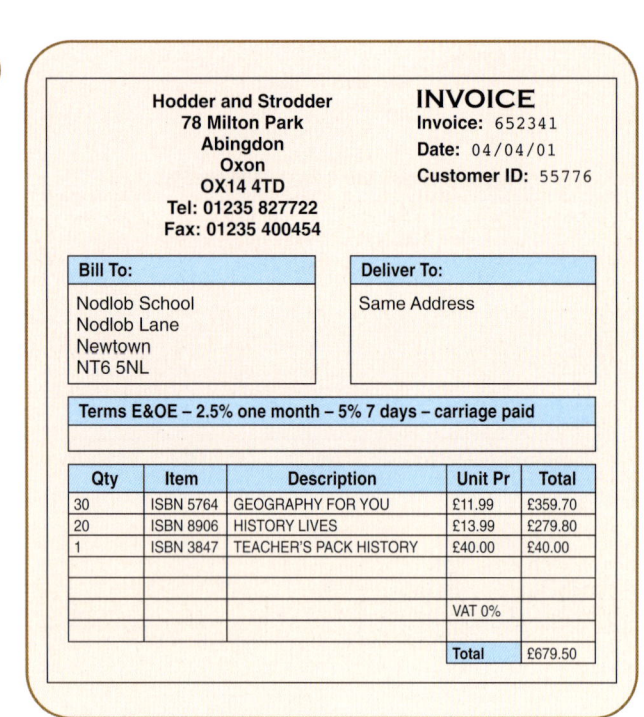

Figure 17.3 An invoice

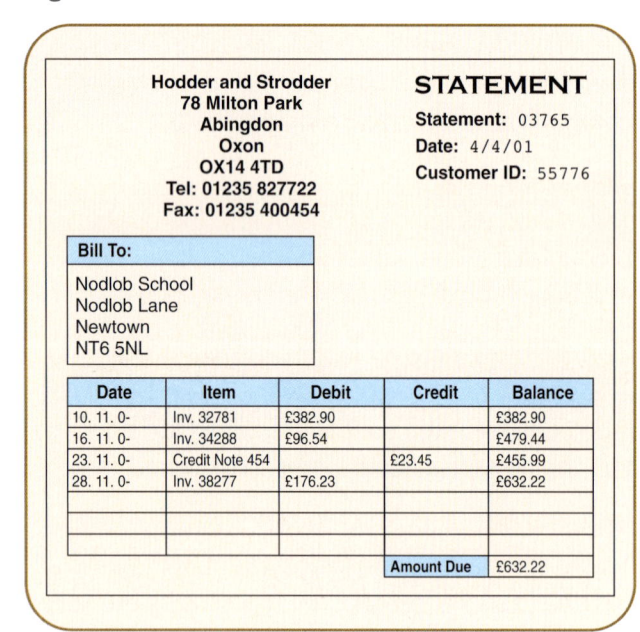

Figure 17.4 A statement

The statement of account

This is sent to the purchaser, usually each month, detailing all transactions between the seller and the purchaser during the month (it is a copy of their account). It is a reminder to the purchaser to pay what they owe.

A cheque

This is sent by the purchaser to the seller to settle the account.

It is important that accurate records of these documents are kept so that the accountant can prepare the **final accounts** from the book-keeping records. These final accounts will show whether the business has made a profit, is trading successfully and what the business is worth. The final accounts are:

- the profit and loss account
- the balance sheet.

PROFIT AND LOSS ACCOUNT

Businesses calculate their profit at regular intervals during the year. This information can help the managers in running the business. At the end of the year the final profit is calculated and appears in the profit and loss account. The profit and loss account is divided into three parts:

The trading account

The trading account shows the difference between sales revenue (what the goods were sold for) and what the goods cost to make; this is the **gross profit**.

sales revenue − cost of goods sold = gross profit

> ⚠️ **Exam tip**
>
> Remember that gross profit is **not** the final profit, as there are still other costs to be deducted.

Sales revenue	£15 000
less Cost of goods sold	£10 000
Gross profit	£ 5 000

This simply means that goods bought for £10 000 were sold for £15 000, leaving a gross profit of £5000. If the cost of goods sold figure was more than sales revenue, then the business would have made a loss because it means that the business paid more for the goods than they were able to sell them for.

Figure 17.5 Checking stock

In order to calculate cost of goods sold, a business needs to look at its stock of goods and know what stock it started with at the beginning of the year – this is called its **opening stock**. Any purchases of stock made during the year are added to the opening stock. A count of stock remaining at the end of year is made – this is called the **closing stock**. Closing stock in one year becomes the opening stock for the next year because the stock is sitting there waiting to be sold or turned into some other product for sale.

The Trading Account for C Smith Ltd for the year ended 31 March 2004

	£	£
Sales revenue		15 000
less Cost of goods sold		
Opening stock	2000	
add Purchases	7000	
	9000	
less Closing stock	1500	7500
Gross profit		7500

If C Smith Ltd was a manufacturing business, the cost of goods sold figure might include any wages paid to employees making the goods. Wages and salaries paid to employees who are not directly involved in making the goods are dealt with as expenses in the profit and loss account. We will be including all wages and salaries in expenses.

Exam tip

Sometimes you will be given the cost of goods sold figure, and sometimes you may be required to calculate it using the opening stock/purchases/closing stock figures.

opening stock + purchases – closing stock = cost of goods sold

Task

Complete the Trading Account for S Corner from these figures for the year ended 31 March 2004. His sales revenue was £25 000, his opening stock was £4500, he bought £8000 worth of stock during the year and his closing stock was £6000. What is his gross profit?

Figure 17.6

UNIT 17: FINAL ACCOUNTS

The profit and loss account

The profit and loss account follows on from the trading account. It shows the **net profit** (or loss) of the business. Net profit is the profit made by the business after all its **expenses**, sometimes called **overheads** have been deducted. These expenses might include:

- wages and salaries
- rent of premises
- rates
- insurance costs
- gas
- electricity
- interest payable on loans
- stationery costs
- advertising costs
- transport and distribution costs
- depreciation
- cleaning costs
- administration costs
- telephone costs.

Depreciation is shown as an expense in the profit and loss account. The assets which a business owns gradually wear out and are worth less each year. The amount by which a business calculates its assets will reduce in value each year is called **depreciation**. The business needs to show that the value of its assets is diminishing each year, so it does this by charging the annual loss in value or depreciation as an expense in the profit and loss account. This actually means that it is reducing its profit by the depreciation figure.

By deducting all its expenses from gross profit, a business will know its net profit. The business will want the profit to be:

The Profit and Loss Account for C Smith Ltd for the year ended 31 March 2004

	£	£
Gross profit		7500
less Expenses		
Wages and salaries	3000	
Rent and rates	1000	
Other expenses	2000	6000
Net profit		1500

- higher than the previous year
- high enough to satisfy shareholders, with enough left over to reinvest in the business.

Exam tip

You will not be expected to construct a trading and profit and loss account from scratch; you will only be expected to insert missing figures.

Task

1. Copy out the profit and loss accounts for EMS Ltd for 2003 and 2004, and fill in the missing figures.

	£ 2004	£ 2003
Sales revenue	238 000	215 000
less Cost of goods sold	120 000	105 000
Gross profit	?	?
less Expenses		
Wages	40 000	30 000
Depreciation	10 000	10 000
Heating and lighting	50 000	48 000
Other expenses	?	15 000
	112 000	?
Net profit	?	7 000

2. In which year do you think EMS Ltd performed better? Give your reasons.
3. During 2004, sales revenue increased by 15% and cost of goods sold increased by 10%. Wages, heating and lighting and other expenses also increased by 10%. Rewrite the profit and loss account for 2005 with these new figures.
4. What are the new gross and net profit figures?

The appropriation account

This shows what happens to the net profit. Net profit can be distributed in three ways:

- part of it has to be paid to the government in taxes – a limited company will pay corporation tax; a sole trader or partner will pay income tax
- part of it will be paid to shareholders in the form of dividends if the business is a limited company
- the remainder can be retained in the business to pay for new investment in the business.

> **Exam tip**
>
> This retained profit, which we saw earlier, is an internal source of finance. This is the main way in which businesses tend to pay for new investments.

The Appropriation Account for C Smith Ltd

	£
Net profit (profit before tax)	1500
less Corporation tax	500
Profit after tax	1000
Dividends paid	500
Retained profit	500

> **Task**
>
> Use the 2003 profit and loss account from the previous task. EMS Ltd:
> - has to pay tax at 22%, and
> - is going to pay dividends of 50% of the profit after tax.
>
> Complete the appropriation account.

We can now put the full profit and loss account together as follows:

The Profit and Loss Account for C Smith Ltd for the year ended 31 March 2004

	£	£
Sales revenue		15 000
less Cost of goods sold		
Opening stock	2000	
add Purchases	7000	
	9000	
less Closing stock	1500	7500
Gross profit		7500
less Expenses		
Wages and salaries	3000	
Rent and rates	1000	
Other expenses	2000	6000
Net profit (profit before tax)		1500
less Corporation tax		500
Profit after tax		1000
Dividends paid		500
Retained profit		500

> **Exam tip**
>
> A sole trader will not need an appropriation account as any profits belong to the owner; a partnership will show the profits split between the partners as agreed in the Deed of Partnership.

> **Task**
>
> 1. A business distributes its profit in three ways. Explain what these are.
> 2. Explain why a business would choose to increase the dividends it pays to shareholders.
> 3. Why does a business retain some of its profit?

UNIT 17: FINAL ACCOUNTS

Extension task

Jenny Thompson owns a hairdressing salon. She has been trading for two years. Her trading and profit and loss account for the last two years are shown below.

	2002 £	2003 £
Sales	50 000	55 000
Less Cost of sales	12 500	15 400
Gross profit	37 500	39 600
Less Expenses	7 500	6 600
Net profit	30 000	33 000

1. Using the above information, evaluate Jenny's success.

2. Explain why Jenny cannot judge the success of her business by using only the above information.

Task

The following balances of Bega Manufacturing Ltd have been extracted at the end of the financial year on 31 March 2004.

Sales revenue	£950 000
Cost of goods sold	£450 000
Expenses	£330 000

Corporation Tax is 24%; dividends paid are 45%.

Prepare the trading and profit and loss account.

THE BALANCE SHEET

The balance sheet shows what a business is worth at a precise point in time, usually the end of the financial year. We saw earlier that the profit and loss account shows how much profit the business has made, but it does not tell us very much more. The balance sheet shows what the business *owes* and *owns* and is sometimes said to be a 'snapshot' of the business at a particular point in time.

The balance sheet is made up of three parts:

1. assets
2. liabilities
3. capital.

Assets

These are what the business owns. They can be further divided up into:

1. **Fixed assets**, which might be land and buildings such as factories, offices, depots and yards; vehicles like cars and trucks; machinery and equipment such as machine tools, computers and furniture. All of these will stay in the business for some time because the business uses these – they are not for resale.

Figure 17.7 Balance sheet equation

2. **Current assets** are held in the business for a short time. They include **stock** (which might be raw materials, goods waiting to be processed and finished goods ready to be sold), **debtors** (customers of the business who owe money) and **cash**. These assets are said to be current because they can change on a daily basis – the business buys stock, sells it, receives payment and buys more stock.

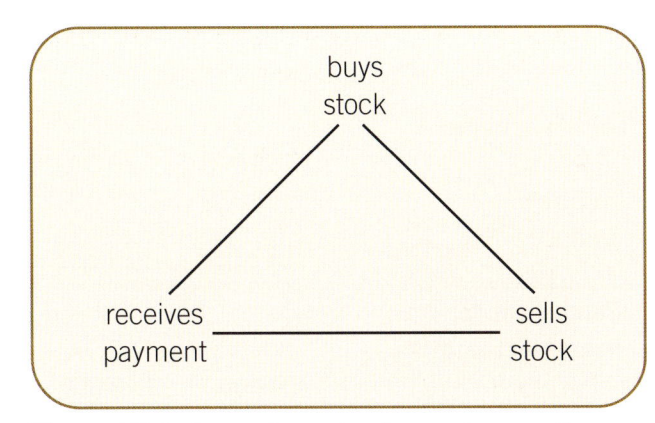

Figure 17.8 Current assets change frequently

Current assets appear in the balance sheet in order of liquidity, which means that the assets which will take longer to turn into cash (ie sell) appear at the top, and the easiest to turn into cash appear at the bottom (eg cash or money in the bank).

Liabilities

Liabilities are what the business owes. They too can be further divided up into:

1. **Long-term liabilities** – consist of money owed by the business, usually loans, which have to be repaid in more than one year's time.
2. **Current liabilities** – consist of money owed by the business which has to be paid within the next 12 months, eg tax owed to the government, dividends owed to shareholders, overdrafts owed to the bank and creditors. Creditors are those people and businesses usually suppliers that the business owes money to. Just as a business gives credit to its customers, so it receives credit from its suppliers.

Capital

This consists of the money which the owner or owners have put into the business. If it is a limited company the owners are shareholders. These shareholders put money into the business when the shares are first sold, so the business owes this money to its shareholders.

The business will also probably have some profits from previous years. This is called its **reserves**. There may also be profit which has been retained in the current year.

The structure of a balance sheet

A balance sheet does exactly what it says – it balances as follows:

Assets = Liabilities + Owners' capital

or

Net assets = Capital employed

You might wonder why owners' capital is on the same side as liabilities – which are what the business owes. The reason for this is because the business does not own the capital; it simply uses the capital to run the business. The capital belongs to the owners – the business owes its owners.

Figure 17.9 Balance sheet equation

Balance Sheet of Devenney Ltd

	£
Fixed assets	50 000
Current assets	30 000
Total or net assets	80 000
Total capital or capital employed	80 000

Task

1. What is the difference between fixed assets and current assets?
2. What are long-term liabilities?
3. Who might the debtors be of a business making windows?
4. Who might their creditors be?
5. Why is capital a liability for a business?
6. Explain the term 'reserves'.
7. What might a business use its retained profit for?

The structure of a balance sheet for both sole traders and limited companies will be more or less the same. However, limited companies, whether they are private or public, will have a wider range of assets, owners' capital and liabilities. Opposite is a typical balance sheet.

Working capital or net current assets is very important as it is the value of current assets left over when all current liabilities have been paid. For example, if you have £2 in your pocket, these are your current assets. If you owe £1, this is a liability. When you have paid your debt of £1, you have working capital of £1. A business needs enough working capital to be able to pay its day-to-day expenses, otherwise it will have a cash flow problem and be in danger of not being able to survive.

Balance Sheet for Bega Manufacturing Ltd as at 31 March 2004

	£ 2004	£ 2003
Fixed assets		
Premises	650 000	540 000
Machinery	100 000	90 000
Vehicles	95 000	84 000
	845 000	714 000
Current assets		
Stock	185 000	150 000
Debtors	140 000	110 000
Cash	55 000	59 000
	380 000	319 000
less		
Current liabilities		
Creditors	160 000	130 000
Overdraft	50 000	50 000
Dividends	66 000	40 000
	276 000	220 000
Working capital		
(net current assets)	104 000	99 000
Net assets	**949 000**	**813 000**
Financed by:		
Shareholders' funds	498 000	450 000
Reserves	190 000	140 000
Retained profit	80 000	50 000
Long-term liabilities		
Bank loan	181 000	173 000
Capital employed	**949 000**	**813 000**

Extension task

Fitness First Ltd is a gym and fitness centre that has been trading since 2000. It was started by three brothers who each bought £100 000 of shares. They converted an old church and this is now valued at £250 000. Their equipment is valued at £200 000 and the computer system they use is valued at £7000.

The business has a loan of £150 000. It has £40 000 in the bank. The business sells clothing and sports equipment and this stock is valued at £70 000. Some members owe their membership fees and these amount to £18 000. The gym owes £35 000 to their creditors. Their retained profit is £40 000 and their reserves are £60 000.

1. Draw up a balance sheet for the year ended 31 March 2004.
2. In 2003 their fixed assets were valued at £400 000. Explain the difference in the fixed assets figure.
3. Capital employed in 2003 was £515 000. Do you think the business is doing better or worse? Give your reasons.

Revision Questions

1. Customers who owe money to Gillen Ltd are called:
   a) creditors
   b) debtors
   c) directors
   d) partners

2. Fixtures and fittings owned by Gillen Ltd are:
   a) liabilities
   b) assets
   c) objectives
   d) responsibilities

3. A financial statement prepared by the accountant of Gillen Ltd is a:
   a) balance sheet
   b) bank statement
   c) person specification
   d) job description

4. Machinery owned by Gillen Ltd reduced in value each year. This is known as:
   a) mortgage
   b) dividend
   c) interest
   d) depreciation

5. The difference between costs and revenue is called:
   a) profit (or loss)
   b) turnover
   c) capital
   d) debt

6. Each year Flyaway plc has to pay corporation tax to the:
   a) shareholders
   b) bank
   c) employees
   d) government

7. What is working capital?

UNIT 17: FINAL ACCOUNTS

Revision Questions (cont.)

8. Calculate the working capital from the following:

Stock	10 000
Debtors	12 000
Cash	2 000
Premises	50 000
Creditors	20 000

9. List three examples of assets that would appear in a balance sheet.

10. Circle the odd one out:

    rent　　　　　rates
    advertising costs　　raw materials
    telephone

11. Circle the odd one out:

    loan　　　　overdraft
    dividends
    debtors　　　tax

12. State two reasons why a balance sheet is prepared.

13. Fill in the gaps using the following words:

    capital　　stock　　current
    creditors　　assets

    Fixed …………
    Land
    Buildings
    Machinery
    Current assets
    …………
    Debtors
    Cash
    ………… liabilities
    …………
    Overdraft
    Working …………

14. Calculate the sales revenue if a business sells 250 units at £7 each.

15. If its total costs are £1500, what is its profit?

Summary

- Final accounts consist of three parts – the trading account showing the gross profit, the profit and loss account showing the net profit, and the appropriation account which shows what has happened to the profit.
- A profit and loss account shows the business how much profit or loss it has made.
- It shows how the business has performed over the year.
- A balance sheet shows the worth of a business – what it owns and what it owes.
- It shows the assets, liabilities and capital of a business.
- It is important because it shows the strengths and weaknesses of the business.
- It allows decisions to be made on the performance of the business.

Key terms

Accounts – the financial records of a business

Accountant – the qualified person responsible for preparing the final accounts

Appropriation account – shows how the profit has been distributed

Balance sheet – shows the value of a business, what it is worth

Cost of goods sold – what the goods cost

Creditors – people to whom the business owes money (suppliers)

Current assets – stock, debtors, cash

Current liabilities – debts which have to paid within 12 months

Debtors – people who owe the business money (customers)

Depreciation – the reduction in value of an asset

Dividend – a share of the profit paid to shareholders

Expenses – sometimes called overheads and deducted from the gross profit (eg rent/rates)

Fixed assets – premises, machinery, vehicles

Final accounts – produced at the end of the financial year

Gross profit – sales revenue minus cost of goods sold

Liquid assets – assets of the business which can easily be turned into cash or which are already cash

Long-term liabilities – debts which do not have to be paid within 12 months

Net profit – gross profit minus expenses

Owners' capital – money put into the business by the owners

Profit and loss account – shows how net profit is calculated

Reserves – profits built up over years

Retained profit – profit kept in the business from the current year, which is added to the reserves

Sales revenue – income gained from selling goods or services

Trading account – shows how gross profit is calculated

Working capital – current assets minus current liabilities. This is used for the day-to-day running of the business

UNIT 17: FINAL ACCOUNTS

UNIT 18

BUSINESS PERFORMANCE AND RATIOS

> **What you will learn**
>
> At the end of this unit you should understand:
> - what business ratios are
> - what financial information the ratios show
> - how ratios are used in analysing business performance.

BUSINESS PERFORMANCE – WHO CARES?

In the last unit we looked at the figures in the final accounts of business. These figures allow businesses to:

- judge their own performance over time
- compare trends
- compare themselves with their competitors.

It is worth having another look at the different people interested in how well a business is doing.

The owners
They will be interested to see whether they are getting a good return for risking their money in the business – Is the business profitable?

The managers
These are the people who run the business for the owners and have a responsibility to ensure that the business performs well. A manager will also be personally motivated to run the business well, because this will improve his or her own personal reputation. In addition, managers will use information from the accounts to make business decisions.

Figure 18.1 Owner

Figure 18.2 Manager

The employees
They will want to know how well the business is doing, particularly if they are seeking a pay increase or are due bonuses. They would also want to know if their jobs are secure.

Figure 18.3 Employees

Creditors
These people will want to know if the business is able to repay any debts or loans. A successful business will probably be able to do this.

The government
Most government revenue comes from tax – the more profitable businesses are, the more tax is collected. In addition, successful and profitable businesses provide jobs which help local economies and the UK's export trade with the rest of the world.

How is performance measured?
Accountants use **ratio** analysis to compare business performance. Financial ratios are an arithmetical way of comparing different figures in the accounts. Sometimes it is difficult to make comparisons, and saying that a 'business is doing well' is not really telling us very much. Look at the following example:

Which one of the companies in the table seems to be performing best? You would probably say Hartlepool Textiles, but is this true? We will find out later.

There are quite a few different ratios, but we need only look at five. These five can be divided up into:

- **profitability ratios**, which measure how well profits compare with sales and capital employed
- **liquidity ratios**, which measure whether a business can pay its debts.

We will be using the profit and loss account and balance sheet for Bega Manufacturing Ltd for 2003 and 2004.

Profit and Loss Account for Bega Manufacturing Ltd for the year ended 31 March 2004

	£ 2004	£ 2003
Sales revenue	950 000	800 000
less Cost of goods sold	450 000	400 000
Gross profit	500 000	400 000
less Expenses	330 000	272 000
Profit before tax (Net profit)	170 000	128 000
less Corporation tax	42 000	32 000
Profit after tax	128 000	96 000
Dividends	68 000	46 000
Retained profit	60 000	50 000

	Boldon Textiles plc	Baverstock Textiles plc	Hartlepool Textiles plc
Sales revenue	£40 000	£70 000	£200 000
Gross profit	£10 500	£16 000	£40 000
Net profit	£4000	£8000	£18 000
Net capital employed	£15 500	£32 000	£77 000

Balance Sheet for Bega Manufacturing Ltd as at 31 March 2004

	£ 2004	£ 2003
Fixed assets		
Premises	550 000	550 000
Machinery	100 000	110 000
Vehicles	90 000	59 000
	740 000	619 000
Current assets		
Stock	185 000	150 000
Debtors	140 000	110 000
Cash	55 000	59 000
	380 000	319 000
less		
Current liabilities		
Creditors	160 000	130 000
Overdraft	50 000	50 000
Dividends	64 000	40 000
	274 000	220 000
Working capital		
(net current assets)	106 000	99 000
Net assets	**851 000**	**718 000**
Financed by:		
Shareholders' funds	450 000	450 000
Reserves	160 000	140 000
Retained profit	60 000	50 000
Long-term liabilities		
Bank loan	181 000	173 000
Capital employed	**851 000**	**718 000**

PROFITABILITY RATIOS

There are three profitability ratios:

1. gross profit margin
2. net profit margin
3. return on capital employed (ROCE).

Gross profit margin

The figures for this ratio are obtained from the trading account. This ratio measures the gross profit made from the sales revenue.

$$\frac{\text{Gross profit}}{\text{Sales revenue}} \times 100$$

Using Bega Manufacturing Ltd's 2004 figures, this ratio is:

$$\frac{500\,000}{950\,000} \times 100 = 52.6\%$$

Figure 18.4

This figure shows that for every £1 of sales Bega Manufacturing Ltd was making, nearly 53p was gross profit. The higher the profit margin or percentage, the better. If the ratio falls from one year to the next, it may mean that the cost of raw materials has increased or that stocks have been stolen or damaged. If Bega Manufacturing Ltd wanted to improve this margin it could:

- try and increase sales revenue but keep cost of goods sold the same, or
- reduce the cost of goods sold (by perhaps trying to buy raw materials cheaper elsewhere or getting a discount from suppliers) but keep sales revenue the same.

Net profit margin

The figures for this ratio are obtained from the profit and loss account. This ratio measures the net profit made from the sales revenue. It shows how good the business has been in keeping its expenses down.

$$\frac{\text{Net profit before tax}}{\text{Sales revenue}} \times 100$$

$$\frac{170\,000}{950\,000} \times 100 = 17.9\%$$

This figure shows that for every £1 of sales Bega Manufacturing Ltd was making, nearly 18p was net profit. Again, the higher the profit margin the better. If the ratio falls from one year to the next, it means that the managers are not controlling their expenses very well and they need to reduce these expenses. If Bega Manufacturing Ltd wanted to improve this margin it could:

- try selling more products and increasing sales revenue while keeping expenses low, or
- try reducing expenses while keeping the same level of sales.

Return on capital employed (ROCE)

The figures for this ratio are obtained from the profit and loss account and the balance sheet. It measures the profitability of the business by comparing its profit with the amount of capital invested by the owners. The higher the return, the better the business is performing, therefore the owners are receiving a better return on their investment.

$$\frac{\text{Net profit before tax}}{\text{Net capital employed (the balance sheet total)}} \times 100$$

$$\frac{170\,000}{851\,000} \times 100 = 19.98\%$$

This figure shows that for every £1 invested in the business, nearly 20p is earned, or for every £100 invested, nearly £20 is being earned. It shows how efficient the business is at generating profits from the money invested. Anyone thinking of buying shares in the business would look at this ratio before making a decision.

To decide whether this is a good return for the business, it will compare this year's figure with the:

- ROCE for previous years
- ROCE earned by competitors
- interest an investor might earn if they put their money into a savings account. If the interest paid was higher then it would be better investing in a bank or building society. Why invest in a business which would be more risky than investing in a bank or building society account which might be a safer alternative?

Figure 18.5

We can now look at the textile company examples on page 170. We can calculate their ratios and see how each business is performing.

Initially we might have thought Hartlepool Textiles plc would be the best performing business because its sales revenue, gross profit, net profit and net capital employed were all higher than the other two businesses. Is this the case? No it is not!

	Boldon Textiles plc	Baverstock Textiles plc	Hartlepool Textiles plc
Gross profit margin	$\frac{10\,500}{40\,000} \times 100$ $= 26.3\%$	$\frac{16\,000}{70\,000} \times 100$ $= 22.9\%$	$\frac{40\,000}{200\,000} \times 100$ $= 20\%$
Net profit margin	$\frac{4000}{40\,000} \times 100$ $= 10\%$	$\frac{8000}{70\,000} \times 100$ $= 11.4\%$	$\frac{18\,000}{200\,000} \times 100$ $= 9\%$
ROCE	$\frac{4000}{15\,500} \times 100$ $= 25.8\%$	$\frac{8000}{32\,000} \times 100$ $= 25\%$	$\frac{18\,000}{77\,000} \times 100$ $= 23.4\%$

Overall Boldon Textiles plc is the better performing business because for two out of the three ratios, it has the highest percentages. It has the highest gross profit margin and the highest ROCE, which means it gives its owners the best return on their investment.

Task

Use the 2003 figures for Bega Manufacturing Ltd.

1. Calculate the gross profit margin.
2. Calculate the net profit margin.
3. Calculate return on capital employed (ROCE).
4. Compare and comment on the figures for 2003 and 2004.

Exam tip

Don't forget to show all your workings – you may get the actual answer wrong but if you show the examiner you can use the formula, then you will still gain some marks.

Task

Headland Computer Supplies Ltd sells computer hardware and software. Extracts from their trading and profit and loss account for 2004 are shown below.

	£
Sales	180 000
Cost of goods sold	150 000
Gross profit	?
Overheads/expenses	20 000
Net profit	?

1. Calculate the gross and net profit figures.
2. Calculate the gross and net profit ratios.
3. Comment on Headlands's performance.

LIQUIDITY RATIOS

These ratios are concerned with the working capital of the business. In the previous unit, we looked at working capital. It is the difference between current assets and current liabilities, and it is the money which the business has to use on a day-to-day basis. If the business has not got enough working capital, it may not be able to pay its debts. If it has too much working capital then this is not sensible as the business is not making the most efficient use of these assets, eg it has too much stock or too much money in the bank.

The ratios which measure the business's ability to pay its debts are:
- the current ratio
- the acid test ratio.

Current ratio

This ratio is also known as the working capital ratio. It shows whether a business can pay its current liabilities from its current assets using the following formula which is shown as a ratio. We will use Bega Manufacturing Ltd's figures for 2003:

current assets : current liabilities

$$\frac{319\,000}{220\,000} = 1.45 : 1$$

This ratio shows that for every £1 Bega Manufacturing Ltd owes, it has £1.45 of assets. The ideal ratio is said to be 1.5 : 1 to 2 : 1. Below

Figure 18.6

1.5 : 1 indicates that Bega Manufacturing Ltd may have difficulty paying its creditors or paying off its overdraft. A low current ratio, say 0.7 : 1 shows the business only has 70p for each £1 it owes, which is worrying.

If Bega wanted to improve this ratio, it should increase its cash figure by selling some of its fixed assets.

Acid test ratio

This is a tougher ratio than the current ratio, because it does not include the stock (because stock is the hardest asset to turn into cash quickly). The stock is still there to be sold, but it is not included.

current assets − stock : current liabilities

$$\frac{319\,000 - 150\,000}{220\,000} = 0.77 : 1$$

This ratio shows that for every £1 owed the business has 77p. The ideal ratio is said to be 1 : 1. Bega Manufacturing Ltd therefore will have difficulty paying its debts, which is worrying. It must be remembered though that there is still the stock to be sold.

Let's have another look at the three textile companies.

We can see that Boldon and Hartlepool have healthy current ratios of more than 1.5 : 1, which means they would be able to pay their debts. Baverstock, on the other hand, has a ratio of below 1.5 : 1, which means it might have difficulty paying what it owes.

The same pattern is repeated with the acid test ratio. Boldon and Hartlepool both have ratios above the ideal of 1 : 1. Baverstock would, once again, have difficulty because for every £1 it owes, it only has 50p.

Task

Use the 2004 figures for Bega Manufacturing Ltd.

1. Calculate the current ratio.
2. Calculate the acid test ratio.
3. Compare and comment on the figures for 2003 and 2004.

Exam tip

As well as calculating the ratios, you will be expected to know how to use them, what they mean and what they tell you about the business.

	Boldon Textiles plc	Baverstock Textiles plc	Hartlepool Textiles plc
Current assets			
Stock	3800	2500	15 500
Debtors	4000	1500	12 000
Cash	300	500	10 000
Current liabilities			
Creditors	4000	4000	18 000
Current ratio	$\frac{8100}{4000} = 2 : 1$	$\frac{4500}{4000} = 1.13 : 1$	$\frac{37\,500}{18\,000} = 2.08 : 1$
Acid test ratio	$\frac{4300}{4000} = 1.08 : 1$	$\frac{2000}{4000} = 0.50 : 1$	$\frac{22\,000}{18\,000} = 1.22 : 1$

Task

Extracts from the balance sheet of Headland Computer Sales Ltd for 2004 are below.

Fixed assets	28 000
Stock	70 000
Debtors	22 000
Creditors	40 000
Bank overdraft	13 000

1. Calculate the liquidity ratios.
2. Comment on Headland's performance.

Exam tip

You will be given any formulae you need on the examination paper – all you have to do is put the correct figures into the formulae.

Task

Extracts from Headland Computer Supplies Ltd's final accounts for 2005 are shown below.

Sales	195 000
Cost of goods sold	165 000
Gross profit	30 000
Net profit	5 000
Fixed assets	30 000
Stock	75 000
Debtors	24 000
Creditors	42 000
Bank overdraft	11 000

1. Calculate gross and net profit ratios and liquidity ratios.
2. Compare its performance from 2004 to 2005.
3. What action, if any, would you recommend to Headland?

Past Paper

Below are the sales revenue and cost of sales (or cost of goods) figures for Flyaway plc and two of its rivals.

	QuickFlight plc £m	British Eastern plc £m	Flyaway plc £m
Sales revenue	44.5	139.0	58.0
Cost of sales	22.6	72.6	30.0
Gross profit	21.9	66.4	?
Gross profit ratio (margin)	49.2%	47.8%	?

1. a) Calculate the gross profit margin for Flyaway plc. Show your workings. (2)
   b) Which of the three companies above seems to be performing best? Give your reasons. (4)

2. The two objectives of Flyaway plc are profitability and survival.
   a) Explain two ways in which Flyaway plc might meet its stated objective of profitability. (4)
   b) Survival is an objective for all businesses. Explain how the merger between Kilverton Air Services (a regional airport) and ExHols (a tour operator) to form a new company, Flyaway plc, will help Flyaway plc to survive. (4)

(adapted from Edexcel 2001, Foundation and Higher)

Past Paper

An accountant has produced the financial information shown below for the partners of Louisa Designs.

Louisa Designs Sales and Net Profit

(Bar chart showing Sales and Net Profit in £000 for years 1993, 1994, 1995: Sales approximately 180, 200, 200; Net Profit approximately 25, 25, 25)

1. a) State two groups of people who will also be interested in the financial information of Louisa Designs. (2)
   b) Explain why each group is interested in this information. (2)

2. Calculate for Louisa Designs the:
   a) net profit percentage (net profit margin) (2)
   b) current ratio (2)

3. a) Identify one trend shown in the accountant's information.
   b) Explain the likely effect on Louisa Designs of this trend. (2)

Louisa Designs: Summarised Balance Sheet as at 31 December 1995

	£000	£000
Fixed assets		53
Current assets	36	
Curent liabilities	40	
		(4)
		49
Capital		39
Long-term loan		10
		49

(Edexcel, 1996, Foundation and Higher)

UNIT 18: BUSINESS PERFORMANCE AND RATIOS

Revision Questions

1. Give two groups of people who would be interested in the performance of a business.
2. Which two financial documents are used for looking at business performance?
3. $\dfrac{\text{Net profit}}{\text{Sales}} \times 100\%$ is the .... ratio.
4. What is the formula for the gross profit ratio?
5. What does ROCE mean?
6. Is it better to have a higher or lower ROCE?
7. Is the current ratio a profitability ratio?
8. What is thought to be the ideal current ratio?
9. The acid test ratio is measured as a percentage. True or False.
10. If a business has liquidity problems, what does this mean?

Summary

- There are different groups of people interested in the performance of a business.
- Accounting ratios are calculated using figures from the final accounts.
- Profitability ratios measure gross/net profit against sales.
- Liquidity ratios measure the business's ability to pay its debts.
- Ratio analysis lets the business analyse its performance, make comparisons and spot trends.
- Ratio analysis is useful for decision-making and planning.

Key terms

Acid test ratio – current assets − stock : current liabilities

Current ratio – current assets : current liabilities

Gross profit margin – $\dfrac{\text{gross profit}}{\text{sales}} \times 100$

Net profit margin – $\dfrac{\text{net profit}}{\text{sales}} \times 100$

Ratio – a formula that helps assess the financial performance of a business

Return on capital employed (ROCE) – $\dfrac{\text{net profit}}{\text{net capital employed}} \times 100$

GCSE BUSINESS STUDIES for Edexcel

Section 4
MARKETING

UNIT 19

THE MARKET

What you will learn

At the end of this unit you should understand:

- the market
- marketing objectives
- product orientation
- the marketing mix
- marketing
- market orientation
- market segments
- marketing strategy.

THE MARKET

A market is a place where buyers and sellers come together to exchange products and services for money. This means that it is necessary for the sellers to have something which the buyers are prepared to buy. Sometimes when we think of a market, we think of a lot of stalls in the middle of a town, but this is only one kind of market. Anywhere where goods are exchanged for money is a market. Let's look at a few examples:

- We have already mentioned a town market; this can either be outdoors or under cover, and the stalls will sell a wide variety of goods. At the end of the day, the stallholders will pack away their goods and perhaps move to another market the next day.
- Any kind of shop is a market, whether it is, for example, a supermarket, a department store, a row of local shops, or the shops in a large out-of-town shopping mall.
- Goods can be bought over the phone, or the internet, or by using catalogues. These are all examples of markets where there is no face-to-face contact between the seller and the buyer.

Figure 19.1 A town market

Figure 19.2 A shopping mall

- Another type of market is the world market, where goods are bought from other countries, eg oil, gold, diamonds, food products. In Britain, we buy these types of goods because we cannot produce or grow them ourselves.

All of these markets depend on having goods which the customers want to buy and attracting the customers to buy *their* products in *their* market. This is where marketing comes in.

Task

Give two examples of the type of product you might expect to buy from each of the following markets:

1. a market stall
2. a department store
3. a catalogue.

MARKETING

There is no point in having goods for sale if they are not wanted by the customers or the customers do not even know that they exist. Marketing means finding out what customers want, providing it and making sure that the public is aware of it and where they can buy it.

Marketing activities include:

- carrying out market research to find out what customers need and want
- developing products to meet these needs and wants
- finding out what types of customers are likely to buy the products
- deciding where the products should be sold
- working out what price should be charged
- advertising and promoting the products so that customers are aware of them and persuaded to buy them.

It is very important that a business considers each of these points before it launches a product onto the market. It may otherwise find that it has wasted its money, because the product does not sell.

Marketing objectives

A business will have various **objectives** it hopes to achieve through its marketing. These could include:

- to introduce a new product
- to increase sales of an existing product
- to target a new market segment
- to halt a decline in market share
- to change the image of a brand.

Task

Figure 19.3

Jim's DIY store is a small friendly shop in the High Street of a little market town. He has a good range of stock but loses customers to the branch of a large nationwide store in a nearby local town. He has had colourful brochures, showing the goods he stocks, delivered to all the houses in his town.

What do you think the marketing objectives for this action might be? Explain your answer carefully.

Market orientation

Most businesses nowadays cannot afford to produce products and just hope that customers will buy them. They will use market research to find out what the consumers really want and need, and then produce a product to suit the consumers. This is called **market orientation**.

Product orientation

However, there are some products (eg newly developed hi-tech goods) where it is important to produce a product and then persuade customers to buy it, because they may not realise that they need it until it has been developed. This is called **product orientation**.

> **Task**
>
> It often helps your understanding of different but similar concepts if you explain them in your own words. Let's have a try here.
>
> Explain in your own words the difference between market and product orientation.

Figure 19.4 Different types of bread for different parts of the bread market

- Age – many products are aimed at particular age groups. For example, different magazines are published for small children and teenagers. Package tour holidays can be aimed specifically at families or at groups of young people.
- Income – businesses produce goods and services aimed at groups earning different incomes. For example, most car manufacturers produce a range of models, some aimed at top income earners and others aimed at lower earners.
- Geographical – this considers the region of the country that consumers live in. Certain products are traditionally popular in particular areas, eg faggots and mushy peas in the Black Country area of the West Midlands, or haggis in Scotland.
- Interests – products are aimed at customers' interests and hobbies. For example, in a newsagent's shop there will be magazines about every different sport you can think of.

MARKET SEGMENTS

Segmenting a market means dividing the market for a product into different types of consumers who share similar characteristics. A business can then target these groups with particular products that are attractive to them. For example, bread manufacturers will produce different types of products for different parts of the bread market. There will be white bread, brown bread, wholemeal bread, granary loaves, speciality breads. Each of these products will appeal to a different segment of the overall market for bread, which will hopefully maximise sales for the company.

We will look at some of the ways in which a market can be segmented:
- Gender – male or female. For example, products such as clothes vary for males and females. Perfume manufacturers produce different ranges for men and women.

> **Exam tip**
>
> Remember that consumers will appear in more than one market segment; eg gender (boy), age (teenager), living in London (geographical), football fan (interests).

Points for market segmentation
- Sales can be increased by producing versions of goods or services targeted at various segments of a market.
- Segmentation helps to target advertising and promotion more effectively at the relevant market segments. We will look at advertising and promotion in more detail later in this section.
- It ensures that products are on sale in the right place to attract the target market segment.
- Sometimes a company will identify a segment of a market whose needs are not being met; this is called a 'gap in the market'. The company can increase their sales if they develop a product to fill the gap.

Points against market segmentation
- It is more expensive to produce and market several different products, rather than just one.
- Smaller amounts of a product may be produced, causing unit costs to rise.

Exam tip
You need to remember the influence that different market segments will have on the image of a product, the price that is charged for it, the place it is sold in and the way it is advertised and promoted.

MARKETING MIX
The marketing mix describes all the activities that go together to make a customer decide to buy a product. The business should ensure that the **product** is the right one, the **price** matches the product, the **promotion** tells the customer about the product, and the product is on sale in the right **place** at the right time. If a business gets all these factors correct, they should be successful in selling their products. Because all these activities begin with the letter P, they are often referred to as the '4 Ps'.

- **Product** – it is important that a firm finds out what consumers need and want through market research, and produces products and services to match. This includes its design, its appearance, its special features, its quality, and its reliability.
- **Price** – this is based on how much customers are prepared to pay, how much the product or service costs to produce, how much competitors are charging and how much profit the company wishes to make.
- **Promotion** – this comprises the methods used to bring a product to the attention of the customers and to sell it to them. This means advertising and promoting the product.
- **Place** – this involves making sure that the product is in the right place at the right time, so that potential customers can buy it.

However, the most important thing to remember about the marketing mix, is that it is different for every product. For example, for a very expensive car, the product would be of a very high quality both in terms of design and workmanship. There would be few places where it could be sold. The price would be high and it would only be promoted in places where the target market would see the promotion. On the other hand, a mass-market product, such as a chocolate bar, would be on sale

Figure 19.5 Marketing mix

UNIT 19: THE MARKET

in many different types of outlets. The price would match those of the competitors. Promotion would be seen everywhere, not just by a targeted audience, and the product would attract a number of different target markets.

To be successful, all the elements of the marketing mix must work together and match each other, thus ensuring that the product sells and makes a profit for the company.

needs to be altered to achieve the objective. The strategy might be to increase the advertising and promotion of the product, while making sure that the product is available for sale in more outlets. The price might also be altered, to attract more customers. All these factors need to be carefully integrated to produce an overall strategy for increasing sales.

Exam tip

If you are asked to discuss the marketing mix for a product in an examination question, it is important to think carefully how to market that particular product. You need to make sure that the '4 Ps' are closely linked together in your answer and that they match the product and the target market who might buy it.

Task

Taking the two products mentioned above, an expensive car and a chocolate bar:

1. How you would expect to see each one promoted?
2. Where would you expect to see each one on sale to the public?

Make sure you explain your reasons carefully.

MARKETING STRATEGY

A marketing strategy is a medium- to long-term plan for meeting marketing objectives. For example, if a business has an objective of increasing the sales of an existing product, it will decide how the marketing mix of that product

Past Paper

Nocha Ltd's second factory will specialise in a new range of luxury ice cream. It is planned to sell the range to major UK supermarket chains and freezer centres but **not** directly to the general public.

Discuss a suitable marketing strategy for the new range. (9)

(Edexcel, 1999, Higher)

Extension task

Pretty Cosmetics has developed a new, cheap liquid eyeshadow that is guaranteed to last all day without fading or smudging.

1. Which market segment(s) do you think they should aim the product at? Explain your choice.
2. Do you think this product was market or product orientated? Explain your answer carefully.
3. How do you think they should market the product? Your answer needs to consider the '4 Ps' of the marketing mix.

Revision Questions

1. The market is a place where buyers and sellers come together to exchange products and services for:
   a) gain
   b) barter
   c) customers
   d) money

2. Finding out what customers need and want is called:
   a) product orientation
   b) market orientation
   c) market research
   d) marketing strategy

3. What are the '4 Ps' of the marketing mix?

4. Explain what is meant by the phrase 'a gap in the market'.

5. Explain why market segmentation is important to a business.

6. Why do businesses need to be market orientated?

7. What is a marketing strategy?

8. How could the market for the following products be segmented?
   a) soap
   b) books

Summary

- A market can only work when it allows buyers and sellers to meet and exchange goods and services.
- A business needs to know what the segments of its market are and respond to these with products, services and promotion.
- A business that combines the '4 Ps' of the marketing mix appropriately for its products or services should be a successful business.

Key terms

Market – a place where buyers and sellers come together to exchange products and services for money

Market orientation – developing products or services after analysing market research results to find out what the consumer needs and wants

Market segmentation – breaking the total market for a product into different parts

Marketing – finding out what customers need and want, providing it at the right price, making sure the public is aware of it and where they can buy it

Marketing mix – the '4 Ps' (product, price, promotion, place) that combine to make a customer decide to buy a product or service

Marketing objectives – the goals which a marketing department hopes to achieve

Marketing strategy – a medium- to long-term plan for achieving marketing objectives

Product orientation – developing a product and then finding the market for it

Target market – the people a product is aimed at according to factors such as gender, age, income

UNIT 19: THE MARKET

UNIT 20

PRICE

What you will learn

At the end of this unit, you should understand the meaning of the following pricing strategies:

- supply/demand
- penetration
- skimming
- cost plus
- competition
- promotional

WHAT IS A PRICING STRATEGY?

Before we start to look at the various ways in which a business might price its goods, we need to understand what is meant by the term '**strategy**'. A strategy is a medium- to long-term plan of how to achieve an objective.

For example, a business might have an objective of bringing out a new product onto the market, and part of the planning for this will be about how they price the product. The strategy for the pricing will include looking at the kind of price they want to use when the product first comes onto the market. This will need to be attractive to customers so that they want to buy something which is new to them: it might need to be quite low to make them interested. The next part of the strategy could look at how they might change the price once the product has become well known and is selling well. At this stage, customers might be prepared to pay a higher price.

Finally, the strategy might include planning for when the product has reached the stage when the public are no longer buying the product in such large amounts. The firm might change the price again to interest them once more.

Now we can look at some of the pricing strategies that a business could use.

SUPPLY AND DEMAND

To explain how this works, let's take the example of a business growing tomatoes. In the summer months, there will be plenty of tomatoes in the market; from other growers, imported from abroad, grown by people in their own green houses. Prices will be quite low because there is

Figure 20.1 Tomatoes waiting for harvesting

enough supply of tomatoes to meet the demand of the customers. However, around Christmas time, when the supply of tomatoes will be much lower because of the weather conditions, but the demand might be high, the prices will rise. Therefore, from this we can see that when there is a good supply of a product, the price will be lower, but if the supply reduces and the demand stays high, the prices can be set much higher.

This law of supply and demand means that a businesses have to work out what the patterns of supply and demand are in their particular market, and they have no alternative but to change their prices to match. Otherwise, no one will be prepared to buy their products.

Figure 20.2

Exam tip

It is important to remember that with supply and demand a business has little control over the market price.

Task

Can you think of two more products, apart from the tomatoes mentioned above, where the business could use supply and demand pricing? Make sure you explain the reasons for your answer.

COST PLUS PRICING

This pricing strategy means that a business works out the total cost of producing a product by adding together all the fixed and variable costs. Then it adds an amount for profit, often called the **mark up**, to give the selling price. The mark up is usually expressed in the form of a percentage.

For example, a company producing mountain bikes works out that the total cost for producing a bike is £700. They decide that they want to add on 10% mark up to create a profit for them. This would give the following calculations:

Total costs per bike = £700

Percentage mark up per bike 10% of the total costs = $\dfrac{£700 \times 10}{100}$ = £70

Selling price per bike to the retailer = £770.

This is a very simple pricing strategy and is also often used by retailers to give them a profit on the price they have had to pay the manufacturer for the goods. Therefore, to continue our example of the mountain bike, the retailer buys the bike from the manufacturer for £770 and then adds his mark up of, for example, 7%.

Cost of bike to retailer = £770

Percentage mark up per bike 7% of total cost = $\dfrac{£770 \times 7}{100}$ = £53.90

Selling price to the customer £823.90.

Points for cost plus pricing
- It is quick and simple to calculate.
- This strategy ensures that all the costs of producing the product by the manufacturer are covered and a profit is made.
- It ensures that the retailer covers the costs of buying the product from the manufacturer and makes a profit.

Points against cost plus pricing
- The amount of mark up which a business can add will be affected by the amount they think the customers will be prepared to pay for the product.
- Goods may not sell if the company adds a mark up which makes their goods more expensive than their competitors'.

PENETRATION PRICING

A penetration pricing strategy involves setting a low price for a product to persuade customers to buy it. This method can be used to introduce new products into a market where there are already similar goods, eg when bringing out a new chocolate bar. Another occasion when penetration pricing might be used, is if a company is launching an already successful product into a new market, eg English rugby shirts being sold in America.

In both cases, the hope is that a good market share can be gained quickly. Once this has happened and the products have gained customer loyalty, which will mean they will continue to buy the products, the producer can increase the price to gain larger profits.

However, there are problems to this pricing strategy. It is not really suitable for products which are likely to have a short product life cycle, eg fashion clothing, because there may not be time to recover the lost revenue from the lower prices before the product goes out of fashion. In addition, if a product has high research and development costs before it comes onto the market, these will not be recovered while penetration prices are being charged to the customers.

Points for penetration pricing
- It attracts customers to the product and makes them more likely to try it.
- It helps to increase the market share of the product more quickly.

Points against penetration pricing
- Revenue is lost while the product is selling at a lower price.
- It is not suitable for products with short product life cycles.
- It does not help to recover research and development costs.

Task

Fred McKintosh owns a small garden centre. He grows many of his own plants. To set his prices, he takes all his costs into account (eg seeds, compost, pots, time), and then he adds a percentage mark up.

Each year he sells many geranium plants. His costs for producing each plant are 30p and he adds a 10% mark up.

1. What price does he charge for each plant?
2. If he sells 500 plants, how much profit does he make?

He also buys the trays of winter pansies from another grower. He buys the trays at £1.50 each and sells them at £2.00 each.

3. How much profit is he making on each tray?
4. What percentage is this mark up?

Exam tip

Make sure you can work out percentages before you go into an examination!

185

UNIT 20: PRICE

Task

Figure 20.3

Fun Time Confectionery Co makes chocolates and sweets. They are about to introduce a new chocolate bar, and to attract customers, they intend to use a penetration pricing strategy. The cost to make each bar is 20p and they will sell them at 25p each.

1. If they sell 1000 bars, how much profit will they make?
2. At the end of three months, they raise their price to 30p per bar. What profit will they make on the sale of 1000 bars now?
3. Explain in your own words why you think this strategy might be a good idea for Fun Time Confectionery.

COMPETITION PRICING

Competition pricing means a business setting the price for a product based on the price charged by their competitors. A company introducing a new digital camera into a market which already has a number of similar digital cameras made by other manufacturers, would have to charge a price in line with the competitors' price. If they charged a much higher price, no one would be prepared to try their

Figure 20.4 An example of a digital camera

camera. On the other hand, if they charged a much lower price, customers might think the camera is of a lower quality, and therefore would be less likely buy it.

Points for competition pricing
- This is a safe strategy because it avoids price competition which can be damaging to a company.

Points against competition pricing
- Businesses have to find other ways of attracting customers to their product, such as increasing their advertising.
- The competitive price may only just cover the costs of the product, resulting in low profits.

Task

BP and Shell are both companies which sell petrol. They charge competitive prices for their products. Explain why you think they have to do this.

SKIMMING

The pricing strategy of skimming is the opposite of the penetration pricing we looked at earlier. With skimming, the price for a unique product when it is first introduced will be set high. We have all seen this happen with many hi-tech products, eg DVD players. When they first appeared on the market, they were very expensive and only trendsetters, enthusiasts and well-off people bought them. This is because they were prepared to pay a high price to own a new product before other people. Later, in order to get other customers interested in DVD players, the manufacturers bought their prices down and now there is a mass market for them.

Points for skimming
- While the price is high, the business can make large profits to help pay for the research and development costs of the product.
- High prices can give a product a good image, which is helpful for a new product.

Points against skimming
- Some possible customers may be put off buying the product because of the high price.
- Competitors may bring out a lower-priced imitation and snatch the market.

> **Task**
>
> Charles Crabtree Ltd is an old established bakery firm. They have developed a new type of wholemeal loaf. Do you think they should use a penetration or skimming pricing strategy when they introduce the loaf onto the market? Make sure you explain your answer carefully.

PROMOTIONAL PRICING

Promotional pricing means reducing the price of a recognized product for a certain amount of time to interest customers in buying it. For example, the manufacturers of a breakfast cereal may find that their sales are falling, possibly because new products have come onto the market. To try to remind customers how enjoyable their cereals are, they need to persuade them to start buying them again.

Figure 20.5 Looking for bargains in the sales

Selling the product more cheaply for a period of time may do this. Once sales have increased, the price can then go up again.

Another example of when it is useful to use a promotional pricing strategy is for getting rid of stock that has gone out of fashion. Clothes retailers often do this at the end of the summer to clear the summer stock which customers have stopped buying. This means that although they will not make the profits they do at the full prices, they will at least gain some revenue from the sales.

Points for promotional pricing
- It can help to renew customers' interest in products with falling sales.
- It earns revenue on goods that are no longer popular.

Points against promotional pricing
- Sales revenue will be lower on each item and therefore profits will be lower or non-existent.
- When used to renew interest in a product, it can be a very risky venture if sales do not rise.

Revision Questions

1. Charging a low price to get consumers interested in a new product is called:
   a) strategy
   b) cost plus
   c) penetration pricing
   d) supply and demand

2. Setting a high initial price to cover research and development costs is called:
   a) promotional pricing
   b) skimming
   c) competition pricing
   d) cost plus

3. A medium- to long-term plan to achieve an objective is called
   a) marketing
   b) price
   c) promotional pricing
   d) strategy

4. Cost plus pricing means that a .... is added to .... to arrive at a price that gives a ....

5. What kind of pricing is a company using if it checks to see what other companies are charging for their goods?

6. Explain, using examples, two reasons why a company might introduce promotional pricing.

Summary

- It is important to remember that price is a vital part of the marketing mix.
- Price can attract customers or turn them away.
- Prices give customers an image of the quality of a product.
- It is necessary for prices to cover the costs of a product and make a profit.
- Competitors and the prices they charge affect prices.

Key terms

Competition pricing – setting prices based on what competitors are charging

Cost plus pricing – covering the costs of a product and adding a percentage mark up to make a profit

Penetration pricing – setting a low price to introduce a new product to a market

Price – an element of the marketing mix; the amount of money a business charges consumers for a good or service

Promotional pricing – special price reductions for a set period of time

Skimming – setting a high price for an exclusive new product

Strategy – a medium- to long-term plan of how to achieve an objective

UNIT 20: PRICE

UNIT 21

PROMOTION

What you will learn

At the end of this unit, you should understand:
- the aims of promotion
- types of advertising media
- personal selling
- advertising campaigns
- types of advertising
- below the line promotion
- public relations
- the controls on advertising

THE AIMS OF PROMOTION

What we mean by promotion in the marketing mix, is the promotion of a product or service by the use of advertising, sales promotion and public relations. It would be pointless for a business to produce a new product or service without promoting it in some way; unless the customers know it exists, they will not consider buying it. Promotion is about communicating with the customers to tell them what the product is, where they can buy it and how much it will cost.

However, this is simply **information**. The other function of promotion is to *persuade* customers to buy your product, not those of your competitor. Therefore, promotion also has to make the product look so attractive to the consumer that they will choose to buy that product rather than another. This is called **persuasion**.

Promotion does not just stop at advertising new products and services. It also has to keep the product in the customers' minds, by continually reminding them that this is the product they should buy.

Promotion also has another function, which is to develop and improve the image of a business. This is so that the customers come to regard the whole range of products which the business produces as trustworthy.

We can summarise these aims as:
- making consumers aware of a new product
- reminding customers of an existing product
- persuading consumers to buy a product rather than those of a competitor
- developing the image of a business.

In this unit, we will look at the ways in which businesses use promotion to achieve the aims we have just considered.

TYPES OF ADVERTISING

The main purpose of advertising is to communicate, and businesses have to pay for this. It is sometimes called '**above-the-line**' promotion and uses media such as television, magazines, radio, cinema, newspapers, posters, leaflets and the internet.

⚠️ Exam tip

If an exam question asks you to discuss above-the-line promotion, you should consider the various media available for advertising products.

SOFA bed, green, converts to double bed, hardly used, £35. Ring 01296 336047

SOLID pine distressed table and 4 chairs, vgc, 5 x 3.6ft £175 Tel 01645 797907

STAINLESS steel loft bed with desktop underneath, bargain at £75 ono. Tel 07793 876927

Tumble dryer white, excellent condition £40 01257 474566

TWO seater settee, cream & pale blue, immaculate condition £85 0121 678456

TYRES 185/65/r15, 88h x 2 brand new, unused, fit zantia, bought in error £50 Tel 0121 554617

Figure 21.1

Advertising can be **informative**, which means that it gives information. For example, the government advertises on the television to inform families about benefits that are available, such as tax credits. Another example is a classified advertisement in a local newspaper which gives information about a product for sale. It will state what it is, how much it costs and how to contact the buyer. Car manufacturers produce informative advertising about the cars they make. This will give the specifications of the car, so that the prospective customer knows exactly what the performance of the car is.

Exam tip

Informative advertising is very important when new technical products are coming onto the market, so the potential customer is able to compare one product against another.

On the other hand, advertising can be **persuasive**. This means it tries to influence the potential customer and convince them that they ought to buy the product or use the service. Persuasive advertising tries to appeal to the emotions of consumers, eg by telling them that life will be better or they will be more attractive if they buy a product. Most of the advertisements we see try to persuade us in some way, but of course they also give us information about the product.

Task

1. Look in a newspaper or magazine and see if you can find examples of three informative and three persuasive advertisements. Using examples from the adverts, explain in your own words the difference between the two types.

2. Take one of the persuasive adverts and examine it closely.
   a) Explain which emotion it is trying to appeal to.
   b) How well do you think it does it?
   c) What is the information in the advert?
   d) Which is more prominent, the persuasion or the information?
   e) Why do you think this is?

TYPES OF ADVERTISING MEDIA

There is a wide range of advertising media that firms can choose from to advertise their products or services. We will look at each of them in turn.

National television

Advertising on commercial terrestrial and satellite television channels such as ITV and Sky can reach a vast audience. By using colour, movement and sound, they can attract attention and make an impression. The advertising can be targeted. For example, adverts for children's toys will be shown during children's programmes in the afternoon and early evening. However, television advertising is very expensive and the message is short-lived, and may not be remembered. There is also a tendency for viewers to use the advertising breaks to pop into the kitchen to make a cup of tea, so they miss the adverts altogether.

Figure 21.2 Television advertising attracts attention

Radio
Commercial radio stations such as Virgin Radio, carry advertisements that employ sound to communicate their message. They will often make use of a tune, known as a jingle, to grab the attention of the listener. They can be targeted in the same way as television adverts, by making sure that the adverts match the audience for a particular programme, eg adverts for gardening products during a programme about gardening. They are cheaper to produce and to broadcast than television advertising. But, they have a smaller audience and because they are not visual, may not attract attention.

Cinema
As with television, cinema advertising can use sound, colour and movement to make an impact. There is a captive audience but this will be a limited number of people, compared with television or radio. Cinema adverts are often for local firms and because they are usually only seen once, may not be remembered.

National newspapers
Newspapers such as the *Times*, the *Sun* and the *Mirror* can reach a very large audience and advertising is relatively cheap compared with national television. Papers are useful because there is something for the reader to refer back to at a later date. Also, specific details can be included. Because national newspapers tend to be read by certain social groups, it is possible to target these with relevant advertisements. On the other hand, newspaper adverts are usually limited to black and white and there will be many advertisements competing with one another for attention.

Regional/local daily newspapers
Local papers, such as the *Birmingham Post*, serve a certain area of the country, and the advertising can be linked to local events and conditions. In addition, many homes in the UK have free weekly newspapers delivered to them that carry a large number of adverts as well as local news. The cost of advertising in these is usually relatively cheap.

However, there are a great number of adverts in local newspapers, particularly the free ones because they rely on the advertising revenue for their existence. Therefore, there is less likelihood of an advertisement being noticed. In addition, newspapers are only read once (if at all, in the case of free newspapers), so the adverts may not be noticed.

Magazines
These usually have a clear target audience, such as teenagers, males, females, car enthusiasts, football supporters, skateboarders, etc: the list seems endless. Therefore, it is easy to target advertising to the relevant readership group and also to link advertising to the features in the magazine. For example, in a women's magazine, a feature on different methods of using make-up would be an ideal place for make-up manufacturers to advertise their goods. This means that the adverts are only seen by the target market and this makes the money spent very cost effective.

Advertisements can be in colour and frequently take up whole pages, making them more striking. However, even though there is the use of colour, there is no movement or sound, and competitors' products are also being advertised.

Posters and billboards

These are excellent for short, sharp messages, and can contain eye-catching colour and features. Because many are situated where they will be seen by motorists and passengers on public transport, who will only see them briefly, they have to communicate their message very quickly. This means they cannot contain detailed information, only persuasive pictures or slogans. However, they can stay in place for a long time, as long as they are not damaged by wind and rain. Therefore, many people can see them repeatedly, so that the message is reinforced continually. This is a relatively cheap form of advertising that can be seen by everyone.

Other sites for posters are the sides and backs of buses and taxis, which move around, so spreading the message of the advert. Many local businesses will put posters in the street or by the side of the road. This is method is often used to advertise the opening of a new business, for example.

Figure 21.3 Advertising on a taxi cab

Leaflets

Leaflets can be given out in the streets, which means it is impossible to target a particular segment of the population. Also, many of them will be thrown away without even being read. Leaflets and direct/junk mail can also be put through letter boxes, which makes it easier to target an audience. For example, a new restaurant opening in the centre of a town would deliver leaflets in that town rather than all over the country. Leaflets are cheap to produce and can be kept for future reference, but they are easy to ignore.

Directories

Companies pay for space to advertise in directories such as Yellow Pages and Thompson's Directory to advertise in these publications. These publications are sorted alphabetically according to different trades and professions.

The internet

Internet sites are relatively cheap and easy to set up and to update, and it is possible to monitor the number of 'hits' which the site receives. A large amount of information can be put on the website. It can be interactive, allowing customers to place orders and pay for their goods from the comfort of their own homes. On the other hand, not everyone has internet access, so the audience may be limited. Also, the advert is competing with a vast number of others worldwide and unless it is really attention-grabbing, it may be missed.

Choosing advertising media

Businesses have to decide which would be the best media to use to advertise their products. There are a number of factors that they have to consider:

Cost

A small firm will probably not be able to spend a large amount on advertising, and might choose to use relatively cheap methods such as local newspapers or leaflets. Larger companies will be able to afford more expensive methods, such as national television or national newspapers. But they will look carefully at how cost effective each

Task

Copy the following table and from the information given above, fill in the points for and points against each form of advertising.

Type of advertising media	Points for	Points against
National television		
Commercial radio stations		
Cinema		
National newspapers		
Regional/local newspapers		
Magazines		
Posters and billboards		
Leaflets		
Internet		

Task

We all carry advertising for companies every day, on carrier bags, branded clothing, pencil cases, shoes and trainers, school bags, etc. Take a typical day in your life and make a list of all the advertising you are doing for different companies in your daily life.

Exam tip

It is very important to read exam questions about advertising very carefully and decide whether the product needs to be advertised nationally or locally, and how much the company is likely to be able to afford for their advertising campaign.

method is. For example, an advertisement in a national newspaper will be less expensive than an advert on national television. However, the television advert will potentially be seen by a greater number of people and because it includes sound and movement, is more likely to be noticed.

Firms have an advertising budget and they will have to plan their advertising to fit into this budget. They will need to take into account the cost of making the advertisement as well as the cost of the media they use.

Advertising by competitors

Businesses will be looking at the advertising done by their competitors, and as far as possible ensuring that they advertise using the same media.

The target audience

A business has to decide what market segment it is trying to reach, and as far as possible use appropriate advertising to reach the market, eg advertising in specialist magazines, because they will only be read by people likely to be interested in the product. One the other hand, television advertising reaches the largest number people, but it is much harder to target the advertisements at potential customers.

Figure 21.4 Deciding on advertising media

Task

Decide which media would be best to advertise each of the following products. Take into account the factors discussed above and carefully explain your reasons for your choice.

1. A new hot chocolate drink produced by a multi-national drinks company.
2. The reopening of a local Indian restaurant after it has been refurbished.
3. A new skateboard park in a local park.
4. A day coach trip to France by a local coach firm.
5. A rise in the price of postage stamps.
6. The Glastonbury Festival.
7. The opening of another McDonald's restaurant.

Arguments for advertising

- Advertising provides information for consumers so that they are able to make a better informed choice about what they buy.
- Advertising earns revenue for the media and keeps down the cost of newspapers and magazines.
- Advertising encourages competition and should lead to lower prices for the consumer.
- Advertising employs a great many people in the advertising industry.

Arguments against advertising

- Advertising can tempt people to buy products they do not really need and cannot afford.
- Advertising can encourage people to buy products which may damage their health.
- Advertising can lead to higher prices for the consumer, particularly if sales do not increase, but the cost of the advertising still has to be covered.

BELOW-THE-LINE PROMOTION TECHNIQUES

'Below-the-line' refers to promotional methods that do not involve using the media. Below the line methods include procedures such as price reductions, gifts, point-of-sale displays, after-sales service, free samples, competitions, trade fairs and exhibitions. These are all techniques which directly encourage consumers to buy by tempting them on the spot. They are often short term and therefore, will have an influence on buying habits for a limited period of time. We will look at these methods in a little more detail:

Price reductions

Reducing the price or offering money-off coupons are both ways of tempting consumers to try a product that they might not otherwise buy. Price reductions are frequently seen on food products on the shelves in a supermarket or in dump bins at the end of the aisle. Money-off coupons give a price reduction on the next purchase. They are often found, for example, on the back of cereal packs or in magazines and newspapers.

Free gifts

These are regularly given away on the front of magazines. They could be small objects like lip gloss on a fashion magazine, or a free CD on a music magazine. Other examples include posters or calendars. Cereal manufacturers put items aimed at children inside the packets. These often come in sets to encourage the children to persuade their parents to buy the same type of cereal until the whole set has been collected.

Buy-one-get-one-free (BOGOF) is another example. Many food and beauty products carry a BOGOF offer, to persuade customers to buy that particular brand of product.

Point-of-sale displays

These are placed at the point where products are sold, eg a shop, a petrol station or a hairdresser's. Attractive displays are used to exhibit and promote a product so that it stands out amongst all the rest. Some manufacturers provide special stands on which to put their products; eg for displaying chocolates and sweets or hair and beauty products.

An alternative method often used with food and drink products, is to have a free sample of the product for the customers to taste. This will usually

Figure 21.5 After-sales service

be connected with a special price reduction on the product to entice them to buy some.

After-sales service
Companies sometimes provide this to reassure the customer that if anything goes wrong with their product, friendly help and advice will be given by the business. This is particularly important when the product is an expensive or highly technical one, such as cars or computers. Customers are far more likely to purchase from the business again if the after-sales service has been good.

Competitions
These are often used to attract customers to buying a product by having an entry form on the back of the packet or inside a newspaper or magazine. Prizes can range from holidays, to cars or cash.

> **Exam tip**
>
> It is important to remember that all these below-the-line methods of promotion are designed to tempt people into buying something. They all cost money for the producer or the retailer, but if it means more customers who may then remain loyal to your product, it is worth it.

> **Task**
>
> Match and write out the following definitions with the correct description.
>
> 1. Friendly help and advice to reassure a customer.
> 2. Getting two products for the price of one.
> 3. Toys inside cereal packets to encourage repeat purchases.
> 4. Gives a price reduction on the next purchase.
> 5. Attractive displays used to exhibit and promote a product.
> 6. A way of winning a prize of a holiday.
>
> money-off coupon, free gift, buy-one-get-one-free, after-sales service, competition, free gifts, point-of-sale display.

PERSONAL SELLING
Personal selling involves talking directly to potential customers, usually through a sales team, using the telephone, meetings or by knocking on doors. This method is often used when products are expensive and individual, eg when a house needs new windows, which will cost many thousands of pounds. These need to be made specially for that house, so measurements, etc have to be taken.

Personal selling is also used when companies sell products to other companies rather than the public. Sales representatives who have a great deal of specialist knowledge about the product they are selling, will visit the buying company to explain the technical functions of the product and take orders.

Using personal selling means that a producer will receive rapid and individual feedback from the customer. This should help them to improve or develop their products to attract more customers. It also means that the customer feels that the product has been tailored to suit their needs, and they have been given advice and help in making their choice.

However, personal selling is expensive, because of the cost of employing a large number of staff to sell the product. This raises the costs of marketing. Also, many consumers do not like door-to-door selling or telephone marketing techniques.

PUBLIC RELATIONS

Public relations deal with a business's relationships with its stakeholders, such as employees, shareholders and customers. It is important that a favourable image is achieved by the company so that sales increase. Public relations activities are aimed at obtaining good and positive publicity. This can be done by making use of the press, television or radio broadcasts. For example, a new business like a hairdresser, would produce its own advertising, but would also like the local newspaper to write a review of the salon, to increase the publicity.

Large organisations have a public relations department whose job it is to promote the image of the company in a favourable light. One of their functions may be to arrange press conferences to give journalists information about a new product, eg a new model of a car. If a company wishes the public to know about something they have done, (eg cutting pollution), they will issue a press release that can be used by television and radio stations.

Another type of public relations activity is to provide sponsorship, eg on a local level, for a youth football team. Multi-national organisations sponsor worldwide events, such as the Coca Cola sponsorship of the Olympic Games. Sponsorship means that the name of the company will be prominently displayed by the team or throughout the sporting occasion, keeping it in the public eye.

Making donations to charity is another form of public relations. This may take the form of donating products such as blankets or food in the case of a natural disaster. Or, they may give money to an event such as the Children In Need Appeal.

Successful company visits can raise the profile of the company in the eyes of the visitors. An example of this is Cadbury World, which shows the public the process of chocolate making in a fun but informative way, and is aimed at children of all ages.

Figure 21.6 Examples of sponsorship

Exam tip

Remember the main function of public relations is to give a good image of a company and to improve relations between the company and the public.

Extension task

Sheltbury is a medium-sized country town. It has a thriving theatre which attracts audiences from many miles around. They put on plays, musical events, pantomimes and ballets. These are performed by local, national and international orchestras and companies. They have booked a Russian ballet company to perform Swan Lake in two months' time.

UNIT 21: PROMOTION

Choose two methods of advertising and two methods of below-the-line promotion they could use to publicise this performance. Describe the advantages and disadvantages of each of these. Remember to take into account cost and the target audience when you make your choices.

3. The directors of Happy Ideas Ltd are using the internet to advertise the Millennium Bear. Discuss whether this is an appropriate method. (4)

(Edexcel, 2000, Higher and Foundation)

ADVERTISING CAMPAIGN

Any business that intends to advertise and promote a new or existing product should organise what it intends to do by creating an advertising campaign. This is a planned programme which should:

- clearly define the purpose of the advertising, eg to capture a new market or to increase market share
- ensure the advertising and promotion is clearly focused to attract the target audience
- select relevant media and methods of promotion
- set a timescale over a specific period of time
- set a budget and remain within it
- produce results which can be measured to evaluate the effectiveness of the campaign.

? Past Paper

Wheatfields Ltd is a family-run farming business. Each year they run a Steam Fair that attracts thousands of visitors.

Organising the annual Steam Fair goes on all year. One of the main tasks is advertising the event. Advertising is used to reach the Steam Fair's target audience.

1. What is a 'target audience'? (2)
2. Suggest two suitable methods of advertising that could be used and explain why they would be best for Wheatfields Ltd. (8)

The income from the Steam Fair is donated to charity.

3. Explain one reason why Wheatfields Ltd spends so much time, effort and money promoting and advertising the Steam Fair. (2)

(Edexcel, 2002, Foundation)

? Extension task

Sheree and her friend Gemma, after working as very successful hairstylists for seven years, have decided they would like to open their own salon. They hope to keep their present clients as well as attracting new ones. They are planning to open in the local town centre in a month's time.

1. Decide which types of media you think they should use to advertise the opening. You will need to consider the target audience and cost in your answers. Make sure you explain the reasons for your choices carefully.
2. Devise an action plan for them, so that during the month before they open, they advertise in the right place at the right time.

? Past Paper

Happy Ideas Ltd's bears are advertised in the United Kingdom at point-of-sale and through specialist magazines.

1. Explain the term point-of-sale advertising. (2)
2. Identify two reasons for using one of these methods of advertising. (2)

CONTROLS ON ADVERTISING

Advertising and promotion are very powerful persuaders, and sometimes it is claimed that advertising misleads or exploits consumers. For this reason there are codes of practice and laws which are designed to protect consumers.

The Advertising Standards Authority (ASA) is responsible for monitoring advertising in the UK. It makes sure that advertisers obey the rules of the British Code of Advertising, Sales Promotion and Direct Marketing. This is a voluntary agreement which stresses that advertisements and promotions must be legal, decent, honest and truthful. Also, they must not cause widespread offence. It covers newspapers, magazines, cinema adverts, leaflets, brochures and posters, but not radio and television advertising.

If consumers feel that adverts have broken the rules, they contact the ASA, who investigate the complaint and can ask the advertiser to either withdraw the advertisement or make changes to it. The Independent Television Commission (ITC) controls the adverts on radio and television in a similar way.

Neither of these organisations can enforce their rules by law, but there are important laws concerning advertising. These include:

1. The **Trade Descriptions Act** 1968, which makes it a criminal offence for traders to make false statements about the goods they sell. This means, for example, that it is illegal to say that goods can do something they cannot, such as saying that a black and white printer can print good colour printouts. Also, it is illegal to say that goods include ingredients that they do not.

2. The **Sale of Goods Act** 1979, which states that goods must be as they are described in any advertising or promotion, eg a waterproof watch sealant must not let water into the watch.

? Past Paper

Customers buying cars from Docdel plc have legal protection. Explain how the following Acts protect these customers.

1. Sale of Goods Act
2. Trade Descriptions Act (6)

(Edexcel, 1997, Foundation)

Figure 21.7

Revision Questions

1. Advertisements that only give information about a product are called:
   a) expensive
   b) informative
   c) persuasive
   d) inexpensive

2. Advertisements that try to influence consumers to buy a product are called:
   a) demonstrative
   b) persuasive
   c) expressive
   d) informative

3. Activities aimed at obtaining good and positive publicity for a company are called:
   a) public sector
   b) private relations
   c) public relations
   d) public limited company

4. The Act that makes it a criminal offence for traders to make false statements about the goods they sell is called:
   a) Sale of Goods Act
   b) Trade Descriptions Act
   c) Weights and Measures Act
   d) Consumer Protection Act

5. Give four aims of promotion.

6. Give one advantage and one disadvantage of personal selling to a business.

7. Why are good public relations important to a business?

8. Explain the difference between advertising and below-the-line promotion.

9. Name the two organisations which are responsible for monitoring advertising in the UK.

Summary

- If businesses do not promote their product, they will not attract custom.
- Advertising is known as 'above-the-line' promotion and other promotion techniques are known as 'below-the-line'.
- The main factors that determine the choice of promotional methods to be used by a business are cost, competitors and the target audience.
- The main concern of public relations is the image of the business.

Key terms

Above-the-line promotion – advertising of a product or service by paying to use media such as television, radio newspapers or posters

Advertising campaign – a planned programme to organise the advertising and promotion of a product or service

Below-the-line promotion – promotional methods that do not involve using the media

Informative advertising – advertisements that describe the features of a product or give information about a service

Personal selling – talking directly to potential customers

Persuasive advertising – advertisements that try to influence and persuade consumers to buy a product

Promotion – publicising a product or service by the use of advertising, sales promotion and public relations

Public relations – activities aimed at obtaining good and positive publicity for a company

Target audience – the market segment a business is trying to reach

UNIT 22
PLACE

>> **What you will learn**

At the end of this unit you should understand:
- the importance of place in the marketing mix
- channels of distribution
- methods of distribution
- the role of IT in distribution.

THE IMPORTANCE OF PLACE

What we mean by 'place' in the marketing mix is the place where the product is to be sold to the final consumer, and also the means used to get the product to the place, which is called **distribution**. It is very important that products are in the right place and at the right time for the target market. If they are not, the customers will look elsewhere.

Imagine you want to buy a new CD by your favourite group, which you have seen advertised on the television and in magazines or on the internet. You know there are various shops and websites where you can buy it. You decide to visit your local record store and find that the product is not on the shelves because it has not been delivered yet. Disappointed, you decide to order it over the internet, and even though you have to wait for it to be sent to you, the CD arrives the next day. Your local shop has lost your custom for this sale and maybe for future purchases. This illustrates how important it is to have the product in the right place at the right time.

CHANNELS OF DISTRIBUTION

A **channel of distribution** is the route taken by a product from the producer to the customer (consumer). This can either be directly to the consumer or through a number of different people. We will look at the three main channels that can be used.

Channel of distribution one

Producer ⟶ Consumer

This is very simple because it means producers selling their products directly to the consumer. An example of this is a village bakery. The bread and cakes are baked by the shopkeeper and sold in the shop directly to the consumers. They do not pass through any other channels.

Figure 22.1 A village bakery

Other examples are mail order or internet sales, where the customer looks either at a brochure or a website to see the products or services provided by a company. Then they order what they want and have the goods sent to them directly.

Factory shops are another example of channel one. Here the public visits a shop owned by the producer and is able buy their goods, often at reduced prices.

In addition, manufacturers who need components for their products from other companies, usually receive them directly through Channel One. For example, a car manufacturer will receive the tyres for his vehicles directly from the tyre manufacturer.

Points for channel one
- The goods are often cheaper because no other companies are involved.
- It is the fastest channel.

Points against channel one
- It is more difficult for consumers to shop around.
- After-sales service levels may not be so good.

> ### ⚠ Exam tip
> Missing out the wholesaler is faster and cheaper.

Channel of distribution two

Producer ⟶ Retailer ⟶ Consumer

In this channel, the producer of the goods sells them directly to a retail outlet, generally a shop. The customer then buys the products from the shop. Many large supermarkets are stocked in this way. The manufacturer produces large amounts of a product especially for the supermarket (eg bread and milk) and delivers them directly to the supermarket. Other more durable goods are delivered to large distribution centres and are held there until the EPOS system (see page 205) indicates that more stock is needed at a particular shop. This method is also often used in the clothes industry, where fashion garments are supplied directly from the producer to the shops.

Another example of channel of distribution two is:

Buyer ⟶ Agent ⟶ Seller

The job of an agent is to bring buyers and sellers together. They are used by sellers to find buyers, eg travel agents and estate agents. These agencies provide advice and guidance for buyers and should have a wide range of products from which the buyer can choose. An agent's income comes from the commission which they make on each sale.

Points for channel two
- Faster than dealing with producers through a wholesaler (see channel three).
- Products should be cheaper for the customer because it cuts out the middleman (the wholesaler, see channel three).
- Retailer can negotiate discounts for bulk buying from the producer.
- Producer receives more direct customer feedback about the products.

Points against channel two
- Retailer has to rent very large premises to store the goods.
- Retailer has to bear the cost of transporting goods from distribution centres to stores.

> ### ⚠ Exam tip
> It is important to remember that how products reach the consumer and where they are sold are two different issues, although they are linked.

> ### ❓ Past Paper
> *Customers of Flyaway plc can book holidays by going into a travel agent.*
>
> Explain the advantages to a customer of going into a travel agent to choose a holiday. (6)
>
> (Edexcel, 2001, Higher)

Figure 22.2 Example of a distribution centre

Channel of distribution three

Producer → Wholesaler → Retailer → Consumer

This channel involves using a wholesaler who buys products from producers in large bulk and then divides the stock up into much smaller quantities for retailers to buy. The wholesaler takes on the cost of storing the products and the risk of not selling them. This is particularly useful for small retailers, such as those in local shopping centres, who do not have the space to store large amounts of stock. They may also find if they had to buy large quantities, that the goods might go past their sell-by date before they could sell them. It also means they have a wide choice of goods to choose from at the wholesalers.

Points for channel three
- The retailer can buy the quantity he thinks he will be able to sell.
- The wholesaler will stock products from many producers, giving more choice for the retailer.
- This cuts storage costs for the retailer.

Points against channel three
- Goods will be more expensive for the consumer because both the wholesaler and the retailer will add their profit margins to the producer's price.
- It can take a long time for the goods to get from the producer to the consumer.

> **Exam tip**
>
> The longer the channel of distribution, the more people will be involved, so the price will be higher for the product.

Choosing a channel of distribution to use

As we said at the beginning of this unit, it is very important that a producer chooses the most efficient channel of distribution to have the product in the right place at the right time. It is also important that this is done as cheaply as possible to keep costs down. Therefore, there are a number of factors that have to be considered to help producers decide which will be the most successful method for their product. We will look at each of these in turn:

The product
- Will it keep for a long time or is it perishable? Products such as fresh fruit and milk need to reach to the customer as quickly as possible and so require short channels of distribution such as channels one and two.
- Is it fragile? Fragile goods need to be handled as little as possible to reduce the chance of breakage, so again short channels are required.
- Is the product complex and will it need installation? Many highly technical products (such as computer networks) need to have a direct channel between the manufacturer and the customer, so would use channel one.

The cost

It may be cheaper to sell a product direct to the customer, because every time a product goes through an intermediary, such as a wholesaler or a retailer, they will take their profit margin. This means that the final price will be higher and the product may not attract customers because it is expensive.

The market
The market segment at which the product is aimed may influence the channel of distribution. For example, goods produced for a mass market, such as chocolate and sweets, can be sold either direct to the public, in retail outlets, or through wholesalers. Therefore, they can reach the customer through any of the channels of distribution. On the other hand, high-quality expensive goods, such as some cars, which are targeted at a much smaller market, would be sold through a high-class showroom using channel two.

The competition
Producers need to take into account where competitors sell their products and make sure they use the same outlets, so that their goods are also available for customers to choose from.

Figure 22.3 A high-class car showroom

> **Exam tip**
>
> It is very important, if you are asked to choose a channel of distribution for a business in a case study, that you think carefully about the product it is producing and take the factors just mentioned into account.

> **Task**
>
> For each of the following products, which channel of distribution would be most appropriate to get the product from the producer to the consumer? Explain your answers carefully for each question.
>
> 1. ice cream
> 2. a television
> 3. a new car
> 4. a skate board
> 5. fresh vegetables
> 6. newspapers

METHODS OF DISTRIBUTION
This term refers to the place where the customer is able to buy products. These range from department stores, chain stores, discount stores, superstores, supermarkets, local shops, direct sales, mail order to the internet. We will look at each type in a little more detail.

Department stores
These are large stores, often with at least two floors. They are made up of a number of departments, each run by a manager and selling different goods, eg menswear, ladieswear or electrical goods. They often sell expensive goods and are usually found in town and city centres or out-of-town shopping malls. Examples include Harrods, Selfridges and John Lewis.

Chain or multiple stores
Businesses with many branches in different towns and cities are known as chain stores. They may be like Marks and Spencer or Boots and sell a wide range of goods from clothes to stationery and food. Alternatively, they may specialise in a particular group of products, such as B & Q for DIY, or River Island for clothes and footwear.

Discount stores
These are stores where goods are sold at reduced prices to the customers. Examples include Matalan and Poundland, which sell a range of branded goods at discount prices.

Figure 22.4 An example of a superstore

Superstores
These are huge stores selling a wide range of goods from food to electrical goods and clothes all under one roof. They are usually found on the edge of towns and cities with large car parks provided. An example is SavaCentre. Another type of superstore is a specialist superstore, such as Ikea, which sells a vast range of furniture and household goods.

Supermarkets
Supermarkets sell mainly foodstuffs, both branded and own-brand goods. They are often situated on out-of-town sites with free car parking provided. Examples include Tesco, Sainsbury's, Safeways and Asda. However, unless they have a bus service running to the shop they are not convenient for people without cars.

Local shops
Small specialist retailers such as butchers, bakers, greengrocers and pharmacies, as well as services such as hairdresser's and post offices, offer convenience, particularly for customers who do not have their own transport to travel to out-of-town stores. They also give personal service and may provide a delivery service. However, because they generally have to use wholesalers to obtain their stock, they may have to charge higher prices than supermarkets.

Direct sales
These are sales made directly to the customer often in their own home. This may be done by door-to-door selling, eg Avon cosmetics, or by telephone selling such as companies selling conservatories or new kitchens. However, many people do not welcome door-to-door salespeople or telephone calls trying to sell them goods.

Internet
On-line shopping happens via the internet where customers browse through a range of products and sellers and make purchases using their credit cards. The goods are delivered to the home of the buyer. However, after-sales service may not be so good as that provided by shops.

Exam tip
It is very important to consider the type of product and where the target market might expect to buy it, when answering questions about which method of distribution might be used by a producer.

Task
Copy the table below and complete the points for and points against columns. See if you can add any other points, apart from those mentioned in the text.

Type of outlet	Points for	Points against
Department store		
Chain or multiple store		
Discount store		
Superstore		
Supermarket		
Direct sales		
Internet		

> **⚠ Exam tip**
>
> *Remember that a company will often use more than one method of distribution to get the product to the customer. By using different methods they may reach different segments of the market.*

Types of transport for distribution

Methods of distribution also include the type of transport used by the producer to move the goods to the place where they will be sold. There are several forms of transport which can be used: air, road, rail, sea, and pipelines. Before deciding which they will use, producers need to take into account the cost, the urgency, and the size of the products they need to move.

Air transport

This is an expensive but quick form of transport. It is mainly used for small valuable products or goods which are perishable and need to be delivered speedily, especially if they are being transported from other parts of the world.

Road transport

Transport on the road is the most common form of transport in the UK, and it is relatively cheap and quick. Goods of all sizes can be moved by road transport, which is flexible because it does not rely on timetables and takes the goods from door-to-door.

Rail transport

This is less flexible than road transport because trains run to timetables. In addition, the goods have to be transferred from the producer to the railway station and then, at the end of the rail journey, to their final destination by another form of transport. However, over long distances it is quicker than road transport and often cheaper.

Sea transport

This form of transport is used to transport goods around the world for international trading to take place. Many of these goods are packed into

Figure 22.5 Types of transport used in distribution

containers which can be carried by wagons or trains to the docks where they are loaded onto ships. This is a relatively secure and cheap form of transport.

Pipelines

Liquids and gas are transported in this way. For example, gas and oil are extracted from the sea and pumped along pipelines to the processing plant or refinery. This means that the products are sent directly from the gas or oil field without the need to use any other form of transport.

Exam tip

When answering a question about the way that goods should be transported, remember that you need to consider the cost, the time taken and the security of the particular item.

Task

Decide what would be the best type of transport to be used by the producer of the following products. Give your reason for each answer. Some products may need more than one form of transport.

1. spring daffodils from the Channel Islands to the wholesale flower market in London
2. steel girders from the manufacturer to building sites
3. Fiat cars built in Italy for the UK market
4. coal from UK mines to power stations in Wales
5. natural gas from the North Sea to the homes of consumers
6. milk from the farm to a processing plant and then to the door-step
7. next-day delivery of parcels from North America to the UK
8. spare parts for Jaguar cars packed into containers in Coventry and sent to car dealers in Germany

THE ROLE OF 'IT' IN DISTRIBUTION

The majority of distribution and stock control is computerised nowadays, using an Electronic Point of Sale (EPOS) system. Goods carry a barcode which is scanned at the checkout point in a shop. The checkouts are linked to a central computer which records all the items that have been sold. If the level of stock held in the shop drops below the reorder level, more stock will be ordered. In the case of goods that are frequently bought, such as bread and milk, the ordering will be done automatically via e-mail or Electronic Data Interchange (EDI) between the shop and the supplier. A delivery is then arranged. This ensures that goods do not run out.

Past Paper

Hotspur & Wren Ltd, a furniture and carpet retailer, has always tried to keep up to date, and part of the refit of the new store included installing EPOS (Electronic Point of Sale) terminals.

Explain how EPOS works and what benefits this might have brought to Hotspur & Wren Ltd. (8)

(Edexcel, 2003, Higher)

Extension task

Jarvis Jones Ltd has just developed a revolutionary new type of pushchair for babies and toddlers. The pushchair is a top-of-the-range model and will be expensive, costing around £450 each. The company is sure that the new features they have incorporated into the pushchair will make it a winner with parents, but they are not sure which channel of distribution to use to get the product to the public.

Decide which channel of distribution you think they should use, taking into account the product, the cost, the market and the competition. You need to include each of these aspects in your answer.

UNIT 22: PLACE

Revision Questions

1. The route taken by a product from the producer to the consumer is called the:
   a) span of control
   b) channel of distribution
   c) chain of command
   d) IT in distribution

2. A company that buys goods in bulk from producers then sells them in smaller quantities to retailers is called:
   a) retailer
   b) wholesaler
   c) agent
   d) consumer

3. Mail order and internet sales are examples of channel of distribution number
   a) one
   b) two
   c) three

4. List the four factors a business has to consider when choosing which channel of distribution to use for their goods.

5. Give one advantage and one disadvantage to a retailer of buying goods directly from the manufacturer.

6. Give one reason why a customer might choose to go to an estate agent when they are considering buying a house.

7. What is the main difference between a department store and a chain store?

8. Give one advantage and one disadvantage to the customer of internet shopping.

9. Explain the factors that would be important to a company transporting precious jewellery from the UK to Australia.

Summary

- Producers must ensure that their goods and services are available where and when customers require them.
- The channel of distribution chosen to deliver goods from the producer to the consumer will be affected by the product, the costs, the market and the competition.
- Methods of distribution refers to the outlets where the customer is able to buy goods and services, and the form of transport used to get the goods to the outlet.

Key terms

Buying in bulk – buying large quantities of a product with the aim of gaining a lower price per unit

Channel of distribution – the route taken by a product from the producer to the consumer

Methods of distribution –
a) the place where a customer is able to buy a product;
b) the type of transport used to deliver goods from the producer to the consumer

Retail outlet – a shop which sells goods to the general public

Wholesaler – a company which buys products from producers in bulk and divides this into smaller quantities to sell to retailers

UNIT 23

PRODUCT

What you will learn

At the end of this unit you should understand the terms:
- goods and services
- product life cycle
- product mix
- branding and packaging.

Product is the initial element of the marketing mix, which does not mean it is always the most important, but without the product or service, there would be no sales. Therefore having the right product is the foundation of all good marketing.

GOODS AND SERVICES

When we talk about products, we mean goods and services. Goods are physical products that have a value and can be bought and sold, eg a pair of trainers costing £60.

Some goods can be classified as **consumer goods**, which are produced for the use of the public. Some consumer goods will not last long, eg burgers, sweets, flowers. Others, such as cars and computers, will last for much longer.

The other classification of goods is **capital goods**. This refers to goods owned by a company and used in the making or providing of other goods and services, eg tools, machinery and equipment.

Services are non-physical products which help to improve our lifestyles and can also be bought and sold. Examples of services include hairdressing, healthcare, education, and tourism.

Exam tip

It is important to remember when we are talking about products, we must include services as well as goods.

Task

1. Think about a typical day in your life. Make two lists: one of the goods you *buy* in a day and one of the services you *use* in a day.
2. Which is the longer list? Why do you think that is?

WHAT MAKES A PRODUCT SUCCESSFUL?

To be successful, a product needs to satisfy the customers so that they will buy it and advise other people to buy it as well.

Figure 23.1 Examples of consumer and capital goods

Some of the factors that make a product successful are:

- attractive design and packaging – so the customer is attracted to buy that product
- efficiency – the product does what it is expected to do efficiently
- reliability – the product does not break down and lasts for a reasonable length of time
- quality – the quality of the product matches the price which the customer paid for it
- good after-sales service and advice – so that the customer feels reassured that they will receive help if they need it
- a unique selling point (USP) – the feature that makes it different from similar products, thus making the customer want to buy that product rather than others.

The more of these factors that can be provided in one product, the more likely it is to sell.

PRODUCT MIX

Many companies produce a range of products to try and reach different segments of the market. This is called their product mix or product range. For example, an ice cream manufacturer could have a range of different ice creams: luxury ones with full fat milk; others with additions of fruit or chocolate; half fat ones for people who are concerned about their diet; lollies and cornets for children. By having a variety of products they hope they will appeal to most segments of the market.

It is useful for a company to know where their product range is in terms of their share of the market and market growth. This can be done by using the **Boston Matrix** shown in Figure 23.2. This divides products into four different sectors. To use the matrix, the company would need to examine their range of products and decide which sector each product falls into.

1. **Stars** – are potentially very profitable products for the company, but they may require a great deal of investment in promotion to make them sell well.
2. **Problem children** – their future is uncertain, they may become stars if the company invests large amounts of money in them, or they may turn into dogs.
3. **Cash cows** – these are highly profitable products. The money they make can be 'milked' to help stars and problem children.
4. **Dogs** – products which are in decline with falling sales. The company will probably drop them soon.

Figure 23.2 The Boston Matrix

The Boston Matrix allows a business to see if they have a balanced product mix that does not have too many dogs and problem children. They also need enough cash cows to develop the stars.

> **Exam tip**
>
> It is important that products in a company's mix do not compete with each other.

PRODUCT LIFE CYCLE

The product life cycle shows the progress of a product from its development to its decline. It also shows the sales that can be expected at each stage in the life cycle. All products go through the same life cycle, but it is likely to be different for every product. The stages are:

- **Development** – the product is being designed, developed and tested. This may take years, eg a new aircraft, or a few hours like a new dish in a restaurant. At this stage, there are no sales and the costs of research and development are high. Therefore, the product will be making a loss.

- **Introduction** – the product is launched and put on the market. It will be relatively unknown, and generally sales will be quite low. There will be heavy advertising and promotion costs. Losses are often made at this stage.

- **Growth** – sales begin to grow rapidly as the product becomes more established in the market. The promotional costs will have dropped and the product may now be making a profit. However, it is likely that competitors will launch their version of the product.

- **Maturity** – the product is well established on the market, and making good profits. Sales will be good, but only growing slowly, if at all. There will be more competition, and promotion will need to point out the difference between this product and competitors'. The firm will try to develop brand loyalty.

- **Saturation** – as more firms come into the market, it becomes flooded with products. Competition is high and prices may have to be reduced to attract sales.

- **Decline** – sales and profits are falling. This is often due to changes in fashion or consumers' tastes, or a new and better product has appeared on the market. It is probable that the company will soon remove the product from the market.

A diagram of a typical product life cycle looks like this:

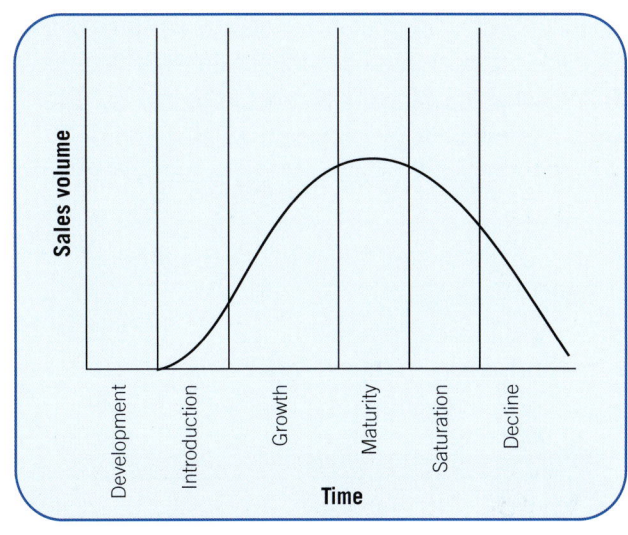

Figure 23.3 A product life cycle

The life cycle may last for a few months or many years, depending upon the product. Fashion clothing will have a short life cycle, while Kellogg's cornflakes have been around for many years and would still be considered to be in the stage of maturity.

Exam tip

It is important to remember that product life cycle does not mean how long a product lasts: it refers to the stages which a product passes through.

Task

Think about the following well-known products. At which stage in the product life cycle is each one?
- Mars bars
- audio cassettes
- skate boards
- 3G mobile phones
- mini disc players

Extension strategies

In order to keep the product on the market for longer when it reaches the maturity or saturation stage of the life cycle, companies could adopt extension strategies. This means changing the product in some way. There are a number of ways in which this can be done:

- change the appearance or packaging of the product
- encourage the customer to use the product more frequently
- develop a wider product range
- find new uses for the product
- find new markets for the product.

> ⚡ **Exam tip**
>
> It is often cheaper for a company to extend the life cycle of an existing product than to develop a completely new product.

> ✏️ **Task**
>
> Figure 23.4
>
> The Scented Perfume Co has a number of different products. They try to keep a balanced product mix. One of their perfumes which has sold very successfully for a number of years has now reached decline stage. They are very keen to continue to produce this perfume, but realise that without adopting some extension strategies, it may not be possible.
>
> Select two extension strategies you think they could adopt, giving your reasons for your choice.

Functions of the product life cycle

Identifying the life cycle of a product has a number of uses:

1. It will identify the volume of sales that might be expected from the product at each stage in its life cycle.
2. It will indicate when a product might become profitable.
3. It may help to identify when a business should stop producing and selling a product.
4. It can identify when extension strategies might be introduced.
5. It helps a business to identify the different methods of promotion that a product might need during the life cycle.

> ⚡ **Exam tip**
>
> If an examination question asks you about the likely product life cycle for a particular product, you must think carefully about how long you think each stage is likely to last. Remember, this will vary for every product.

BRANDING AND PACKAGING

If you think of any type of product, such as computers or trainers, there are many examples of each on the market. How can a business make their product seem different from their competitors? One way is to give it a **brand name**. This is a unique name and identity that makes the product easily recognisable, and differentiates it from others. It needs to be short, and easily

Figure 23.5 Different types of packaging, with brand names

remembered by the public. Examples of well-known brand names are Heinz, Nescafé, Adidas, MicroSoft, Kleenex, Walkers and Ferrari. All these names have an image which makes them individual in the eyes of the consumer. They know what they expect from a product with that name, and if they trust the product they will buy it again.

There are many benefits to branding:

- Businesses will hope that this leads to brand loyalty, where customers will repeat-buy because they prefer the look, taste, quality or image of their products.
- If the company's name becomes established with one product, it may encourage customers to buy different products bearing that name.
- Customers can be reasonably sure about the quality they will get with branded goods.

Many large retail organisations have 'own-brand' goods. These are products made by manufacturers to specifications laid down by the retailer, and will often be sold at prices below the well-known brands. All the major supermarkets carry own-brand goods on their shelves.

Branding and packaging go hand-in-hand, because packaging will display the product's brand name which, because it is easily recognised, should catch the consumer's eye.

Packaging is the way that goods and services are presented to the consumer. It is very important because a product that is unsuitable or unattractive probably will not sell very well. This is because consumers link the quality of the packaging with the quality of the product itself.

Packaging serves a number of functions:

- It protects the goods – many goods are fragile and could break if not packaged. It also keeps products clean and hygienic.
- It promotes the goods – the design should be eye-catching and make the goods distinguishable from others. This can be done by colour, shape and size.
- It provides information – this may be about how the product should be used. Food products have to carry certain information on the packaging by law, eg details of the ingredients.
- It makes the goods easy to buy and use – many products could not be purchased unless they were packaged for consumers. For example, how would we buy shampoo or toothpaste if they were not packaged in handy containers?

However, there are criticisms of packaging:

- It can add to the cost of production and make goods more expensive for the consumer.
- Many goods seem to have more packaging than is necessary. This can be seen as a waste of resources that then have to be disposed of, which contributes to environmental problems.

Task

Visit a supermarket and select five products where the packaging instantly catches your eye. In the case of each one, explain what the product is, and what made the packaging so noticeable to you.

Exam tip

Packaging is so important in marketing a product, it is often referred to as the fifth 'P' in the marketing mix.

Revision Questions

1. Giving a product a unique name and identity is called:
   a) packaging
   b) branding
   c) developing
   d) clarifying

2. The four stages a product passes through between development and decline are called ...., ..., ... and ....

3. Goods which are produced for the use of the public are called .... goods.
   a) consumer
   b) capital
   c) service
   d) physical

4. In the Boston Matrix, highly profitable products are called:
   a) stars
   b) problem children
   c) cash cows
   d) dogs

5. Why do manufacturers have a range of products?

6. What happens to a product in the decline stage of its life cycle?

7. What would a manufacturer have to consider when designing packaging for:
   a) a television set?
   b) toilet cleaner?

8. Give six examples of brand names.

Summary

- Getting the product right is the foundation of all good marketing.
- Product means both goods and services.
- Many companies have a product mix (range) to try to reach different segments of a market.
- All products have their own life cycle – the different stages through which the product passes.
- Branding and packaging make products recognisable and help to sell them.

Key terms

Branding – giving a product a unique name and identity

Goods – physical products that have a value

Packaging – the way that goods or services are presented to the consumer

Product life cycle – the stages through which a product passes in its progress from development to decline

Product mix – the range of goods and services produced by a company

Services – non-physical products that can be bought and sold

Unique selling point – the feature that makes a product different from similar products

UNIT 24

MARKET RESEARCH

What you will learn

At the end of this unit you should understand:
- the role of market research
- methods of market research
- the design, use and presentation of questionnaires
- the analysis and evaluation of findings from questionnaires.

THE ROLE OF MARKET RESEARCH

Businesses need to find out from their customers whether they like their existing products and if they would be prepared to buy a new product. If they do not ask their customers what they think and act upon the information they gain, they risk producing goods and services that are not what the consumers want. To avoid this they carry out market research. This helps a business to find out answers to questions such as:

- Would customers be prepared to buy new products?
- Who are their customers likely to be?
- How much are customers willing to pay for products?
- What makes customers buy one product rather than another?
- In which ways can their products be improved?
- Does their promotion and packaging work to attract customers?
- Who are their competitors, and what do they produce?

There are two methods of market research:

1. **Primary research** – often called **field research**, which collects information directly or first-hand.
2. **Secondary research** – often called **desk research**, which means looking at information that has already been collected and published.

Figure 24.1 Field research

PRIMARY RESEARCH

Primary data can be collected in a number of ways, such as surveys, personal interviews, focus groups, consumer panels, observation, and product sampling.

However, before an organisation decides which method of primary research it is going to use, it must make a decision about the sample it is going to take. This is because it would obviously be impossible for a company to collect the views of every member of the population as it would cost too much and take too long. Therefore, a smaller group that is representative of all the potential buyers of a product is asked instead. This is called a **sample**. There are two main methods of choosing a sample:

1. **random sampling** – all members of the population have an equal chance of being selected as part of the sample. You might think this means just standing in the street and asking passers-by to answer your questions. However, there would be many members of the population who would not be in the street at the time you are there, therefore, they do not stand any chance of being part of your sample. To pick a random sample, it is necessary to take all the names on the electoral register (a list of all the people who live in a particular area) and pick out, for example, every fiftieth name. This particular person then needs to be interviewed to make the sample truly random. Random sampling is very expensive and time-consuming, but gives a true sample of the population.
2. **quota sampling** – the interviewers select people within the population who meet set criteria. This means they may choose to speak to 300 males and 300 females, all aged between 14 and 18. Therefore, if they are conducting street interviews, they pick whoever they want as long as they are within the correct age range, and they interview 300 people of each sex. This is much cheaper than random sampling, and is far easier to complete.

Exam tip

Random sampling sounds like picking people at random by asking them in the street. This is exactly what it is not. It involves making sure that everybody has the same chance of being picked.

Surveys

The most common form of survey is to use a questionnaire. This is a list of questions which are carefully planned to find out what customers think. A questionnaire can be carried out in the street, by telephone, by post, by e-mail or through a newspaper.

Points for questionnaires
- The business can decide exactly which questions it wants to ask.
- Everyone is asked the same questions.
- If they are used face-to-face or over the telephone, there is two-way communication, which helps to make sure that the respondent understands the questions.
- It is easy to analyse the replies using Information Technology.

Points against questionnaires
- They often do not allow people to express their own opinions.
- They are brief and impersonal.
- There is a very low return rate for postal and newspaper questionnaires.
- They are quite expensive and time-consuming.

Designing a questionnaire
A successful questionnaire will:
- have simple, clear questions that cannot be misunderstood
- have questions that link directly with the information needed
- not ask too many questions
- ask the questions in a common sense order
- record the data quickly and conveniently.

The most important question to ask yourself when you start to design a questionnaire is 'What do I want to find out?' It is a good idea to jot down the information you need to find out before you start to design the questions. This will focus your mind and make sure you do not miss out anything vital. Remember, you will not have a second chance to ask any missing questions!

Next you need to decide what kind of questions you are going to ask. Most questionnaires use closed questions, where the person answering

Figure 24.2 Designing a questionnaire

chooses from pre-set answers, often by ticking a box. An example of a closed question about the taste of a product might be:

Do you find the taste of this product:
very pleasant ☐ unpleasant ☐
pleasant ☐ very unpleasant ☐

Points for closed questions
- People may be more willing to answer them because tick boxes are quicker and easier to complete.
- They are easy to analyse because there is a limited choice of answers.

Points against closed questions
- There may not be the 'right' answer for some people in the choices they have been given.
- There is no possibility for people to give their individual opinions.

It is also possible to use open questions where people can answer them in their own words and give their own opinions, but it is much more difficult and time-consuming to analyse this sort of reply. An example of a open question about taste might be, 'What do you like about the taste of this product?'

Points for open questions
- They allow people to express their own opinions.
- They give businesses a chance to find out more about people's feelings.

Points against open questions
- Each answer is different.
- Answers are very hard to change into statistics.

Task

Compose a questionnaire to find out the following: what are the most popular soft drinks; what influences people to buy a particular flavour and brand; how many drinks people buy; where they buy the drinks from.

Think carefully about the types of questions you ask, the order in which you ask them and how the answers will be recorded.

Using a questionnaire
Once you have designed your questionnaire, you have to think about how you are actually going to conduct the research. You need to make decisions about:

- where you are going to carry out the questionnaire
- on which day or days of the week
- at what time of day
- how many people you are going to question.

All of these factors will affect the people who will be available for you to ask. For example, if you want to question people between 20 and 30 years old, you would not find many of them on a weekday between 9.00 in the morning and 5.30 in the afternoon. So, you might have to try a Saturday instead.

UNIT 24: MARKET RESEARCH

It might also be helpful to work out what you are going to say to introduce yourself before you do your survey. You need to explain why you are carrying out the market research and how long the questions will take. Also, remember to thank people for their time.

The analysis and evaluation of findings from questionnaires

You have completed your survey and now you need to make sense of the data you have obtained. You need to put the answers into a form that is easy to understand. This can be done by displaying the information as tables, charts or graphs.

- **Tables** can be used to present data neatly. For example, suppose a question in a survey has asked about the number of times customers of different ages buy goods in a particular shop. The data could be presented in a table.

Age group	At least once a day	At least once a week	At least once a month
13–15	5	10	20
16–18	7	12	22
19–21	4	9	15
22–24	6	7	18

The table has been used to collate the data and put it into an organised order. However, looking at the table does not quickly make it clear how many customers might be expected to use the shop. This could be done by using a chart.

- **Charts** show information in a form that is easily and quickly understood. The most common forms of charts are bar or column charts and pie charts.

By putting the data into a chart we can see at once that the largest number of customers in this age group visits the shop at least once a month.

We can also present the information in a pie chart, which again gives a clear picture of how often customers visit the shop.

If you use a spreadsheet to collate your data from a survey, it is very easy to produce charts.

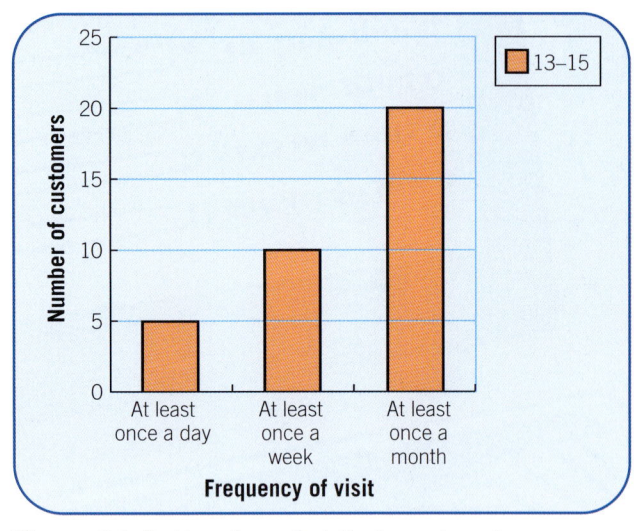

Figure 24.3 Number of visits to a shop by age group 13–15 (bar chart)

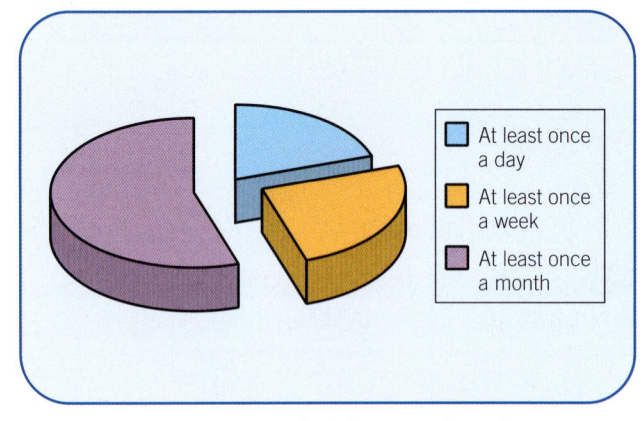

Figure 24.4 Number of visits to a shop by age group 19–21 (pie chart)

Task

Look at the two types of charts shown above and decide which one shows the information more clearly. Write down exactly why you have made your decision.

- **Graphs** provide another way of presenting information. A line graph enables you to compare two sets of data against each other.

By looking at the graph below we can quickly see that the age group 16–18 visits the shop more frequently overall.

Figure 24.5 Graph to compare visits to a shop by age groups 16–18 and 19–21

Now we have put the information into a form that is easier to understand, we can begin to draw some conclusions from it. As we said, the age group 16–18 are the more frequent visitors to the shop. If the shopkeeper has asked the question in a survey, so that he could find out which age group he needed to try and attract, he could see it is the 19–21 year olds. His next step would be to devise some kind of strategy to encourage this age group to visit his shop.

Interviews

Interviews might be used for primary research, eg to find out whether a member of the public liked a product, such as soap powder, that had been placed in their home for them to try out. The interviewer will have a set of ready-prepared questions to ask the interviewee, many of which will be open questions to allow them to express their own opinions.

Points for interviews

- It is easier to obtain detailed information about the person's views.
- If any of the questions are difficult to understand, the interviewer can explain them.
- If the interview is in the person's home, packaging can also be shown and the person's views recorded.

Points against interviews

- Interviews are an expensive way of gathering information, because they are time-consuming to conduct.
- The interviewer may have to travel some distance between one interview and the next, taking up time and costing money.

Focus groups

This is where a group of people meet together to provide information about a product or service that they have experienced. An example might be a company that provides package holidays which invites a group of their clients to discuss their holiday. The group would contain a range of individuals and they would be asked questions prepared by market researchers. This is cheaper than conducting individual interviews, but there is the possibility of people being swayed by the opinions of others in the group.

Task

Joe and Vanessa have done a survey as part of their Business Studies coursework. One of the questions they asked was about methods of advertising:

Which of the following methods of advertising would you use to advertise a fast food outlet?

They collected the following data.

Television 2	Local radio 7
National newspapers 0	Local newspapers 20
Leaflets 15	Posters 10
Yellow Pages 8	

Using the data, construct a column chart and a pie chart. Make sure your charts are fully labelled.

Remember, if you use a spreadsheet to collate your data from a survey, it is very easy to produce charts and graphs.

UNIT 24: MARKET RESEARCH

Figure 24.6 A focus group

Points for focus groups
- They are a relatively cheap way of gaining the views of customers.
- Customers are more likely to respond to this than a postal questionnaire.

Points against focus groups
- Customers may have their opinions changed by other members of the group.
- This will only be a small number of customers, who may not reflect the views of the majority of customers.
- It may be difficult to find people prepared to give up time for a focus group session.

Consumer panels
This is where groups of consumers give their views about a product or service over a period of time. Most television and radio stations make use of consumer panels to monitor the popularity or otherwise of their programmes. Panels may also be asked to give their views on new products. For example, before an advertisement is presented to the general public, it may have been viewed by a consumer panel who will give their views on it first.

Points for consumer panels
- They can give detailed information about a product.
- They can measure how consumers' opinions change over time.

Points against consumer panels:
- It can be difficult to keep the same panel available over a period of time.

Observation
This is often used by retailers who observe the behaviour of customers in their store. They may watch how customers wander around the store and how long it takes them to make a decision on buying a product. They may also want to know whether a display attracts their attention. Another form of observation is counting the number of vehicles per hour that pass a billboard or poster.

Points for observation:
- A large number customers can be observed over a period of time.
- It is a relatively cheap way of gaining information.

Points against observation:
- It only gives customer reactions, it does not give the reasons for those reactions.

Product sampling
This is where samples of new products are offered, in a supermarket, for example. The customers are asked to taste or drink the product and then answer questions about it.

Points for product sampling:
- It is easy to set up and carry out.
- Customers usually respond well, because they are getting something for nothing.

Points against product sampling:
- The customers in a shop are unlikely to be representative of the population as a whole.
- People may be reluctant to give their real opinions for fear of causing offence.

Figure 24.7 Product sampling

> **Exam tip**
>
> Make sure you know the strengths and weaknesses of each method of research, and can give examples.

Points for primary research
- It is specific to the product or service and what the firm wants to find out.
- It is up to date.
- It gives an insight into the market, which can be used to gain an advantage over competitors.
- It can be kept private by the company.

Points against primary research
- It is often expensive to collect.
- It is time-consuming.
- It needs a large sample to make sure it is accurate.
- The data has to be analysed to give meaningful information.

> **Task**
>
> What method of primary research would be best for a company introducing a new type of carpet shampoo? Give your reasons for your choice carefully.

Remember, primary research may also be referred to as field research.

SECONDARY RESEARCH

Secondary research uses data that has already been collected. This could involve looking at sources such as:

- government publications, eg the *Family Expenditure Survey* or *Regional Trends*
- articles in specialist magazines, eg the *Grocer*
- articles and special reports in newspapers, eg the *Financial Times*
- the internet which has information about every item imaginable.

Remember, secondary research may also be referred to as desk research.

Points for secondary research
- It is often obtained without cost so it is cheaper than primary research.
- It is usually instantly available.

Points against secondary research
- It is not tailored specifically to the needs of the company.
- It is available to other firms.
- It may be out of date.

> **Exam tip**
>
> If you are asked whether a company should use primary or secondary research, you need to take into account how much money they have to spend, how quickly they want the information and how specific it needs to be.

UNIT 24: MARKET RESEARCH

Task

Jenny Smith started making quilts two years ago as a hobby. She has decided that she would like to try and sell them instead of just making them for family and friends. She realises that she will have to advertise her quilts, otherwise no one will buy them. She is not sure how the law stands with regard to advertising.

1. Using secondary research, find out as much as you can about the Trade Descriptions Act 1968 and the Sale of Goods Act 1979.
2. Write a letter to Jenny, telling her how these two Acts will affect any advertising she might do.

Past Paper

Mary Li, a wood carver, wants to sell individually hand-carved wooden ornaments. Mary wishes to find out whether there will be a large enough local market for her ornaments.

Explain how Mary could use market research to help her find out. (5)

(Edexcel, 2002, Higher)

Revision Questions

1. To find out what customers think about their products a business will carry out:
   a) promotion
   b) sales
   c) market research
   d) advertising

2. Information which is collected first hand is called:
   a) research and development
   b) primary research
   c) secondary research
   d) word-of-mouth

3. Desk research involves looking at information that has already been:
   a) published
   b) written
   c) added to
   d) added up

4. The most common form of survey is to use a:
   a) answer sheet
   b) questionnaire
   c) interview
   d) test

5. Open questions ask people to express their own:
   a) revelations
   b) opinions
   c) actions
   d) multiple choice

6. The owners of a shopping mall want to find out how many customers visit the mall. How could they find out this information?

7. A sandwich bar in a city centre is planning to bring out a new range of sandwiches, but first needs to find out whether the customers would like them. What type of research would you advise them to carry out? Give reasons for your answer.

8. Why might the information gathered by primary market research be inaccurate?

Summary

- Businesses use market research to find out what consumers think about a product or service.
- Market research is either primary – first hand, or secondary – second hand.
- Questionnaires need to be carefully created and the sample of respondents needs to be worked out to give a representative sample of the population.
- The results of market research should be presented in a form that allows analysis and evaluation of the information.

Key terms

Closed questions – questions with pre-set answers

Market research – the collection of information about existing or potential products

Open questions – questions which allow respondents to give their own opinions

Primary (field) research – collection of first-hand information

Questionnaire – a list of carefully planned questions to find out what consumers think

Secondary (desk) research – looking at information that has already been gathered

UNIT 24: MARKET RESEARCH

GCSE BUSINESS STUDIES for Edexcel

Section 5
PRODUCTION

UNIT 25

ECONOMIES AND DISECONOMIES OF SCALE

> ## What you will learn
>
> At the end of this unit you should understand:
> - the ways in which businesses expand
> - economies and diseconomies of scale
> - the benefits and drawbacks of economies of scale
> - the benefits and drawbacks of diseconomies of scale
> - how they both have an effect on the use and management of resources in the production of goods and services.

BUSINESS SIZE

One of the objectives which the owners of businesses will have is to see their business grow to be big and powerful. The shareholders will want this also, because bigger companies have greater financial resources and are, therefore, less likely to go out of business. The dividends which they receive from profits will probably also be higher.

The directors and managers will want the business to grow because this means they will have much greater power, influence and possibly reputation in the business world. Their views are more likely to be listened to by other business leaders.

Deciding on whether a business is large or small is not that simple to establish. How do we measure the size of a business? We can use the following as indicators:

- the physical size of the business – How many branches does it have, or how much land does it occupy?
- the number of employees – How many people work in the business?
- the total value of its assets – the capital employed which is used to create profit.
- the turnover – or what the business receives from its sales revenue.

When these indicators are combined then we can reliably measure the size of the business. Some businesses will be very small, employing only one or two employees, whereas others will be large public limited companies, employing thousands of employees.

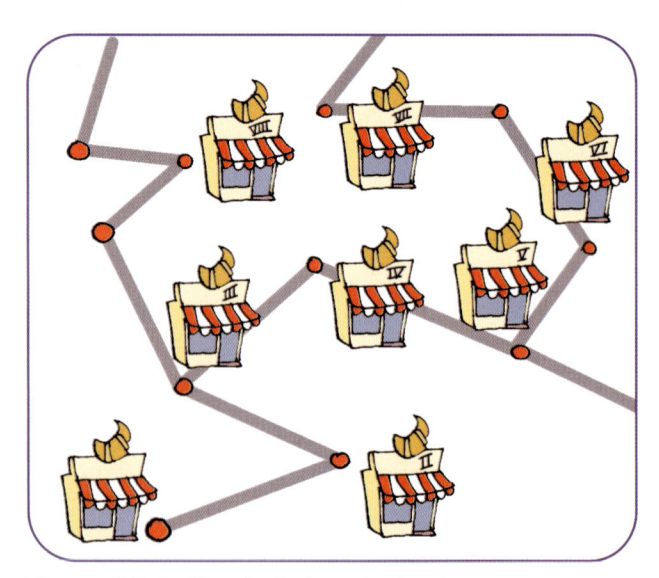

Figure 25.1 Physical size of a business

How can businesses expand?

A business can expand in two main ways:

1. Through a **takeover**, which occurs when one business buys enough shares in another business to allow it to take control. If the shareholders of the first company are agreeable to the takeover it is said to be a **friendly takeover**; if they are opposed to it, then the merger is said to be a **hostile takeover**.
2. Through merging with another company: the owners of two businesses agree to join together to become one business. This is called a **merger**.

There are three main kinds of merger (sometimes also known as integration):

1. horizontal
2. vertical
3. conglomerate.

Horizontal merger

This occurs between businesses in the same industry and at the same stage of production.
The main advantages are:

- economies of scale (see page 231)
- less competition in the industry
- greater share of the market which should result in greater market power.

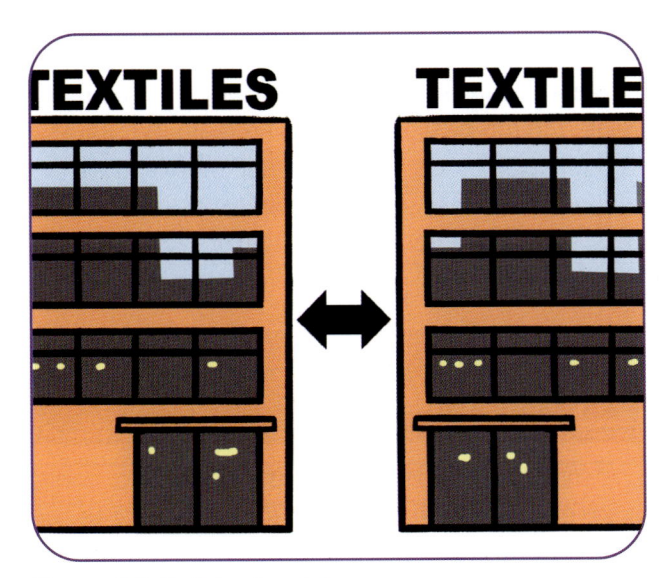

Figure 25.2 A horizontal merger

Vertical merger

This occurs between businesses in the same industry but at different stages of production.

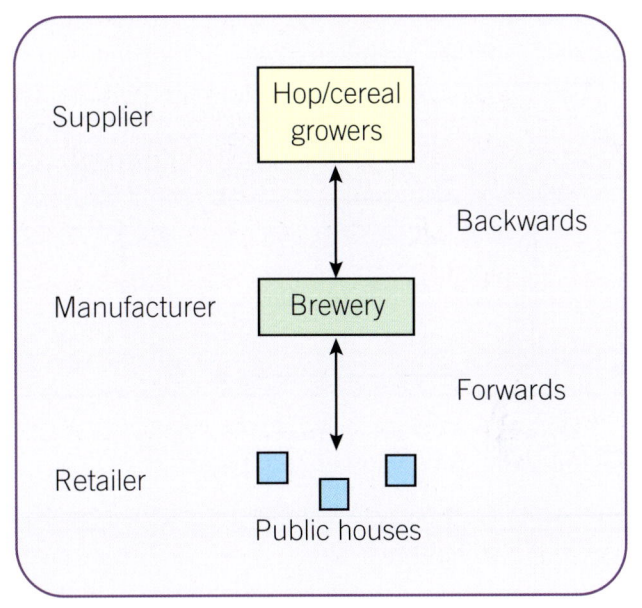

Figure 25.3 A vertical merger

Vertical mergers can be backward or forward mergers. **Backward mergers** occur when a business takes over another business *further back* in the chain of production, eg the brewery above taking over the hop/cereal grower. The main advantages are:

- there is a guaranteed supply of raw materials
- costs of the raw materials can be controlled
- quality of the raw materials can be controlled
- any profits of the raw material grower now belong to the brewery.

Forward mergers occur when a business takes over another business at a *later* stage in the chain of production, eg the brewery taking over the public houses. The main advantages are:

- there is a guaranteed outlet for the product
- any profits of the public houses now belong to the brewery
- the public houses are not allowed to sell any other make of beer.

UNIT 25: ECONOMIES AND DISECONOMIES OF SCALE

Conglomerate mergers

These occur when businesses in completely different industries merge (also known as **diversification**). Their goods or services are not related, eg a publisher, a cosmetics manufacturer, a holiday company and an insurance company.

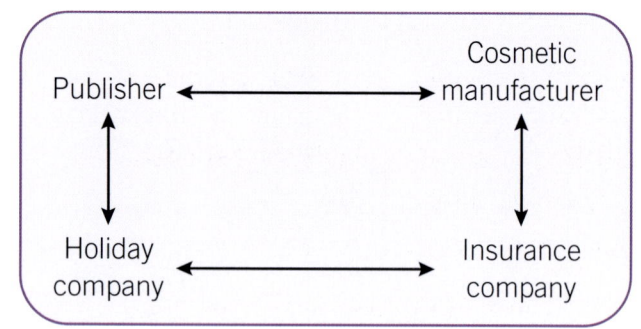

Figure 25.4 A conglomerate merger

The advantages are:

- by diversifying, the risk is reduced because the business is not relying on one single product or service
- if the business's products saturate the market and it cannot expand then it needs new markets.

Task

Use the internet or newspapers to find examples of businesses which have been involved in takeovers and mergers.

Task

1. Explain the difference between a takeover and a merger.
2. Using an example, explain a horizontal merger.
3. Explain a hostile takeover.
4. Explain two reasons why a manufacturer might take over one of its suppliers.
5. Explain two benefits to a business of a forward merger.
6. There is no obvious link between pet food and children's toys. Suggest reasons why a firm might wish to diversify in this way.

ECONOMIES OF SCALE

It is generally accepted that bigger businesses gain some advantages over smaller business through **economies of scale**. As a business grows in size, its costs fall owing to internal economies of scale. This means that the business benefits from a fall in the average cost of the goods it produces.

Internal economies: Production/technical, Purchasing/marketing, Financial, Managerial, Risk bearing

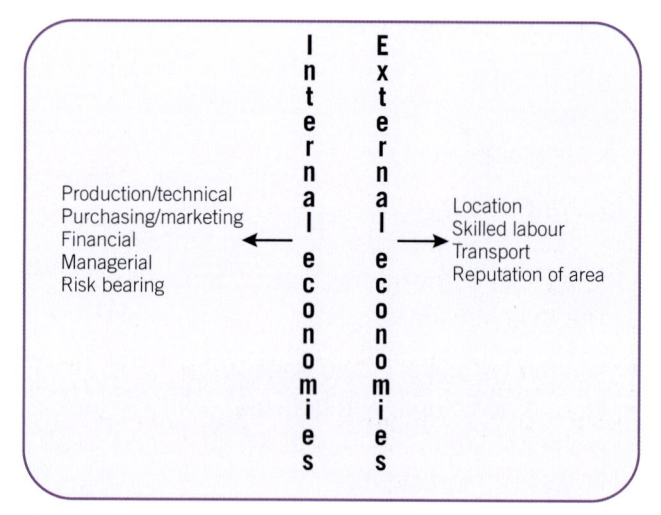

External economies: Location, Skilled labour, Transport, Reputation of area

Figure 25.5 Economies of scale

Internal economies of scale are those specifically related to the business itself. The main internal economies of scale or savings are shown in the table on page 227. **External economies** of scale are advantages that benefit the whole industry, not just individual firms.

Exam tip

Make sure that you know the difference between internal and external economies of scale.

TABLE 25.1 Types of economy of scale

Types of economy of scale	Example
Production/technical economies	• a firm can use computers and technology to replace employees on the production line that would be too expensive or underused by a small firm • able to transport bulk materials • mass production means unit costs are lower
Purchasing/marketing economies	• bulk buying – being able to buy goods in bulk lowers the unit price • employing specialist buyers who negotiate better deals • employing a specialised sales team • advertising costs can be spread
Financial economies	• easier for large firms to raise capital • better lending terms and lower interest rates – easier to borrow • risk is spread over more products • greater potential finance from retained profits • administration costs can be spread
Managerial economies	• more specialised management can be employed; saves money, more efficient • top managers can be employed, attracted by top salaries
Risk-bearing economies	• firms can afford to take risks with new products because other products or parts of the business are still profitable
External economies	• skilled labour in the area – local colleges may run specialist courses • being close to other similar businesses who can work with each other • having specialist supplies and support services nearby • better road and rail networks which often improve as the area develops • reputation of the area improves as it becomes known for a particular industry • attracts other businesses, eg component suppliers • all of these combine to provide a mutual advantage to businesses in the area

Task

Mariam, a sole trader who owns a grocery shop, is in trouble because of a supermarket which has just opened. The supermarket benefits from economies of scale. Select and explain how four of these economies will benefit the supermarket.

Exam tip

Learn the main economies of scale and diseconomies of scale.

DISECONOMIES OF SCALE

A business cannot keep on growing, because there are limits to the amount of growth that can take place. It will not necessarily be in the interest of businesses or consumers for companies to grow and grow. As businesses continue to expand, they may reach a point where they get too big for the market in which they are operating. Their average unit costs of production begin to rise again. If they do grow too large then they start to suffer from **diseconomies of scale**. These diseconomies start to happen because the larger the business becomes, the more difficult it is to manage. Diseconomies of scale can be caused by a number of factors, shown in the table.

TABLE 25.2 Examples of diseconomies of scale

Diseconomy of scale	Example
Decision-making/managerial problems	• decision-making takes longer because there are more people involved in the process; the business can be slow to respond to changes • too many middle managers, so it is not clear who is in charge of what or whom
Communication problems	• communication between employees becomes poor because once again there are more people involved – too many layers in the organisation/hierarchy • lines of communication can become blurred or broken • too much paperwork and bureaucracy
Coordination/control problems	• the business may be trying to do too many things at once, and going in too many directions for anyone to have an overall grasp of what is going on
Staff problems	• employees may not feel part of the business, leading to lower morale and motivation • employees do not feel that they belong to the company because the day-to-day contact might have been lost • industrial relations might not be good, leading to disputes over pay or conditions

The problems of diseconomies of scale are all to do with people. Managers need to appreciate this as the business grows. The following table shows what they can do to manage expansion and hopefully lessen the effects of diseconomies.

TABLE 25.3 Solving problems

Types of problem	Possible solution
Communication	• have regular staff meetings – works councils • keep everyone informed • look at existing communication systems
Coordination	• regular meetings to try to keep everyone focused • ensure that everyone is working to the same objectives
Staff motivation	• delegate more • recognise achievement • involve all staff

Exam tip

Diseconomies of scale tend to be people problems.

All of the effects of diseconomies tend to come from problems of employee motivation. If there is poor motivation, staff will work less hard, show less commitment, be unhappy in their job and be absent from work more. These all lead to higher staffing costs, so it is important for employees to be motivated and feel part of the business.

IS BIG ALWAYS BEST?

Despite the benefits of expanding into a large business, small businesses continue to exist because they have their own special advantages. Some businesses, like hairdressers and newsagents, do not always lend themselves to large-scale operations. Customers prefer the personal service which comes from small businesses. Sometimes the owners prefer to keep their businesses small because they do not want the worry and responsibility of running a large business. They also like the personal aspect of their business which they would not have with a larger business.

Often the only management in a small business is the actual owner or owners. You learned in Section 1 that one of the advantages of being a sole trader is the speed with which decisions can be made because there is no need for consultation. However, you also learned that the sole trader has to be good at a wide range of management skills, unlike someone working in a larger business who has specialised in one particular area.

Figure 25.6 Virgin – a large multinational company

Another disadvantage of remaining a small business is that the business is not in a position to take advantage of the benefits of economies of scale.

⚠ Exam tip

Small businesses can survive without economies of scale because they offer specialist services to their customers for which they can charge higher prices; they operate in niche markets.

✏ Task

The directors of Dudley plc have recently been discussing diseconomies of scale.

1. State what is meant by diseconomies of scale.
2. Explain how diseconomies of scale could affect the work of Dudley plc.

✏ Task

As businesses expand, they start to benefit from economies of scale.

1. List two economies of scale and explain how these economies benefit a business.

However, when companies like Hotspur & Wren become too big, they start to suffer from diseconomies of scale.

2. List two diseconomies of scale and explain how they might affect a business.

Revision Questions

1. How can the size of a firm be measured?

2. Horizontal and vertical are types of:
   a) merger
   b) production
   c) finance
   d) advertising

3. Purchasing and managerial are .... economies of scale.
   a) external
   b) internal
   c) horizontal
   d) vertical

4. An external economy of scale is:
   a) division of labour
   b) integration
   c) location
   d) objective

5. A reduction in a firm's costs resulting from an increase in the size of the firm, is an ....

6. List three economies of scale.

7. List three diseconomies of scale.

8. Explain one reason why employees' motivation can be affected when a firm grows.

9. List three ways in which a business can lessen the effects of diseconomies of scale on employees.

10. Why do some businesses prefer to remain 'small'?

Summary

- A business can expand through mergers and takeovers.
- If a business expands it can take advantage of economies of scale.
- The disadvantages of being too large are diseconomies of scale.

Key terms

Conglomerate – formed when one business takes over other businesses in completely different industries

Diseconomy of scale – something which increases the unit cost

Diversification – when businesses in different industries merge, which spreads risk

Economy of scale – something which lowers the unit cost

Horizontal merger – when one business merges with another in the same industry at the same stage of production

Vertical merger – when one business merges with another in the same industry but at a different stage of production – can be forwards or backwards

Merger – when two businesses agree to join together

Takeover – when one business buys another business

UNIT 25: ECONOMIES AND DISECONOMIES OF SCALE

UNIT 26

METHODS OF PRODUCTION

What you will learn

At the end of this unit you should understand the following methods of production:
- job
- batch
- flow.

A method of production is the way in which a product will be made. There are three main methods:

JOB PRODUCTION

Job production means producing high-quality products or services one at a time. It is usually used for unique or one-off products, often made to the customer's order. Examples might be a craftsman making ornamental picture frames, or an architect designing an extension for a house.

Figure 26.1 Job production – ship building

The goods may be made by one person working alone, or by a team of people. Job production also involves undertaking large one-off projects such a building a ship or the Channel Tunnel. This is called **project production**.

Job production frequently uses highly skilled craftsmen or specialist workers, and the use of labour saving machinery is limited. This makes it **labour intensive**, meaning that the labour costs are a high proportion of the total costs of production. Goods also take a comparatively long time to make. This, along with the fact that materials are often bought in small quantities for each order, makes it the most expensive method of production.

However, the workforce is likely to be well motivated because the products are all individual, which makes the work more interesting and varied. It is also easier for them to take pride in their work since they will work on the product from beginning to end.

Points for job production
- Unique, high quality goods or services are produced to the requirements of the customer.
- Tasks are more interesting as the products vary.
- Workers are well motivated and take pride in their work.

Points against job production
- Selling prices are higher because it is labour intensive.

- Materials are bought in small quantities, making them more expensive.
- Goods take a long time to make and it is difficult to speed up production.

> **⚠ Exam tip**
>
> Remember, job production produces exclusive, highly priced goods and services.

BATCH PRODUCTION

Batch production means making a number of identical or similar products in a set or batch. An example might be a furniture factory, which will make 20 chairs of a certain model and then change to making 10 bookcases, then 15 dining tables. In this case, the chairs might all be identical, or there could be decorations on some and not on others, but the overall model is the same. Each batch will be finished before the workers go on to the next one. Changing to a new batch often means resetting the machinery that is being used. This causes delays in production and loss of output.

In a factory, batch production involves a group of workers, each of whom specialise in one job, such as welding, machining, painting and assembling. The batch of products passes through each worker who performs their part of the process until they are finished.

Batch production is most suitable for producing relatively small amounts of a product. It often involves workers who specialise in one particular part of the process, so the work can become repetitive.

Points for batch production
- It allows for the use of machinery which speeds up production.
- Producing in larger numbers lowers unit costs.
- Materials can be bought in larger quantities.
- Overall, costs are lower, resulting in lower selling prices.
- It allows for some flexibility, with batches being made to customers' requirements.
- Employees concentrate on one part of the process, reducing the need for highly skilled labour.

Points against batch production
- Goods made in batches need storage space until they are sold. This is costly.
- Resetting machinery between batches causes delays in production and loss of output.
- Workers may be less motivated because the work is more repetitive.
- Partly finished goods have to be moved frequently from one worker to another.

> **⚠ Exam tip**
>
> If a question asks whether a business should use job or batch production, look carefully at what you have been told about the product to help you to decide.

Figure 26.2 Batch production – welding

FLOW PRODUCTION

Flow or mass production means producing large numbers of goods continuously. The products being made pass straight from one stage of production to the next, usually down a conveyor belt. This is called a **production line**. Large numbers of identical items can be made, which

UNIT 26: METHODS OF PRODUCTION

means that the costs of production are lower per unit. Flow production is highly automated, which means it uses a great deal of very complex and expensive machinery and relatively little manpower. This is called **capital intensive**.

In flow production, the aim is to keep the process going at all times. If a part of the production line breaks down, the whole line has to stop while repairs are carried out. This is extremely expensive for the business, because no one is working and no goods are being produced.

Examples of products made in this way include computers, televisions, sweets and chocolates, cars, cameras, mobile phones; in fact, any product with a large and constant market.

Another form of flow production is used in the oil and chemical industries. This is called **process production**, where the materials pass through pipes and a series of processes are carried out to change them (eg changing crude oil into petrol).

Points for flow production
- Labour costs are low and materials can be purchased in large quantities.
- Low unit costs mean relatively cheap goods.
- Continuous, often 24-hour production is possible, producing large numbers of goods.

Points against flow production
- Machinery is very expensive and the costs of setting up the production line are very high.
- If one part of the line breaks down, production has to be halted until it can be repaired or replaced.
- It is very inflexible as a production line is difficult to adapt.
- The work is repetitive and boring with little job satisfaction.

A business must decide which is the best method of production for it to use. This depends on a number of factors, such as:

- the amount likely to be sold
- the nature of the product to be made
- what the costs will be
- the variety of goods expected by the customer.

If, for example, a company is going to produce high-quality, handmade suits, the obvious method of production would be job production. On the other hand, if the demand for a product is huge, for example bags of crisps, they would be mass-produced using flow production.

> **⚠ Exam tip**
>
> *Flow production is only appropriate for goods with a high and constant demand.*

> **⚠ Exam tip**
>
> *Remember, the nature of the product being made and the amount that can be sold will be the main factors in determining the method of production.*

Figure 26.3 Flow production – an oil refinery

Task

For each of the following products decide which would be the most appropriate method of production. Explain your reasons in each answer.

1. tubs of different types of ice cream
2. tins of baked beans
3. dental care
4. pairs of trainers
5. baking loaves of bread
6. a jeweller making an exclusive brooch

Past Paper

Louisa Designs is an haute couture fashion house. At present she employs:

- one cutter who is responsible for cutting patterns to her design
- three machinists who sew the garments
- one hand-finisher who is responsible for all the work which cannot be done on a sewing machine
- one presser who is responsible for pressing the finished garments.

1. At present Louisa Designs uses job production. Explain what this is. (2)

2. Explain the differences between batch and flow production. (4)

3. Explain the possible effects on employees if Louisa Designs moves from job to batch or flow production. (4)

(Edexcel, 1996, Foundation)

Task

Explain why printing newspapers involves elements of both batch and flow production. Make sure you explain your reasons carefully.

Past Paper

One of the craft shops at Wheatfields Ltd is vacant. Mary Li, a wood carver, wants to lease this shop and sell individually hand-carved wooden ornaments.

Explain the main features of the method of production used by Mary. (2)

(Edexcel, 2002, Higher)

Exam tip

Remember a company may use more than the method of production. For example, Cadbury produces batches of chocolate bars using flow production, but also produces hand-made chocolates using job production.

UNIT 26: METHODS OF PRODUCTION

Revision Questions

1. Batch production makes a number of identical or similar items in ………. or ……….
2. The method of production that undertakes one project at a time is called:
   a) batch
   b) flow
   c) job
3. Using your own examples, suggest a product which might be suited to each type of production.
4. At Land Rover UK, each vehicle coming off the assembly line has different specifications and accessories. Explain which two methods of production are combined to produce these vehicles.
5. Linda worked on the production line in a large chocolate factory for two years. Then she moved to the department that produces individually hand-made chocolates. What differences would she find in her new job?
6. Sara Evans makes wedding cakes for a baker's shop in Manchester. Explain whether job, batch or flow is the most suitable form of production for her business.

Summary

- There are three main methods of production: job, batch and flow
- The method of production used will depend on the product, the demand, the costs and the variety required.

Key terms

Job production – undertaking one product or project at a time to produce high-quality goods or services

Batch production – producing a number of similar or identical items in batches or sets

Flow production – producing large numbers of goods continuously

UNIT 27

PRODUCTIVITY

» What you will learn

At the end of this unit you should understand:
- the term 'productivity'
- methods of production and technology to improve productivity
- the importance of EPOS, EFTPOS, CAD, CAM and CIM.

WHAT IS PRODUCTIVITY

Productivity is the output measured against the inputs used to create or make something. To work this out, divide the output over a given period of time by the number of employees. When the employees become more efficient and can work faster at their job, then the output should be improved and the costs should decrease. Productivity can also be measured against the amount of money spent to make the item, eg purchasing machinery. A calculation can be made as to how cost-effective is the item purchased.

The method of production depends entirely on what the product to be made is. Methods of production such as batch and job have been mentioned in the previous unit. An aeroplane is a very large product, and has many many parts that make up the whole product. It requires a great deal of skill and many craftsmen who will spend months making their particular part of the aeroplane. Everyone will have to work as a team, from collating the parts to assembling them. When they do assemble the parts they must have somewhere large enough for the aeroplane to fit in. Productivity would therefore be very difficult to work out, and ways of improving would be complicated.

However, producing a car is very different from producing an aeroplane. The majority of cars are made on a production line, where workers or robots add parts to the car as it moves along the line. Several cars can be made in a day. Productivity can therefore be worked out, and companies can become more productively efficient, gaining more profit.

LEAN PRODUCTION

Mass production is concerned with producing large quantities of items on a production line. The employees are either very skilled at working the machines or have a job which can be extremely monotonous, such as watching the production line to check for errors or faults. The Japanese have been the forerunners in trying to devise a method of lean production.

The sole aim of lean production is to reduce the waste of resources during production, which in turn improves efficiency. It also aims to reduce the time it takes for the product to progress from the development stage to being for sale in the shops. One of these methods is **JIT (Just in Time)**.

In lean production, every single method is looked at to try to find ways of improving the method of production. The company may decide to look at competitors to see how they are working; they may travel to different parts of the world to see how a product is produced there. The company will then find the best method, by copying and adapting what other companies do, in order to improve their efficiency. The benefits of doing this are:

- better quality products
- faster and more efficient production
- increased output but at a lower cost
- less waste of resources during production.

Just in Time (JIT)

Just in Time is a Japanese management philosophy. It was first developed by Toyota many years ago at its automotive manufacturing plants in Japan, in order to reduce the number of items that have to be kept as stock. Today this method has been applied in many companies. It is where a company receives materials and components immediately prior to production beginning, and no earlier.

For the company to have a large amount of stock sitting in a warehouse on the plant is expensive and very wasteful of their resources. Money is being tied up on the stock items, and valuable space on the premises is being wasted. Just in Time systems try to keep the stock to the minimum by having replacement stock arriving at the point when it is required, just before it is needed. This reduces wastage of time, storage and money. Computers should be keeping a check on the number of items needed, and informing the supplier when the stock is required.

The onus is now being placed on the supplier, and very complicated agreements are made between customer and supplier with regard to arrangements for delivery. Penalties are given if goods are delivered late. Satellite suppliers are companies located close to the manufacturer, who can deliver goods quickly.

Supermarkets are another area of business where they use JIT; perhaps this is why some items are not on the shelves. They have to rely on the transport of goods and delivery systems. If there is a breakdown of a vehicle or traffic jam it can hold up deliveries.

Buffer stock

Buffer stock is where a company will keep a small amount of stock to enable the workforce to keep working until the next delivery arrives. Quite often the buffer stock is used up very quickly, such as in supermarkets, and this is one reason why there are sometimes items missing from the shelves.

Figure 27.1 Car manufacturing using the JIT method

Exam tip

Visit your local supermarket or talk to students in your school who work in a supermarket. How important to the company is stock control? How much room in the supermarket is dedicated to stock?

Task

1. Why do businesses hold a 'buffer' stock?
2. What benefits does the business gain by adopting a JIT system?
3. What dangers are there for a business adopting a JIT system?

Stock control

There is nothing more frustrating that going into a supermarket to purchase some goods, only to find that they are not in stock. Why have they run out? It may be that more people than expected have been buying the product. It may also be that the delivery is late.

Supermarkets have to make sure that there is sufficient stock to keep the customers satisfied, or they may go to a competitor.

When stock levels reach a certain point (**reorder point**), then they will be reordered so that the item is back to the maximum level of stock.

Figure 27.2 Stock control

Shops must reorder stock before it sells out. They must also ensure that they do not keep too much stock on the premises; as mentioned earlier, this is expensive and the company could be putting the money to better use.

TECHNOLOGICAL METHODS OF PRODUCTION

Other methods of technology can help a business to become more efficient and cost-effective.

EPOS (Electronic Point of Sale)

There are very few items that we buy nowadays which do not have a barcode on them. The barcode is a set of thick and thin parallel lines, which represent a 13-digit number that is usually printed above or below the bar. The coded number identifies the product uniquely and indicates the country or origin, the company that made the product, the product code number and package size. The last digit is a check digit that acts as an accuracy check to ensure that the barcode is read or keyed in correctly. The barcode will usually not include the price of the product because the price can change frequently; also, different shops charge different prices.

Figure 27.3 Example of a barcode

Task

1. Collect four or five different barcodes from items you use daily.
2. List the advantages and disadvantages to the customer and company of having barcodes on items.

When shopping in a supermarket a customer will put the items in the basket or trolley. Once they have finished the shopping they take the goods to the checkout point. Here the goods are passed over a laser scanner that reads the barcodes. The scanner is linked to an **Electronic Point of Sale** terminal (EPOS), which has a keyboard, a screen and a small dot matrix printer. The data from the barcode is sent to the store's main computer, which immediately returns information about the product name and price to the checkout, where they are printed on the customer's receipt and the amount added to the total.

The same details also appear on the screen of the EPOS. Sometimes the scanner cannot read the barcode, so the numbers are keyed into the EPOS using the keyboard. When all the goods have been recorded the EPOS produces an itemised receipt for the customer showing the names and prices of all the products, the total amount to be paid, the date and time.

Most supermarkets are now adding many details onto the bottom of their receipt, such as your loyalty points, discounts at an affiliated petrol station, special offers.

All the checkouts in the supermarket are linked to the main computer, which records the items that have been sold at any given time. Details about the amount of stock held in the shop's warehouse are also recorded in a stock control file. At the end of each day, the main computer produces a report showing the total amount that has been sold of each item, and this number is taken away from the overall amount recorded in the stock control file.

If any item has fallen below the reorder level, an order will be sent for the required goods, with the shop or departmental manager deciding how much stock should be ordered. Sometimes the computer may be set up automatically to do this without the departmental manager having to do anything.

The order is normally sent through EDI (**Electronic Data Interchange**) which is sent via e-mail to the supplier, thus saving time.

EFTPOS (Electronic Funds Transfer at Point of Sale)

As computers are becoming more sophisticated, paper is being used less and less; rather than sending cheques in the post, banks and companies are increasingly using a payment system called EFT (**Electronic Funds Transfer**) to make payments between account holders.

BACS (**Bankers Automated Clearing System**) is used by an enormous number of companies to pay monthly salaries directly into employees' accounts. It is also used to pay direct debits, standing orders, mortgages and most types of regular bills. This is another method of technology improving the efficiency of transferring money.

Other examples of electronic funds transfer are debit cards, credit cards and smart cards.

The payment for goods by this method is much easier for the customer and easier for the supplier. The plastic card is swiped through an Electronic Funds Transfer at Point of Sale (EFTPOS) terminal which is similar to an EPOS terminal with additional features. The details of the sale and the card are stored in the terminal.

```
            PADSCO'S
            21-23 Leicester Road
            London
            SE12 6PM
            Tel: 020 7654 3212
            VAT no: 998 9988 99

ORANGES                           £0.54
BREAD                             £0.79
YOGURT                            £0.99
BANANAS                           £1.49
BALANCE DUE                       £3.81
CASH                              £4.00
         Total number of items sold = 4
CHANGE                            £0.19
---------------------------------------
PADSCO CARD STATEMENT
  5656 2000 8525 844647*
  PADSCO QUALIFYING BILL          £3.81
  YOUR ACCOUNT WILL BE
    CREDITED WITH
  POINTS EARNED                       7
---------------------------------------
CO1379  #00436  16:33:32  24 MAR 2004

   *goodbye, and thank you for shopping with us*
```

Figure 27.4 Example of a receipt

> ⚠️ **Exam tip**
>
> Technology is always changing – new methods are always being introduced to help both business and the consumer. Look through the newspapers and cut out articles that may be of interest with regards to technology and the way it affects us.

Computer Aided Design (CAD)

Computers are now used in all stages of production of almost everything we buy. They are involved in the initial stages of designing the product, through to its construction or manufacture.

Computer Aided Design has completely changed the way in which products are designed. Instead of making an expensive model of a car or bridge, the whole project can be designed on the computer screen. Thus any small amendments or changes can be made very easily without having to rebuild a new model. The accuracy with which the computer can draw the item is much better than a person sitting at a desk making sure that the lines are exactly the correct lengths or shaped in the correct way.

With computer technology, it is easy to make changes to a design, such as the colour of an item or the style of a garment. When designing a bridge, various effects can be simulated to check whether it can withstand certain weather conditions. In the past, changes of any kind to any item would have taken considerable time and effort to check and alter; yet now it is carried out in seconds.

Computer Aided Manufacture (CAM)

Computer Aided Manufacture enables a product designed on the screen to be made by a computer. An example of this could be a desk; designed on the computer, the measurements and dimensions are then transferred to the computer on the shop floor, which will cut the wood. Another computer will then ensure that the pieces of wood are glued or stuck together, which makes up the desk.

This production method is now used in many industries. For example, in the mixing of dyes for fabrics, computers control the whole production process including temperature, mixture and rate of flow. As computers can now be programmed and reprogrammed so easily, it is possible to produce even the smallest quantity of dye without having to halt production.

Figure 27.5 Cutting metal using CAM

Computer Integrated Manufacturing (CIM)

Computer Integrated Manufacture is a combination of all of the above methods. Computers now play a very active part in all forms of manufacture, from the initial design of the product and its components, through all the various stages of production, including quality control, to the delivery of the finished goods.

Computers can be reset at short notice, thus reducing the time that production is halted. For example, when a customer orders a car at a showroom, the salesperson can actually request a particular car with the exact specification the person wants, and have the vehicle delivered in a short time. The computer is set to include all the extras or additional items the customer wants, together with the colour of the car required. Before the age of computers, customers had much less choice. The link between the salesperson's computer and the computer at the car manufacturer means that little time is wasted. Many other industries are working in the same way.

Task

1. Explain the term point of sale.
2. Explain the advantages and disadvantages of using CAD/CAM:
   - to a business
   - to a customer of the business.
3. Why would a car manufacturer wish to use JIT?

Summary

At the end of this unit you should be able to understand:

- the importance of productivity
- the different methods of production
- the reasons for trying to improve production
- the implications of new technology on production.

Revision Questions

1. A barcode is a set of lines of different thickness, which are:
   a) parallel
   b) diagonal
   c) identical
   d) horizontal

2. When all the goods have been scanned, an EPOS terminal produces an itemised:
   a) bill
   b) receipt
   c) credit note
   d) debit note

3. Cars are normally made on an assembly line. Explain why a company may use this method and why this method of production is suited to the car industry.

4. State how robots can benefit a local firm producing garden furniture.

5. How can this help the workers, and how can it help the company?

6. Explain the Just in Time method of stock control.

7. What does the success of this method depend upon?

8. What are the dangers of adopting this method?

Key terms

CAD/CAM – Computer Aided Design/Computer Aided Manufacture

CIM – Computer Integrated Manufacture

EPOS – Electronic Point of Sale

Just in Time – keeping stock to a minimum

Lean production – a method of production to cut down on waste

UNIT 28

QUALITY

What you will learn

At the end of this unit you should understand:
- the importance of quality control
- total quality management
- the consequences of poor quality control in production.

WHAT IS QUALITY?

When we talk about quality goods and services, we generally mean a product that works well, is reliable, looks good and does what we expect it to do. If we buy something that does not reach these expectations, we will probably make a complaint and be very unlikely to repeat the purchase. Furthermore, we may advise other people not to buy the product. Therefore, it is very important that a business finds out, through market research, exactly what customers regard as quality for their particular product(s) and ensures that it produces this standard consistently.

A quality product does not have to be highly priced, eg a pen costing 50p should be reliable and work correctly. On the other hand, a very expensive car should also be a quality product. If it breaks down or performs poorly, it is not meeting customer expectations. So, how can a business try to ensure that it is producing quality products? This can be done by introducing quality control systems.

⚠ Exam tip

Remember, a product does not have to be expensive to be a 'quality product'. It has to meet the quality expectations of the customers, so that they feel they have value for money.

Figure 28.1 Quality products

QUALITY CONTROL

Quality control systems check the quality of a product. However, before a company can start to introduce such systems, it must first set the standards of quality it wishes to achieve. Standards for design and production methods will need to be set. In addition, there may be legal safety standards; if so, these must be met. Once this has all been decided, the business knows what it is looking for when it sets up the checking processes.

Traditional methods of quality control

Traditional methods of quality control depend on inspecting the goods after they have been made, by taking samples or spot-checking. This means having a quality controller at the end of the production process, when the goods are finished, who will take out a sample of items. These will be checked against a list of standard requirements. If any of the items are found to be faulty, they will either be sent back to be reworked or thrown away. In either case, this means the firm will be wasting time, materials and therefore, money.

This method of quality control also means that other products which did not get chosen for testing could be faulty. These may reach the consumer, resulting in dissatisfied customers and complaints. To try to ensure that this does not happen, modern methods of quality control have been developed.

Points for traditional quality control
- It reduces the number of faulty goods produced.

Points against traditional quality control
- It only checks a sample of the products.
- Faulty goods have to be destroyed or reworked, meaning time, materials and money are wasted.

Modern methods of quality control

Total Quality Management (TQM)

This is a Japanese concept based on the idea that quality is not just the job of a quality controller at the end of the production process, but of every single person who works for an organisation. This means the production workers, the office staff, the cleaners, the maintenance staff and the management team are all equally responsible for making sure that the work they do is of a suitable quality.

To make this idea easier to understand, everyone is asked to think of what they produce as being the right quality for a customer, whether the customer is a fellow employee or the final purchaser. For example, the customers of the maintenance staff are the people who use the machines; the customers of the cleaners are the rest of the workforce. Therefore, every worker should try to do their work correctly the first time, thus maintaining quality throughout the business. The result should be lower costs and satisfied final customers.

Kaizen

Kaizen is another Japanese concept aimed at improving quality. Kaizen means continuous improvement, and like TQM it involves everyone throughout an organisation. Employees are asked to put forward their ideas on how the quality of the product and the methods of production can be improved to the benefit of the company and the customers. This is often done by using Quality Circles which meet regularly to discuss quality issues and recommend solutions. The Quality Circle is usually made up of members of staff of all levels from each department of the organisation.

The main problem with TQM and Kaizen is that they can only work if the whole workforce is motivated to make them do so. It only needs a handful of employees to let the quality of their work

Figure 28.2 Quality control in a Japanese factory

drop, and mistakes and defects will begin to occur. Therefore, it is necessary for these concepts of quality to become part of the culture of the organisation. This requires training and the goodwill of the workforce and will probably take time to put into effect.

Points for TQM and Kaizen
- It makes every employee feel responsible for quality.
- It results in jobs being done correctly the first time.
- It reduces wastage.
- It aims to make continuous improvements.

Points against TQM and Kaizen
- It only works if every employee is motivated to play their part.
- It takes time and money to put into practice.

Consequences of poor quality/quality control

It is very important to businesses that they maintain their share of the market, but this will not happen if the goods they produce are of a poor quality. As we have already discussed, customers will not keep buying shoddy goods. A firm can only continue to be successful if it produces items with zero defects. Otherwise, customers will become dissatisfied and turn to the products and services of competitors. Therefore, quality control is of paramount importance.

Task

Figure 28.3

Purcey's Pies is a small company which produces sausage rolls and pasties using batch production. Their products, which have been very popular, are sold in local supermarkets and cake shops. However, just recently they have had a number of complaints which suggest that the quality and reliability of their goods has fallen. In fact, one supermarket is threatening to stop buying from them and to change to another supplier. Up until now, Purcey's Pies has not felt that they needed to check their quality, but now they feel they must introduce a system, otherwise they could lose customers.

1. Advise Purcey's Pies on a suitable method of quality control, giving your reasons for choosing this method.
2. Explain to them how this should be put into practice.

UNIT 28: QUALITY

Revision Questions

1. The concept of continuous improvement by all of the workforce is called:
   a) quality assurance
   b) quality circles
   c) total quality management
   d) Kaizen

2. The concept that quality is the responsibility of everybody in an organisation is called:
   a) total quality management
   b) total costs
   c) total float
   d) quality circles

3. Checking for faults at the end of the production process is called:
   a) quality circles
   b) quality assurance
   c) traditional quality control
   d) poor quality

4. Explain two ways in which better quality might be of advantage to a firm.

5. Explain two effects of poor quality in production.

Summary

- Quality is of paramount importance to a business, otherwise it will not sell its goods or services.
- Quality control tries to ensure that faulty goods do not reach the final customer.
- Traditional quality control relies on checking goods when they reach the end of the production line.
- Total Quality Management depends on every employee in a business being responsible for the quality of his or her own work.
- Kaizen follows TQM by looking for ways to make continuous improvements.

Key terms

Kaizen – concept of continuous improvement by all of a workforce

Quality circle – group of employees who meet to discuss quality issues

Total Quality Management (TQM) – concept that quality is the responsibility of everybody in an organisation

Traditional quality control – checking for faults at the end of the production process

GCSE BUSINESS STUDIES for Edexcel

Section 6
ASSESSMENT

UNIT 29

COURSEWORK

WHAT IS COURSEWORK?

Coursework is work that you complete during your Business Studies course that, when it is marked, goes towards your final GCSE grade. The coursework element of Business Studies is worth 25% of the marks available at GCSE. It is compulsory; every student must complete one piece of coursework. Of course, you may complete more than one piece, as you may want to use one as a practice piece.

The benefits of coursework

- Your coursework goes towards your final grade, so achieving the best mark you can means you do not have everything resting on your final examination mark. It gives you a psychological edge, so you do not need to worry as much. The more you put in, the more you get out!
- Coursework can be very enjoyable and can give you a great sense of achievement when it is completed. It is probably the first major piece of work you will have completed on your own that is totally original.
- Coursework will make your work more interesting as you will be involved in activities that are different from ordinary classroom activities; eg going out and doing some field research, interviewing people and perhaps working in groups. It is totally acceptable if you do research in a group, but your coursework must be your own work and not the same as anyone else's work.
- You can show what you can do as it gives you the opportunity to use your skills. It also gives you the freedom to work at your own pace – within reason! You should be suitably proud of yourself when you have completed it.

So what is a coursework assignment?

Five coursework assignments are provided by the examination board, London Qualifications Ltd, and are linked to the five sections of the specification as follows:

1. Business activity and the changing environment
2. Human resources
3. Accounting and finance
4. Marketing
5. Production.

Each piece of coursework sets you a problem to investigate. You will need to prepare an action plan that helps you plan how you are going to tackle your coursework. You will set yourself tasks and deadlines, as well as looking at the various books and resources you might use. An action plan sheet is provided in this unit, which might help you with your planning.

You will be required to carry out some research and collect data. Some research you will do in the classroom using textbooks, notes and possibly the internet. Other research can be collected using questionnaires or surveys or through interviews.

Once this data has been collected, you can analyse your findings and form some conclusions and possibly make recommendations.

You should wordprocess your report and include tables, charts, graphs and illustrations, which will make it easier for the reader to follow and understand, as well as make your report look more interesting. Make sure you refer to any charts and graphs in your text and that they are relevant to the coursework.

You can use the following headings to present your report:

- Introduction – which will include the purpose of the report

- Research – describe your research methods
- Findings – What did you find out?
- Conclusions
- Recommendations and any implications.

How is the coursework marked?

Your coursework is marked out of 36 and these marks are recorded on a record sheet, which is included in this unit for your reference. When you first see this you will probably find it very confusing, but one of the keys to success with coursework is understanding the record sheet and the assessment criteria which are the items numbered 1.1, 1.2, 1.3 etc on the record sheet.

ASSESSMENT CRITERIA

1 Demonstrate knowledge and understanding of the specified subject content

What do you know and understand about business? Show evidence of your knowledge when you are writing about what you are doing or what you have done in your coursework. You will only gain high marks if your work clearly shows that you have considered what might influence how a business works and why and how it might make decisions.

1.1 Demonstrate basic knowledge or identify basic factors

Have you shown basic knowledge about any area of the specification? For example, what is a sole trader?

1.2 Identify sources of knowledge – text, people, organisations, electronic – any two

Where did you get your knowledge? If you interviewed someone, name that person. Include the title and author of any textbooks. State any web addresses you used and name any organisations you used. If you used class notes, name your teacher.

1.3 Identify business aims or objectives

Have you said what the business is working towards or wants to do? For example, make a profit, expand, diversify.

1.4 Recognise constraints

What might stop the business doing what it wants to do? For example, competition, access to site, location, planning permission, lack of finance, staff need training.

1.5 Recognise differences or check availability

Have you shown that you recognise differences? For example, what is the difference between an overdraft and a loan?

1.6 Consider influences

Have you thought about the influences which affect the business? For example, market trends, time of year, industrial action, media, location, competition, finance.

1.7.1 Consider alternatives

Have you shown more detailed knowledge and considered more than one thing? For example, the differences between partnerships and private limited companies, or the differences between different types of advertising.

1.8 Show sound knowledge or recognise relationships

Have you shown that you understand? For example, by writing in detail.

1.9 Show critical understanding or make comparisons

Does your work show that you have a good understanding of business by fully describing what you have thought about? Have you compared different aspects? For example, public and private businesses – with all the differences and influences fully discussed.

2 Apply knowledge and understanding using appropriate terms, concepts, theories and methods effectively to address problems and issues

Have you used what you know? Show that you can use business terms, that you understand how business decisions are made and how ideas are developed. High scores will only be achieved if you have used what you know in planning and justifying decisions. You must

UNIT 29: COURSEWORK

show evidence by presenting a full business plan or report.

2.1 State basic terms or concepts or theories
Have you used specialist terms? For example, profit = revenue − costs.

2.2 Apply basic methods
Did you use a questionnaire for your research? Include a completed questionnaire as proof you used it. This is one method. Another might be a spreadsheet or a break-even chart.

2.3 Prepare basic action plan or business plan
Have you used the action plan sheet to plan your work? You could also use your Marketing Plan if that's the coursework you are doing.

2.4 Consider issues or legislation
Have you thought about any issues? For example, planning permission, training, or laws which affect business like health and safety or equal opportunities.

2.5 Apply methods relevant to topic
Have you used any business techniques or decision-making tools such as cash flow forecasting to estimate sales, or break-even or ratio analysis?

2.6 Develop action plan or business plan
Have you added any dates or changes to your action plan? Or have you shown how your ideas have been taken further by thinking about other factors and developing your business plan (could be your marketing) plan to include more details? For example, costs of advertising, results of research.

2.7 Recognise strengths and limitations of ideas used and make decisions
Have you included strengths and limitations or advantages and disadvantages of something and then made decisions? For example, the advantages and disadvantages of bank loans and then reasons for any decisions you make as to whether a business should use a loan or not.

2.8 Effectively address a problem
Have you completed a thorough piece of work and included all you can? Have you fully explained all aspects of the problem? For example, controlling a budget, staff recruitment and training, reporting to shareholders.

2.9 Present action plan or business plan with supporting documentation
Have you included a really thorough action plan, with all dates, modifications and changes included, which reflects the way you completed your coursework? Does your business or marketing plan fully cover all areas? Have you included graphs, tables or other evidence? Is it written in appropriate business language and presented in an appropriate business style?

3 Select, organise, analyse and interpret information from various sources to analyse problems and issues
Have you gathered information from a range of sources and used different methods? High scores will only be achieved if you have used at least four sources and methods to collect information. Show that you understand and have analysed the information in relation to the task. Consider alternatives and communicate it all in a report or other presentation – perhaps using PowerPoint.

3.1 Select a relevant source or gather basic information
Have you collected any information? For example, any data collected from your research.

3.2 Record information
Have you recorded any information? For example, using text, graphs, charts, application form, data capture sheet.

3.3 Collate information
Have you put your coursework into a sensible order with page numbers, a contents page and perhaps headers and/or footers?

3.4 Gather additional information from a minimum of three sources or show some ability to organise and use
Have you used three sources of information or have you shown you can use software, for example, to produce graphs/charts and insert these into text?

3.5 Review or interpret information
Have you considered your findings? For example, what does your data tell you? That 98% of all businesses asked use e-mail.

3.6 Consider alternatives
Have you thought about different ways of collecting information? For example, desk/field research. Or have you considered different ways of presenting information? For example, pie charts or bar charts.

3.7 Organise a systematic gathering of information from four sources
Have you used all four sources to collect your data and information and can you prove this? Show evidence of letters, questionnaires, interviews, etc and reference your sources.

3.8 Apply information to task and use effectively
Have you analysed your data and any other information you have collected, and is it relevant to your original task? For example, '… as sales are low in the summer we need to offer a different product or service at that time'.

3.9 Prepare a logical and comprehensive report or presentation
Have you prepared a thorough and full report, using report format with an introduction, research methods, findings and analysis, recommendations and possibly implications? Or you could use another method, such as a talk with notes, overhead transparencies and handouts or a PowerPoint presentation.

4 Evaluate evidence, make reasoned judgements and present conclusions accurately and appropriately
Have you considered all that you have done? High scores will only be achieved if you have considered all the factors, thought about the results and justified your ideas giving suggestions for possible improvements. You should have made judgements, drawn conclusions and linked economic, social or environmental effects to the task or problem.

4.1 Make basic comments
Have you stated any conclusions? For example, 'we decided not to borrow from the bank because of the interest rate, and to use retained profit instead, which would not cost the business anything'.

4.2 Relate conclusions to task
Have you stated your original task or problem and then related your conclusions to this? For example, 'in deciding on which methods of communication to recommend, we had to research what other businesses in the local area used'.

4.3 Make basic reference to financial or social or environmental effects
Have you made any reference to any of the above? Have you recommended that decisions or actions might affect prices, profits, world economy, staff, managers, community, local area, ozone layer, green issues? (You do not have to mention all of them.)

4.4 Consider results or make limited attempt at analysis and conclusion
Have you looked at your findings and made any conclusions? For example, 'as 98% of businesses surveyed use e-mail for both internal and external communication, I am recommending this to the new company when they move to separate sites'.

4.5 Distinguish between facts and opinions and draw limited conclusions
Have you shown the difference between facts and your own or others' opinions? Were the results of your research what you expected? If not, why not?

4.6 Consider financial or social or environmental effects
Have you thought about any of the above effects? Have you thought about any effects on prices, profits, local or world economies, staff, managers, the community or green issues?

4.7 Evaluate outcomes and indicate possible improvements
Have you looked at the outcomes of your research or recommendations? For example, 'the result of interviewing staff showed that they wanted more computer training, so introducing a regular training

programme (*outcome*) should result in an increase in confidence using the network (*improvement*) and fewer mistakes being made (*improvement*). You would need to include another outcome to gain this criteria – perhaps talking about financing the training and the need to borrow to pay for the training (*outcome*).

4.8 Produce a detailed evaluation, suggest and justify relevant improvements

Does your report contain a thorough evaluation of the problem, and have you suggested any recommendations or improvements? In order to justify your recommendation, include the benefits that they will bring

4.9 Link financial or social or environmental effects to suggestions

What effects will your suggestions have on the business, the area or the environment? For example, 'I would recommend the company invest in a new computer network system (*suggestion*) because jobs will get completed quicker and more efficiently, resulting in time saved (*financial effect*). If customers can find out more about our products on the internet we will gain more interest and more sales (*another financial effect*). However, staff will need training which could cause stress to our employees (*another effect*)'.

ACTION PLAN

UNIT 29: COURSEWORK

Time/Date/By when	What I intend to do	Resources	Problems/adjustments

GCSE BUSINESS STUDIES for Edexcel

RECORD SHEET

GCSE BUSINESS STUDIES (1503) – RECORD SHEET

Candidate Name: _____ Candidate No: [ ]

SUMMER 200_ EXAMINATION SERIES

Centre Name: _____ Centre No: [ ]

1. DEMONSTRATE knowledge and understanding of the specified subject content (Each ticked box is equal to ONE mark)

1.1	Demonstrate basic knowledge or identify basic factors	[ ]	1.4	Recognise constraints [ ]	1.7	Consider alternatives [ ]
1.2	Identify sources of knowledge – text, people, organisations, electronic – any two	[ ]	1.5	Recognise differences or check availability [ ]	1.8	Show sound knowledge or recognise relationships [ ]
1.3	Identify business aims or objectives	[ ]	1.6	Consider influences [ ]	1.9	Show critical understanding or make comparisons [ ]

2. APPLY knowledge and understanding using appropriate terms, concepts, theories and methods effectively to address problems and issues (Each ticked box is equal to ONE mark)

2.1	State basic terms or concepts or theories [ ]	2.4	Consider issues or legislation [ ]	2.7	Recognise strengths and limitations of ideas used and make decisions [ ]
2.2	Apply basic methods [ ]	2.5	Apply methods relevant to topic [ ]	2.8	Effectively address topic [ ]
2.3	Prepare basic action plan or business plan [ ]	2.6	Develop action plan or business plan [ ]	2.9	Present action plan or business plan with supporting documentation [ ]

3. SELECT, organise, analyse and interpret information from various sources to analyse problems and issues (Each ticked box is equal to ONE mark)

3.1	Select a relevant source or gather basic information [ ]	3.4	Gather additional information from a minimum of three sources or show some ability to organise and use [ ]	3.7	Organise a systematic gathering of information from four sources [ ]
3.2	Record information [ ]	3.5	Review or interpret information [ ]	3.8	Apply information to task and use effectively [ ]
3.3	Collate information [ ]	3.6	Consider alternatives [ ]	3.9	Prepare a logical and comprehensive report or presentation [ ]

4. EVALUATE EVIDENCE, make reasoned judgements and present conclusions accurately and appropriately (Each ticked box is equal to ONE mark)

4.1	Make basic comments [ ]	4.4	Consider results or make limited attempt at analysis and conclusion [ ]	4.7	Evaluate outcomes and indicate possible improvements [ ]
4.2	Relate conclusions to task [ ]	4.5	Distinguish between facts and opinions and draw limited conclusions [ ]	4.8	Produce a detailed evaluation, suggest and justify relevant improvements [ ]
4.3	Make basic reference to financial or social or environmental effects [ ]	4.6	Consider financial or social or environmental effects [ ]	4.9	Link financial or social or environmental effects to suggestions [ ]

TOTAL (Max 36)

NB Candidates may score at any point but Teacher-Examiners and Moderators must be satisfied that the candidate is generally meeting the level indicated. The piece of coursework MUST be annotated with the assessment criteria numbers from the Record Sheet. The piece of coursework must then be attached to the Record Sheet.

Declaration of Authentication: I declare that the work submitted for assessment has been carried out without assistance other than that which is acceptable under the scheme of assessment.

Mark out of 36 [ ] ×2 [ ] +QWC (mark out of 4) [ ] = Total Mark [ ]

Signed (candidate) .... Date ....

Signed (teacher) .... Name of teacher ....

UNIT 30

THE EXAMINATION PAPERS

You have completed your coursework and achieved a good mark; now you can start thinking about the examination. As with most GCSE examinations, there are two tiers:

- Foundation Tier – grades C–G
- Higher Tier – grades A*–D.

Which tier you take will depend on how you have done throughout the year with classwork, homework and your coursework. You and your teacher will decide this during year 11.

Each examination series is based upon a scenario that is based on a real company. You can see the scenario during year 11 so that you can prepare thoroughly for your final exam. The scenario is included as the first page of your exam, so it is the first thing you see when you open the paper.

SOME EXAM ADVICE

- Use a black or blue pen. Do not use a pencil – this can make your examination script difficult to read, which means the examiner might miss something you have written that is worth marks. Do not throw marks away unnecessarily!
- Candidates sometimes lose marks because they do not do exactly what the examiner wants. Therefore make sure that you read the questions properly – answer the question as it is written and not how you want it to be!
- If the question asks for two reasons, make sure you only give two reasons, not one or three.
- Here are some key words used in exam questions:
  1. identify/state/list – usually only requires one-word answers
  2. explain/outline – make a point and develop it
  3. discuss/compare – explain two sides of a point, advantages and disadvantages
  4. assess – make a point, develop it and start to make conclusions
  5. evaluate – after discussion and analysis, make judgement(s).
- There are lines on the paper for your answer – the examiner will expect to see these lines filled.
- Be aware of the marks allocated to each question – make sure you give enough in your answer to gain maximum marks.
- Show any workings in numerical questions.
- Do not answer in statements (unless the question asks for a list of statements). Always try to expand on your answer. For example, *H & W might have advertised through local newspapers and local radio* (this is a statement) *because this would target their local customers. In their newspaper advertisements they might have promoted the move by including special offers, competitions to name the new store or free gifts* (this is an expanded answer showing analysis). *Using these promotion methods means that H & W are drawing attention to the move which will gain them new customers while retaining existing ones, which should see their sales revenue increase because customers would be keen to visit the new store and see the new ranges of products. So any money spent on advertising and promotion would be worth it* (judgements are made).
- Try and use words like *because*, *therefore*, *so* to link statements and expansions/explanations together.
- In questions that require extended writing, you are advised to use some sort of plan (this can be a spidergram or a list of points) because this leads to well-structured arguments. This approach helps you to organise your thoughts, which means that you will not repeat yourself and you will produce a well-planned answer.

Finally, do enjoy the exam. If you do your best it is all anyone can ask.

Good Luck!

INDEX

Note: page numbers in **bold** refer to key terms.

above-the-line promotion 188–93, **198**
ACAS *see* Advisory, Conciliation and Arbitration Service
accountants 154, **165**
accounting documents 155–6
accounts 154–65, **165**, 166
  balance sheet 160–2
  defining 154–6
  final 156, 164, **165**
  profits and loss account 156–9, 164, **165**
acid test ratio 170, 171, **174**
action plan sheets 248, 252
'additional payments' 112–13
administration 64
advertising
  advertising campaigns 196, **198**
  advertising media 189–93
  controls on 197
  job vacancies 90–3, 99
  promotional 82, 179, 188–93, 196–7, 198
Advertising Standards Authority (ASA) 197
Advisory, Conciliation and Arbitration Service (ACAS) 122
after-sales service 194, 208
age, market segmentation by 178
air transport 204
Amalgamated Engineering and Electrical Union 117
Annual General Meeting (AGM) 55
annual reports 55, **64**
appraisal systems 119
appropriation account 159, 164, **165**
aptitude tests 96
Articles of Association 54, **64**
ASA *see* Advertising Standards Authority
assessment 247–54
  coursework 248–53
  examinations 254
assets 160–1, 164
  and business size 224
  current 161, 162, **165**, 170, 171
  fixed 160, **165**, 171
  liquid 161, **165**
Association of Teachers and Lecturers (ATL) 117

baby boomers 37
backward mergers 225
BACS *see* Bankers Automated Clearing System
balance of payments 33, **44**
  deficit 33, 34
  surplus 33
balance sheet 160–2, 164, **165**
  assets 160–1
  capital 160, 161, 164
  liabilities 160, 161
  structure 161–2
ballots 121
Bank of England 59
banked hours schemes 109
Bankers Automated Clearing System (BACS) 240
banks 23, 59
bar charts 216
barcodes 205, 239–40
batch production 233, **236**
BBC *see* British Broadcasting Corporation
below-the-line promotion 193–4, **198**
billboards 191
black legs 121
black markets 8
body language 81, 84
Body Shop 16, 38, 58
bonuses 112

book-keeping systems 155
booms (economic) 32, **44**
borrowing 23
Boston Matrix 208
brand loyalty 211
branding 210–11, **212**
break-even analysis 147–51
  break-even charts 147–53, **153**
  break-even formula 149, 153
  break-even point 147, 148, 149, **153**
brewing industry 45–6
British Broadcasting Corporation (BBC) 17, 59
British Overseas Trade Board 34
British Rail 59, 60
British Telecom (BT) 28, 59, 60
budgets 128–31, **131**
buffer stock 238
bulk buying 201, **206**
bulk-decreasing industries 45–6, **50**
bulk-increasing industries 46, **50**
business activity **10**, 11–14
  and the external environment 22–44
business advice 25, 34
business environment *see* external environment; internal environment
business objectives 15–18, 20
  defining 15–16
  SMART 15
business organisation 51–65, 70–3, 75
business plans 142–3, **144**
business size 18, 224–31
  see also small companies
buy-one-get-one-free (BOGOF) 193

CAD *see* Computer Aided Design
Cadbury World 195
CAM *see* Computer Aided Manufacture

capital 3, **10**, 141, **144**
  balance sheets 160, 161, 164
  free movement of 29
  limited nature 6
  owner's capital 161, **165**
  return on capital employed 168, 169, 170, **174**
  share/equity capital 141
  start-up capital 138, 141, **144**
  working capital 136, 138, **144**, 162, **165**, 170–1
capital expenditure 138, **144**
capital goods 207
capital intensive businesses 3, **10**, 234
careers services 92
cash 161
Cash Cows (Boston Matrix) 208
cash flow 69, 132, **137**
  net 133, **137**
cash flow forecasting 132–7, **137**
  cash in 133
  cash out 133
  causes of cash flow problems 133
  closing balance 133
  improving cash flow 136
  opening balance 133
CBI *see* Confederation of British Industry
central government 8, 9, 23–5, 58, 59
  and accounts 155
  incentives for business location 47
  use of performance measures 167
Certificate of Incorporation 55, **64**
chain of command 71–2, **75**
chain of production 12, **14**
chain stores 202
channels of distribution 199–202, **206**
  Channel One 199–200
  Channel Two 200
  Channel Three 201
  choosing 201–2
charity donations 195
charts 82, 216
check digits 239
cheques 156

China 9
CIM *see* Computer Integrated Manufacture
cinema advertising 190
classified advertising 189
Clean Air Act 29
clocking on/clocking off systems 110
closed questions 214–15, **221**
'closer supervision' 121
closure, company 122
Co-op bank 38
coal miners 118
Coca Cola 195
collective bargaining 117, **125**
column charts 216
commission 112
Common Agricultural Policy 30
communication 76–87, **87**
  barriers to 84, **87**
  defining 76–7
  diagonal 78, **87**
  and diseconomies of scale 228, 229
  downward 78
  electronic 82–4
  external **87**
  good 84, 85
  by the grapevine 79
  horizontal 78, **87**
  internal 78–9, **87**
  non-verbal 84
  oral 79, 81–2, **87**
  poor 84–5
  process 77–8
  purposes of 77
  types 79–84
  upward 78
  visual 82
  written 79–80
communications 46
  see also infrastructure
companies, defining **64**
Companies Act 54
company cars 113
company visits 195
competition 6
  in the European Union 30
  of international trade 33

and the law 28–9
use of accounts 155
use of advertising 192
use of channels of distribution 202
competition pricing 185, **187**
competitions 194
Computer Aided Design (CAD) 40, 241, **242**
Computer Aided Manufacture (CAM) 241, **242**
Computer Integrated Manufacture (CIM) **24**, 241–2
Confederation of British Industry (CBI) 103, 118
conglomerates 225, 226, **231**
Connexions 92, 103, **104**
consultation 117–25
consultative committees 113–14
Consumer Credit Act 27
consumer durable goods **10**
consumer goods 207
consumer panels 218
Consumer Protection Act 27
consumerables **10**
consumers **10**
  and channels of distribution 199–201
  and the law 26–7
  and monetary policy 23
  needs 2, 6, 8, 9, **10**
  satisfaction 15, 19, 207
  tastes 38
  use of accounts 155
  wants 2, 6–7, 8, **10**
contract of employment 96, **99**
control 51, 52, 54, 57, **64**
  see also management
  chain of command 71–2, **75**
  and diseconomies of scale 228, 229
  span of 72–3
coordination problems, and diseconomies of scale 228, 229
corporation tax 24, 159
corruption 8
cost plus pricing 183–4, **187**
costs 143, 146
  see also expenses

actual 6
of advertising media 191–2, 198
and break-even analysis 147, 148, 149, 150, 153
and budgets 128, 129
and business location 45
and channels of distribution 201
cost plus pricing 183–4, **187**
and E-commerce 41
fixed (indirect/overheads) 146, 148, 149, **153**, 158
of goods sold 156, **165**
opportunity cost 6–7, **10**
semi-variable 146, **153**
social 39
total 146, 148, **153**
variable (direct) 146, 149, **153**
council tax 59
councillors 25
councils 27
coupons, money-off 193
coursework 248–53
assessment criteria 249–52
benefits 248
defining 248
marks 249
credit cards 240
credit notes 155
credit transactions 155
creditors **165**
use of accounts 154
use of performance measures 167
currency, devaluation 31
current assets 161, 162, **165**, 170, 171
current liabilities 161, 162, **165**, 170, 171
current ratio 170–1, 174, **174**
curriculum vitaes (CVs) 93, 94, **99**
customer satisfaction 15, 19, 207
Customs & Excise 155
customs duties 24

debentures 142, **144**
debit cards 240
debtors 161, **165**
deed of partnership 52, **64**
deindustrialisation 12, **14**

delegation 73, **75**
delivery notes 155
demand 182–3
government influences on 23, 24
social influences on 36–7
demography 36–8, **44**
Denmark 30
Department of Education and Skills 92
department stores 202
departments of business 68–9, 75
depreciation 158, **165**
design 208
desk (secondary) research 213, 219, **221**
devaluation of currency 31
development areas 47, **50**
diagrams 82
direct controls 23, 24–5
direct sales 203
direct (variable) costs 146, 149, **153**
directories 191
directors 54, **64**
and business size 224
executive 54
Disability Discrimination Act 1995 123
Disability Persons (Employment) Act, The 1944 97
discipline 123–4
discount stores 202
discounts, for prompt payment 136
discrimination 27, 97
diseconomies of scale 228–9, **231**
dismissal 69, 97, 123–4
unfair 28
distribution 199
channels of 199–202, **206**
methods of 202–5, **206**
role of information technology in 205
diversification 226, **231**
dividends 19, **21**, 54, **64**, 141, 154, 159, **165**, 224
Dogs (Boston Matrix) 208

E-commerce 41
e-mail 83

eco-friendly practices 29
economic activity 11–14, **14**, 44
economic growth 32
economic influences on business 22, 32–6
economic problems 6–7
economic systems 7–9, 10
economies of scale 225, 226–7, 230, **231**
external 226, 227
internal 226, 227
efficiency 208
electronic communication 82–4
Electronic Data Interchange (EDI) 205, 240
Electronic Funds Transfer at Point of Sale (EFTPOS) 240–1
Electronic Point of Sale (EPOS) 40, 200, 205, 239–40, **242**
employees
and diseconomies of scale 228, 229
number of 19, 224
rights 123
use of accounts 154
use of performance measures 167
wants 106
employer's action 121–2
employment legislation 27–8
Employment Protection Act 1978 28, 123
Employment Relations Act 1999 119–20, 123
employment structure 12, 14
employment tribunals 124, **125**
enterprise 3
entrepreneurs 3, 6, 8
Environmental Health Departments 27
environmental legislation 29
Environmental Protection Act, The 29
EPOS see Electronic Point of Sale
Equal Pay Act 1970 28, 97, 123
equity capital 141
ethical business practices 38
European Economic Community 29
European Monetary Union 30

European Union (EU) 25, 29–31, 47, 50, 114, 141–2
European Works Council 114, 120, **125**
euros 30–1
examinations 254
exchange rates 30–1, 34–5, **44**
excise duties 24
expansion 18, 224–31
   and diseconomies of scale 228–9, **231**
   and economies of scale 225, 226–7, 230, **231**
expenses 157, 158, **165**, 168–9
see also costs
exports 31, 33–5
external environment 22–44
   economic influences on business 22, 32–6, 44
   political influence on business 22, 23–32, 44
   social influences on business 22, 36–9, 44
   technological influences on business 22, 40–1, 44

face-to-face communication 81, **87**
facsimiles (faxes) 82–3, **87**
Factories Act 27
factoring 140, **144**
factors of production 3, 10, **10**
   see also resources
   limited nature 6
   payments to 4–5, 6
factory shops 200
Fair Trading Act 27, 28
farmers, subsidies 30
feedback 77, 85
field (primary) research 213–19, **221**
films 82
final accounts 156, 164, **165**
finance 51, 52, 54, 57, 64, 127–74
   accounts 154–65, **165**
   break-even analysis 147–51
   budgets 128–31
   cash flow forecasting 132–7
   costs 146

external 138, 144, **144**
final accounts 154–65
internal 138, 144, **144**
long-term 139, 141–3, **144**
medium-term 139, **144**
performance 166–74
ratios 166–74
revenue 145–6
short-term 139–41, **144**
sources of 138–44
finance departments 69
finance houses 140
financial economies of scale 226, 227
fiscal policy 23, 24
fixed assets 160, **165**, 171
fixed (indirect) costs (overheads) 146, 148, 149, **153**
fixed interest rates 140, 142
flat structures 72, **75**
flow production 233–4, **236**
focus groups 217–18
Food and Drugs Act, The 27
footloose industries 46, **50**
Ford 68
forward mergers 225
fragile goods 201
franchisees 57, **64**
franchisers 57, **64**
franchising 57–8, **64**
free gifts 193
free market economy 7–8
Friends of the Earth (FoE) 31
fringe benefits 113, **116**
furniture manufacturing 4–5

gaps in the market 179
GDP *see* Gross Domestic Product
gender, market segmentation by 178
General National Vocational Qualifications (GNVQs) 102, **103**
geography, market segmentation by 178
'go slow' 121, **125**
goods **10**, 207, **212**
   see also exports; imports

capital goods 207
consumer durable goods **10**
consumer goods 207
   and consumer satisfaction 19
   in a free market economy 7, 8
   free movement of 30
   and inflation 32
   perishable 201
   in a planned economy 8
government *see* central government; local government (local authorities)
grants 25, 30, 47, 141–2, **144**
grapevine 79, **87**
graphs 216–17
Greece 30
greenfield sites **50**
Gross Domestic Product (GDP) 32
gross profit margin 168, 169, 170, **174**

Health and Safety at Work Act 1974 27, 123
Herzberg, Frederick 106
hierarchies 71–2, 75, **116**
hire purchase 140, **144**
hiring staff 69
horizontal mergers 225, **226**
human resource department *see* personnel department
human resources 67–125
   communication 76–87
   internal organisations 68–75
   motivation and reward 105–16
   negotiation 117–25
   recruitment and selection 88–99
   training 100–4
hygiene factors 106, **116**

image 77, 195, 198
imports 33–4, 34–5
income
   see also salaries; wages
   market segmentation by 178
income tax 24, 159
incorporation 54
Independent Television Commission

(ITC) 197
indirect (fixed) costs (overheads) 146, 148, 149, **153**, 158
inductions 100–1, **104**
industrial action 120–1, 122
industrial inertia 47
industrial tribunals 97, **99**
inflation 23, 32–3, **44**
information
   collecting 77
   giving 77
   provided through advertising 188, 189, **198**
   provided through packaging 211
Information Technology (IT), role in distribution 205
infrastructure 25, **44**
   see also communications
Inland Revenue 155
installation 201
interest 136, 139, 140, 169, 23, **44**
   fixed rates 140, 142
   variable rates 140
interests, market segmentation by 178
internal environment 22
internal organisations 68–75
   departments of business 68–9
   organisational structure 70–3
international trade 33–6
Internet 203
   see also E-commerce
   advertising 191
   sales 199, 200
interviews
   job 95–6
   market-research 217
investment 32, 159
Investors in People 114
invoices 155, 156
IT see Information Technology
ITC see Independent Television Commission

Japanese business practices 72, 114, 244–5
job analysis **99**

job centres 92
job descriptions 88–9, **99**
job enrichment 108, 109, 114, **116**
job production 232–3, **236**
job rotation 108–9, 114, **116**
job satisfaction 108–9, **116**
job security 105, 114
job specification 89–90, 99
John Lewis Partnership 112
Just in Time (JIT) 40, 237–8, **242**

Kaizen 244–5, **246**
Kentucky Fried Chicken 58
kitemarks 114

labour 3
   availability 46
   free movement of 29
   limited nature 6
   mental 3
   physical 3
   skilled 46
   social influences on 36
labour intensive businesses 3, **10**, 232
land 3
   availability 46
   cost 46
   limited nature 6
leaflets 191
lean production 237–9, **242**
learning skills council (LSC) 92, 93, 103
leasing 136, 140, **144**
legislation 25–9
   for employees 97, 119–20, 123
   and the European Union 30
   regarding advertising 197
letters 79–80
   of application 94
   liability 160, 161, 164
   current 161, 162, **165**, 170, 171
   limited 54, 64, **64**
   long-term 161, **165**
   unlimited 52, 64, **65**
lifestyle 36, 38
limited companies 54, 54–5

balance sheet 161–2
   main features 54
   private 54, 55, **65**, 141
   public 54, 55, 60, 61, **65**, 141
   setting up 55
limited liability 54, 64, **64**
liquidity 161, **165**
liquidity ratios 167, 170–1, 174
   acid test ratio 170, 171, **174**
   current ratio 170–1, 174, **174**
loans 25, 30, 134, 136, 138, 140, 140–1, **144**
   see also debentures
   break-even analysis 147, 151
   security/collateral 141
local authority enterprises 59
local bargaining 119
local councils 27
local government (authorities) 23, 25
local shops 203
location, choosing 45–50
lock-outs 122
London Qualifications Ltd 248
losses 128, 134, 145, 147
   profit and loss account 156–9
LSC see learning skills council

McDonald's 58
magazines 190–1
   specialist 92, 93
mail order 200
management 54, **64**
   and business size 224
   and the chain of command 72
   and communication 85
   and delegation 73
   Japanese methods 72
   in single status companies 114
   and the span of control 72–3
   use of accounts 154
   use of budgets 129, 131
   use of performance measures 166
managerial diseconomies of scale 228
managerial economies of scale 226, 227
Manpower 92

margin of safety 149, 151, **153**
mark up 183–4
market forces 6
market orientation 178, **181**
market place 5–6
market research 143, 177, 178, 213–21, **221**
   primary (field) research 213–19, **221**
   role 213
   secondary (desk) research 213, 219, **221**
market segmentation 178–9, **181**, 192
market share 15, **21**, 184
marketing 175–221, **181**
   see also marketing mix
   defining 177
   market research 213–21
   markets 176–81
   objectives 177, **181**
   price 182–7
   strategies 180, **181**
marketing departments 69
marketing mix 179–80, **181**
   place 179–80, 199–206
   price 179–80, 182–7, **187**
   product 179–80, 207–12
   promotion 179–80, 188–98, **198**
markets **10**, 176, 176–81, **181**
   and channels of distribution 202
   gaps in the 179
   mass 186
   nearness to 45–6
MAs see Modern Apprenticeships
Maslow, Abraham 105–6, 114
mass markets 186
media
   advertising 189–93
   communication 77, 85
meetings 81, **87**
memoranda (memos) 80, **87**
Memorandum of Association 54, **65**
mergers 30, 225–6, **226**
   backward 225
   conglomerate (diversification) 225, 226
   forward 225

   horizontal 225, **226**
   vertical 225, **226**
messages 77, 85, **87**
MG Rover 109
minimum wage 25
mission statements 16
mixed economies 9, 58
Modern Apprenticeships (MAs) 101, 103
monetary policy 23, 33
monetary rewards 108, 109–13, **116**
money-off coupons 193
monopolies 6, 8, 28–9
Monopolies and Mergers Commission 27, 28
mortgages 141, **144**
motivation 105–16
   defining 105, **116**
   and diseconomies of scale 229
motivators 106, **116**
MSX International 92
multiple stores 202
music industry 37

national insurance 24
National Society for the Prevention of Cruelty to Children (NSPCC) 31
National Union of Teachers (NUT) 117
National Vocational Qualifications (NVQs) 102, **103**
nationalisation 59–60, 61, **65**
nationalised industries 59, **65**
needs
   basic 2, 9, **10**, 105
   consumer 2, 6, 8, 9, 10
   employee 105–6, 114
   hierarchy of 105–6, 114
negotiation 117–25
net profit margin 168–9, **174**
New Deal 25
'new style' agreements 119
newspapers
   national 92, 93, 190
   regional/local 92, 93, 190
Nike 38
non-cooperation 121, **125**

non-monetary rewards 108, 113–14, **116**
non-verbal communication 84
notice, length of 96–7
notices 80, 91
NSPCC see National Society for the Prevention of Cruelty to Children
NUT see National Union of Teachers
NVQs see National Vocational Qualifications

objectives, business 15–18, 20
observation 218
off-the-job training 100, 102–3, **104**
office politics 71
Oftel 28
Ofwat 28
on-the-job training 100, 101–2, 103, **104**
open questions 215, **221**
open testimonials 95
opportunity cost 6–7, **10**
orders 155
organisation, types of 51–65
organisational charts 70–1, 75
organisational structure 70–3
output restrictions 28
overdraft limit 139
overdrafts 134, 136, 139, **144**
overheads (fixed/indirect costs) 146, 148, 149, **153**, 158
overtime 109, **116**
overtime bans 121
'own-brand' goods 211
owners
   and business size 224
   use of performance measures 166
owner's capital 161, **165**
ownership 64
   private sector 51–8
   public sector 51, 58–61

packaging 208, 210–11, **212**
pagers 83
partnerships 52, **65**
pay freezes 122
payments, additional 112–13
penetration pricing 184, **187**

performance 166–74
performance-related pay (PRP) 111–12
perishable goods 201
perks 113
person specifications 88
personal recommendations 93
personal selling 194–5, **198**
personality tests 96
personnel department 69, 88, 99, 123
persuasive advertising 188, 189, **198**
Pertemps 92
PEST factors 22–44
picketing 121
pie charts 216
piece rate work 105, 110–11
pipelines 205
place 179–80, 199–206
   channels of distribution 199–202, **206**
   defining 199
   methods of distribution 202–5, **206**
   role of IT in distribution 205
planned economies 8–9
planning permission 25
point-of-sale displays 193–4
political influences on business 22, 23–32, 44
pollution 29
population pyramids 36–7
population structure 36–8
Post Office 58, 59
posters 191
pressure groups 31–2, 118, **125**
price
   deciding on 6
   decreases 145, 193
   fixing 28
   high 145
   increases 32–3, 145
   low 145–6
   and the marketing mix 179–80, 182–7, **187**
   pricing strategies 182, 183–6, **187**
   and the single currency 31

price reductions 193
primary (field) research 213–19, **221**
primary sector 11, 12, **14**
privacy 64
private limited companies 54, 55, **65**, 141
private sector ownership 17, 51–8, **65**
privatisation 59–61, **65**
Problem Children (Boston Matrix) 208
process production 234
producers 199–201
product 179–80, 207–12
   see also goods; services
   branding and packaging 210–11
   and channels of distribution 201
   new products 40
   product life cycle 209–10, **212**
   product mix/range 208, **212**
   successful products 207–8
product orientation 178, **181**
product sampling 218
production 223–46
   batch production 233, **236**
   chain of production 12, **14**
   economies of scale 226, 227
   flow production 233–4, **236**
   job production 232–3, **236**
   lean production 237–9, **242**
   methods of 232–6, 237
   productivity 237–42
   quality 243–6
   technological methods of 239–42
production department 68–9
production lines 40, 105, 233–4, 237
productivity 237–42
   defining 237
productivity pay 105
profit 2, 6, **21**, 64, 145, 147, 150
   and accounts 154, 155
   and budgets 128, 129
   and cash flow 134, 135
   of franchises 57
   in free market economies 7, 8
   gross 156, 164, **165**

   gross profit margin 168, 169, 170
   of limited companies 54
   as measure of business success 18, 19
   net 158–9, 164, **165**
   net profit margin 168–9
   of partnerships 52
   retained 142, **144**, 159, 161, **165**
   and return on capital employed 169, 170, **174**
   of sole traders 51
profit and loss account 156–9, 164, **165**
   appropriation account 159, 164, **165**
   trading account 156–7, 164, **165**
profit maximisation 15
profit-sharing 112
profitability ratios 167, 168–70, 174
   gross profit margin 168, 169, 170, **174**
   net profit margin 168–9, **174**
   return on capital employed 168, 169, **174**
project production 232
promotion 82, 179–80, 188–98, **198**
   above-the-line 188–93, **198**
   advertising campaigns 196
   aims of 188
   below-the-line 193–4, **198**
   and market segmentation 179
   personal selling 194–5
   public relations 195
   through packaging 211
   types of advertising 188–9
   types of advertising media 189–93
promotional pricing 186
Pronto Print 58
PRP see performance-related pay
public corporations 58, 59, 61, **65**
public image 77, 195, 198
public limited companies 54, 55, 60, 61, **65**, 141
public relations 195, **198**
public sector ownership 17, **21**, 51, 58–61, **65**
   business objectives 17
   reason for 59

reasons against 59
types of 58–9
public spending 24, 58
publicity 31, 121

qualifications 102
quality 208, 232, 243–6
defining 243
poor 245
quality control 243–5, **246**
Quality Circles 244, **246**
questionnaires 214–17, **221**
questions
closed 214–15, **221**
open 215, **221**
quota sampling 214
quotas 34, **44**

Race Discrimination Act 1976 97
Race Relations Act 1976 27, 123
radio 92, 93, 190, 197
rail transport 204
random sampling 214
ratios 167–74, **174**
liquidity ratios 167, 170–1, 174
profitability ratios 167, 168–70, 174
raw materials 11, 12
and backward mergers 225
and exchange rates 35
and inflation 32
nearness to 45–6
receivers 77, 85
recession 32, **44**
record sheets 253
recruitment agencies 92, 93
recruitment and selection 88–99
external recruitment 90, 91–3, **99**
internal recruitment 90, 91, **99**
redundancy 41, 97, **99**, 124
Redundancy Payments Act 27
references 94–5
regional policy 24, 47, 142
Registrar of Companies 55, **65**
reliability 208
rent 136
reorder points 239, 240
reports

business 80
coursework 248–9
repossession 140
Resale Prices Act 28
research and development 68, 209
reserves 161, **165**
resources 3, 10
see also factors of production
limited nature 6
ownership 7, 8, 9
Restrictive Trades Practices Act 28
retailers 240–1
observation 218
outlets 200, 201, **206**
retained profit 142, **144**, **165**
return on capital employed (ROCE) 168, 169, 170, **174**
revenue 128, 156, **165**, 168
and break-even analysis 147, 148, 150, 151, 153
defining 145–6, **153**
and promotional pricing 186
revenue expenditure see working capital
rewards 108–16
job satisfaction 108–9, **116**
monetary 108, 109–13, **116**
non-monetary 108, 113–14, **116**
rights, employee 123
risk-bearing economies of scale 226, 227
road transport 204
robots 40–1
ROCE see return on capital employed
role-play situations 96
royalties 57
Russia 9

safety issues 46
salaries **99**, 111–12, **116**, 157, 240
Sale of Goods Act 1979 26, 197
sales revenue see revenue
sales staff 41, 112
samples 214
satisfaction
customer 15, 19, 207
job 108–9, **116**

scanners, bar-code 240
sea transport 204–5
secondary (desk) research 213, 219, **221**
secondary sector 11, 12, **14**
semi-variable costs 146, **153**
senders 77, 85
services **10**, 11, 207, **212**
see also exports; imports
consumer satisfaction with 19
in a free market economy 7, 8
free movement of 30
and inflation 32
in a planned economy 8
Sex Discrimination Act 1975 27, 97
share capital 141
shareholders 19, 54, 55, 141
and business size 224
potential shareholders 154
use of accounts 154
use of balance sheets 161
use of profit and loss accounts 159
shares 19, 54, 112–13, 154
shops 176, 202–3
short lists 94, **99**
single currency 30–1
Single European Market 29
single status companies 114
size of business 18, 224–31
see also small companies
skills tests 96
skimming 185–6, **187**
small businesses 41, 51–2, 224
organisational charts 71
sources of finance 138
staying small 229–30
smart cards 240
SMART objectives 15
social influences on business 22, 36–9, 44
demography 36–8
lifestyle 36, 38
social costs and benefits 39
social security 24
sole traders 51–2, **65**
balance sheets 161, 162
start-up capital 138

staying small 229–30
span of control 72–3, **75**
sponsorship 195
spreadsheets 216
stakeholders 16–17, **21**
Stars (Boston Matrix) 208
start-up capital 138, 141, **144**
statements of account 156
stock 161, 171
   buffer stock 238
   closing 157
   Just in Time (JIT) 40, 237–8, **242**
   opening 157
   stock control 239, 240
   storage 136
Stock Exchange 18, 141, 154
strikes 118, 120–1, **125**
   all out 120
   selective 120
   token 120
   wild cat 121, **125**
subsidies 30, 34, 47
success, judging 18–21
supermarkets 203, 238, 239–40
superstores 203
supervision, closer 121
supply 182–3
Supply of Goods and Services Act 26
surveys 214–17
survival, business 15, 18
Sweden 30
SwitchNet 240

tables 82, 216
takeovers 225, **231**
   friendly 225
   hostile 225
tall organisations 73
tannoys 82
target markets 179–80, **181**, 192, **198**, 199
tariffs 34, **44**
taxation 23, 24, 59, 159, 167
   and accounts 155
   direct 24
   indirect 24

team working 113
technology
   influence on business 22, 40–1, 44
   technical economies of scale 226, 227
   technological methods of production 239–42
telephone conversations 81–2
television advertising 189–90, 197
tertiary sector 11, 12, **14**
TGWU *see* Transport and General Workers Union
'time off in lieu' 109, **116**
time rate system 110, 112
total quality management (TQM) 244–5, **246**
trade barriers 34
trade credit 136, 139, **144**
Trade Descriptions Act 1968 197
trade fairs 34
Trade Union Reform and Employment Rights Act 1993 123
trade unions 117–20, 121, 123, 124
Trades Description Act 26
Trades Union Congress (TUC) 118, 119, **125**
trading account 156–7, 164, **165**
Trading Standards Department 27
training 100–4, **104**, 114
   inductions 100–1, **104**
   off-the-job training 100, 102–3, **104**
   on-the-job training 100, 101–2, 103, **104**
transport 204–5
Transport and General Workers Union (TGWU) 117
TUC *see* Trades Union Congress
turnover 18–19, **21**, 224

unemployment 23, 33
unique selling point (USP) 208, **212**
United Kingdom (UK) 30
United States of America (USA) 9
unlimited liability 52, 64, **65**

Unsolicited Goods and Services Act 27
utilities 47

value added 4, **10**
value added tax (VAT) 24, 155
variable (direct) costs 146, 149, **153**
variable interest rates 140
variance 128–9, **131**
   adverse 129, **131**
   favourable 129, **131**
vertical mergers 225, **226**
video conferencing 83–4, **87**
videos 82

wages 109, **116**
   and appraisal systems 119
   as expenses 157
   and inflation 32
   minimum wage 25
   negotiation 118, 119
wants
   consumer 2, 6–7, 8, 10
   employee 106
warnings, written/verbal 28
water companies 29
wealth creation 4–5, 16
Weights and Measures Act 27
'what if' situations 147, 149, 153
white collar workers 111
wholesalers 201, **206**
Wide Area Networks (WANs) 240
'work to rule' 121, **125**
workforce, protection 96–7
working capital ratio *see* current ratio
working capital (revenue expenditure) 136, 138, **144**, 162, **165**
   liquidity ratios 170–1
working hours, maximum 25
Works Councils 114, 120, **125**
world market 177
written communication 79–80, 94